AN ALGEBRAIC APPROACH TO COMPILER DESIGN

AMAST SERIES IN COMPUTING

AMAST Series in Computing: Vol. 4

AN ALGEBRAIC APPROACH TO COMPILER DESIGN

Augusto Sampaio

Department of Informatics
Federal University of Pernambuco
Brazil

World Scientific
Singapore • New Jersey • London • Hong Kong

Published by

World Scientific Publishing Co. Pte. Ltd.

5 Toh Tuck Link, Singapore 596224

USA office: 27 Warren Street, Suite 401-402, Hackensack, NJ 07601

UK office: 57 Shelton Street, Covent Garden, London WC2H 9HE

British Library Cataloguing-in-Publication Data
A catalogue record for this book is available from the British Library.

AMAST Series in Computing — Vol. 4
AN ALGEBRAIC APPROACH TO COMPILER DESIGN

Copyright © 1990 by World Scientific Publishing Co. Pte. Ltd.

ISBN-13 978-981-02-2391-5
ISBN-10 981-02-2391-9

CONTENTS

PREFACE

This book is mainly devoted to compiler designers who take seriously their obligations to produce *correct* programming language implementations. By correct we mean that the compiler must be proved to preserve the behaviour (or semantics) of the source program when this is translated into a target program.

It is more than 25 years since the first approach to proving compiler correctness was suggested. Now there are several approaches to tackle the problem; they differ both in the semantic style adopted to define source and target languages (operational, denotational, algebraic, attribute grammars, ...) and in the meaning of correctness associated with the translation process. In spite of that, a systematic development of correct compilers still remains one active and difficult research topic in Computer Science.

Here we investigate an innovative approach: the design of compilers for procedural languages, based on the algebraic laws which these languages satisfy. The particular strategy adopted is to reduce an arbitrary source program to a *normal form* which describes precisely the behaviour of the target machine. This is achieved by a series of algebraic transformations which are proved from the more basic laws. The correctness of the compiler follows from the correctness of each algebraic transformation.

This approach has been carefully devised with the ultimate goal of simplifying the task of designing correct compilers by avoiding some conceptual problems which are inherent to the more traditional approaches to compiler correctness. Our main tool is the quality of the logical reasoning used as the basis of such designs; the reasoning framework includes the following features.

- **Uniformity**. The entire process is formalised within a single and uniform semantic framework of a procedural language and its algebraic laws. Defining the behaviour of the target machine by a program (normal form) in the source language itself we reduce the task of compilation to one of program transformation (or refinement).

- **Abstraction**. We define a very general normal form, capable of representing an arbitrary target machine. The purpose is not to show that a particular compiler correctly translates programs from a particular source language to a particular target language, but rather to build a set of transformations that may be useful for tackling the problem in a more general sense. Particular compilers can then be designed as specialisations of the more abstract transformations.

- **Modularity**. Each operator of the language is dealt with by a separate reduction theorem. This should allow incremental extensions in the sense that the compilation of additional features will have no effect on the features already implemented. Reuse of design and proofs arises as a natural consequence of abstraction and modularity.

- **Mechanisation**. This is a more pragmatic but equally important issue. The approach has been carefully structured to simplify its mechanisation. Its algebraic nature allows a relatively simple formalisation using a term rewriting system such as OBJ3. In this way the reduction theorems (compilation rules) can be verified and a prototype compiler is obtained as a by-product of its own proof of correctness.

We will have succeeded in our exposition if, after studying this book, the reader is convinced that this approach to compilation does comprise the above features and that it indeed encourages simple, concise and elegant design of compilers which are correct by construction. Nevertheless, our ultimate goal will have been achieved if compiler writers put these ideas into practice.

Summary of the Chapters

The first chapter of the book motivates the importance of *correct* compiler construction. After a brief discussion of conventional approaches to compiler design and correctness, we give an overview of our approach to compilation. We present the particular characterisation of the compiler, of its interfaces (source and target languages), and of what it means for the compiler to be correct in the new approach. Some examples of the compilation process are included to illustrate our approach; we also draw a comparison between our characterisation of compilation and the more traditional ones.

Chapter 2 presents background material which explains the mathematical foundations of our work. It describes in some detail the view of procedural programs as *monotonic predicate transformers*, in the sense advocated by Dijkstra. We review the mathematical concepts of partial orders and lattices, and show that our procedural language forms a complete distributive lattice of monotonic predicate transformers. We give examples of refinement calculi based on these ideas and address the problem of data refinement. Finally, we link our approach to compilation to the more general task of deriving programs from specifications.

In Chapter 3 we give meaning to the procedural language in terms of equations and inequations which we call algebraic laws. The latter are stated in terms of an ordering relation on programs. The final section of this chapter discusses how the laws can be proved by linking the algebraic semantics to a given mathematical model; for the purpose of illustration we use *weakest preconditions*.

A complete compiler for a small subset of our procedural language (this subset can be considered as a version of Dijkstra's language) is given in Chapter 4. First we describe the normal form as a model of an arbitrary executing mechanism. The reduction theorems associated with this form are largely independent of a particular way of representing control state; we show that the use of a program pointer is one possible instantiation (other alternatives are a stack of program pointers or a set of pointers, for multiprocessing). The design of the compiler is split into three phases: concerns of *control elimination* are separated from those of *expression simplification* (or decomposition) and *data refinement*.

In Chapter 5 we deal with procedures and recursion, and address the issue of parametrisation. We show how each of these can be eliminated through reduction to normal form, but we leave open the choice of a target machine to implement them. Each feature is treated by a separate theorem, in complete independence from the constructions of the simpler language. This illustrates the modularity of the approach.

Chapter 6 is concerned with the mechanisation of the approach. The purpose is to show how this can be achieved using the OBJ3 term rewriting system. There are three main activities involved: The formalisation (specification) of concepts such as the reasoning language, its algebraic laws, the normal form, the target machine, and so on, as a collection of *theories* in OBJ3; the verification of the related theorems; and the use of the reduction theorems as a compiler prototype. The final section of this chapter includes a critical view of the mechanisation, and considers how other systems can be used to perform the same (or a similar) task.

In the final chapter we summarise our approach to compilation, discuss related work and suggest some research topics for further work which may help to improve the practical applicability of the approach.

Apart from the main chapters, there are three appendices. Although the emphasis of this book is on the compilation of control structures, Appendix A illustrates the compilation of data structures through a scheme for compiling arrays. Appendix B contains the proof of a lemma used to prove the reduction theorem for recursion. Appendix C contains more details about the mechanisation, including complete proofs of some of the main theorems.

Advice on Teaching or Selective Reading

This book was designed as a scientific monograph. Nevertheless, judicious selection of the material may allow it to be used for teaching (as well as for selective reading), both at the level of graduate and undergraduate courses. The main prerequisite is some familiarity with a procedural programming language and some acquaintance with the predicate calculus and high school algebra. Some suggestions for selecting material are given below. The choice of further reading in each case is left open; some references can be found in the bodies of the relevant chapters.

- The material covered by chapters 2 and 3 can be used as part of a course on semantics of programming languages. The algebraic laws which describe the essential properties of the various operators provide an extensive illustration of the algebraic approach to semantics. These laws can be exercised by the students, for example, to prove the equivalence of programs or to carry out program optimisations. A deeper study would proceed with the part of Chapter 5 which deals with the algebraic semantics of more complex programming features such as parametrised recursive procedures. If there is an interest in mechanised transformations, the first three sections of Chapter 6 should be useful.

- Chapters 3 and 4 are a suitable basis for a short (say, 16 hour) course on compiler correctness. If more time is available, Chapter 5 could be used to show how to design correct compilers for recursive procedures. If a theoretical basis for the approach is of concern, Chapter 2 should also be studied.

- A course more concerned with rapid compiler prototyping (than with correctness issues) could also benefit from the book. The mathematical theory would be skipped and the emphasis would be on the design of a compiler as a set of rewrite rules. The results (not their proofs) achieved in chapters 3, 4, 5 and 6 would be useful for this purpose.

- Ideally, the book could be adopted in an advanced course on compiler design with some emphasis on the generation of (mechanically) verified prototypes. The modularity of the approach would allow the students to exercise it in a variety of practical projects, such as: instantiating the compilation theorems to a machine different from that used in this book (for example, the transputer), exploring the compilation of more practical expression languages, or even extending the current compiler with additional control or data structures. This would actually be a good test of the approach and would help to improve its practical applicability.

Acknowledgements

This book is based on my DPhil thesis. I wish to thank C.A.R. Hoare for his guidance and for the teaching, advice and encouragement which have helped greatly; he has originated the approach to compilation which is investigated here. No less support I had from He Jifeng. Most of what is reported in chapters 3 and 4 of this book resulted from joint work with C.A.R. Hoare and He Jifeng.

Peter Mosses and Teodor Rus (the editors), Mathai Joseph and Bernard Sufrin (my examiners), David Naumann, Adolfo Socorro and Ignacio Trejos contributed comments, suggestions and corrections which helped to improve this book in various ways. I also thank Peter Mosses and Teodor Rus for helping to bridge the gap between my thesis and the current book, and for their patience and constant support.

Many thanks are due to Joseph Goguen and his Declarative group at Oxford-PRG (in particular to Adolfo Socorro, Paulo Borba, Grant Malcolm and Andrew Stevens) for the discussions about algebra, theorem proving and OBJ.

I am grateful to my colleagues at the Department of Informatics at the Federal University of Pernambuco for making it such an enjoyable environment, and in particular to Silvio Meira for having introduced me to the field of formal methods, for his friendship and for the permanent encouragement. I am also indebted to my friend Danilo Florissi for his invaluable help with LaTeX.

I thank my whole family for their continued support which can never be expressed in words. The most special thanks go to Claudia, Gabi and Debi who, with much love and friendship, provide me with the necessary strengths to continue fighting for achieving my personal and scientific goals; this book is dedicated to them.

Financial support for this work was provided by the Brazilian Research Council (CNPq, grant 521039/95-9) and by the Federal University of Pernambuco (UFPE).

Recife
January, 1997

CHAPTER 1

INTRODUCTION

We must not lose sight of the ultimate goal, that of the construction of programming language implementations which are known to be correct by virtue of the quality of the logical reasoning which has been devoted to them. Of course, such an implementation will still need to be comprehensively tested before delivery; but it will immediately pass all the tests, and then continue to work correctly for the benefit of programmers forever after.

— C.A.R. Hoare

The development of reliable systems has been one of the main challenges to computing scientists. This is a consequence of the complexity of the development process, which usually comprises many stages, from the original capture of requirements to the hardware in which programs will run.

Many theories, methods, techniques and tools have been developed to deal with *adjacent* stages of the development process. For example, the derivation of programs from specifications; the translation of programs into machine code (compilation); and sometimes even a gate-level implementation of the hardware. Nevertheless, the development of a mathematical model to ensure global consistency of the process in general has attracted very little attention, most certainly because of the intricacy of the task.

Perhaps the most significant effort in this direction is the work of a group at Computational Logic, Inc. [9]. They suggest an operational approach to the development and mechanical verification of systems. The approach has been applied to many system components, including a compiler, a link-assembler and a gate-level design of a microprocessor. The approach is independent of any particular component and deals with the fundamental aspect of integration of components to form a verified *stack*.

This work inspired a European effort which gave rise to the Esprit project Provably Correct System (ProCoS) [59, 12]. This project also aims to cover the entire development process. The emphasis is on a constructive approach to correctness, using provably correct transformations between all the phases. It differs mostly from the previously cited work in that abstract (rather than operational) models have been developed to ensure consistency across all the interfaces between the development

1

phases. Furthermore, a more ambitious scope has been attempted, including explicit parallelism and time constraints throughout the development. The reusability of designs and proofs is also an objective of the project.

The work reported in this book was developed in the context of ProCoS. We are concerned with the compilation phase: the translation of programs to machine code. But the emphasis is on an algebraic approach to compilation, rather than in the translation between a particular pair of languages. Although neither the source language nor the target machine we use as examples coincide with the ones of the ProCoS project, the overall strategy described here (and originally in [53]) has been adopted in ProCoS: see, for example, [74]; and hopefully this strategy will be useful to design many other compilers.

1.1. Motivation for a New Approach

A large number of approaches have been suggested to tackle the problem of compiler correctness. They differ both in the style adopted to define source and target languages (operational, denotational, algebraic, axiomatic, attribute grammars, ...) and in the meaning of correctness associated with the translation process. The first attempt was undertaken by McCarthy and Painter [60]; they used operational semantics to prove the correctness of a compiler for a simple expression language. The algebraic approach originates with the work of Burstall and Landin [13]. Both works have been of great impact and many researchers have built upon them.

In traditional algebraic approaches to compilation, correctness is expressed by the commutativity of diagrams such as the one presented in Fig. 1.1 where the nodes

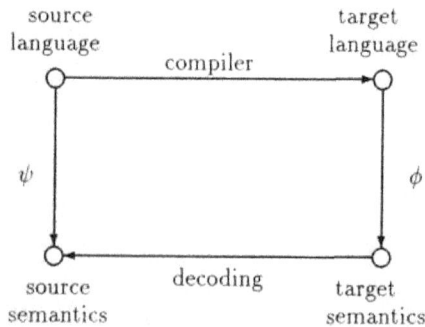

Fig. 1.1. The Morris Correctness Diagram.

are algebras and the arrows are homomorphisms. This kind of diagram was first introduced by Morris [68], building on the original work of Burstall and Landin.

The motivation for a *decoding* arrow (rather than a direct comparison of the two semantics using *equality*) is to allow the meaning of a target program to represent in some adequate way the meaning of the corresponding source program (and not require it to be exactly the same). An alternative is to use an injective *encoding* arrow (mapping source to target semantics) to replace the decoding one. Thatcher, Wagner and Wright [86] reformulated the diagram of Fig. 1.1 in the framework of initial algebra semantics.

Similar commutative diagrams are usually adopted for proving compilation based on denotational semantics. Actually, although the approaches cited above are based on algebra, the semantic definitions of source and target languages can be regarded as denotational definitions (concerning the style adopted). A noteworthy work which uses not only the style but also the notations of denotational semantics is the one carried out by Polak [80]. His characterisation of correctness is slightly simpler than the commutativity of the Morris diagram in that he uses the same denotational model of the source and target languages. Therefore there is no need for encoding or decoding: the bottom arrow of his correctness diagram is just the identity function.

Apart from influencing the early algebraic approaches to correctness of compilation, the work of McCarthy and Painter [60] gave rise to an operational style of verification known as *interpreter equivalence*. In general terms, the semantics of the source and the target languages is given by interpreters which characterise the meaning of programs by describing their effect upon the corresponding *execution environments*. The translation is described by a relation between the execution environments of source and target programs. Again, correctness can be expressed by a diagram with a similar form to that presented in Fig. 1.1.

In spite of the different semantic styles adopted to define source and target languages, all these approaches use very similar characterisations of what it means for a compiler to be correct. Abstracting from what is assigned to the nodes and to the arrows of the correctness diagram in each case, the overall structure is the same. In other words, the components (or interfaces) are the same:

- the syntaxes of the source and target languages,

- their semantics,

- the semantic functions mapping syntax to semantics,

- the compiler itself, mapping the syntax of the source language to that of the target language, and

- a relation to allow the comparison of the semantics of an arbitrary source program with the semantics of the corresponding target program (that is, the one generated by the compiler).

What changes is just the way these components are defined in each case. Even the more recent approaches to compiler design adopt the same general criteria of correctness. For example, Despeyroux [19] characterises correctness using a diagram similar to that of Fig. 1.1, except that she assigns relations (rather than functions) to the arrows; this allows one to deal with nondeterministic languages. Other approaches, for example [17], use the notion of *observational equivalence* to compare the algebras defining the semantics of the source and the target languages.

Experience has shown that, despite all the variations that have been suggested to tackle the problem, the desired simplicity to deal with compiler correctness still remains a challenge. Similar difficulties (apart from many others) arise in the derivation of programs from specifications, where one progressively introduces constructions of a programming language as replacements of certain patterns of specifications. This translation of notations requires checking that an appropriate relation (usually called *refinement*) holds between the semantics of the specification pattern and the semantics of the program introduced in its place. If these semantics are defined using different formalisms, the task is even more complex, since it requires a translation between semantics (some kind of encoding or decoding, as discussed above).

Instead of looking for ways to simplify comparison (or worse, translation) between semantics, a more promising solution seems to be to avoid the problem from the beginning. This is the view followed in recent approaches to program derivation where a mathematical trick is applied: the space of programs is embedded within a more general space of specifications. In this way, a single notation is used both for programming and for specification; programs appear as a subclass of specifications. Therefore the derivation task is reduced to one of transformation of specifications within a uniform framework, with a single semantics. Examples of approaches which adopt this view are the *refinement calculi* by Back [5], Morris [69] and Morgan [66]; a brief presentation of these calculi is given in the next chapter.

The main novelty of the approach to compiler design presented in this book (and originally described in [53]) is that it also benefits from the view described above: the compilation process is completely characterised within a uniform framework of a procedural language whose semantics is given by algebraic laws; we will refer to this language as the *reasoning language*. The source language is a subset of this language, but additional specification operators (such as constructions to model *assumptions* and *assertions*) are useful both for achieving abstract designs of compilers and for reasoning about their correctness.

This uniformity is possible only if we are able to embed the target language within the same framework. We define the behaviour of the target machine by an interpreter-like program (which we call a *normal form*) written in the reasoning language itself. This normal form is basically an iteration which performs a given *action* in each step. Each action will usually be an assignment statement which updates the machine components (represented by program variables); the purpose of each action is to model the effect of a machine instruction. The normal form concept is exemplified in Section 1.3.

Compilation is identified with the reduction of an arbitrary source program to normal form. The reduction process entails a series of semantic-preserving transformations; these are proved from more basic algebraic laws of the language. It is worth observing that in this way the problem of translating between syntaxes (as well as between semantics) is entirely avoided: the product of the compilation process is just a program in the same reasoning language (the normal form) from which we can capture the sequence of generated instructions of the target machine.

All the calculations necessary to assert the correctness of the compilation process are carried out within this single framework of a procedural language whose semantics is given by algebraic laws. No additional mathematical theory of source or target language is developed or used in the process. The relatively simple reasoning framework, its abstraction and modularity are the main features of the approach.

The immediate correctness criterion is to require that an arbitrary source program behaves the same as the corresponding normal form (operationally, as the interpreter executing the corresponding target code). Actually, this is not verified *a posteriori*. As explained above, the normal form is generated by a series of algebraic transformations which are proved from the basic laws of the reasoning language; therefore it is built correctly by construction.

It is possible to simplify the compiler design even further, while still preserving its correctness. The idea is to allow the normal form to be not just the same but possibly better than (a refinement of) the original source code. For this purpose we introduce an ordering relation on programs: $p \sqsubseteq q$ means that q is at least as good as p in the sense that it will meet every purpose and satisfy every specification satisfied by p. Furthermore, substitution of q for p in any context is an improvement (or at least will leave things unchanged when q is semantically equivalent to p). The relation $\sqsubseteq$ is a partial ordering and so is a weaker relation than equality (just like implication is weaker than equivalence in the Propositional Calculus). Therefore refinement is at least as easy to be established as equality, but often easier since the set of algebraic laws which holds for equality is a strict subset of that which holds for $\sqsubseteq$.

The approach to compilation presented in this book comprises some other important features which help to simplify the design of provably correct compilers, as explained in what follows.

- The reasoning language includes some specification operators which allows the definition of a very abstract normal form which can model an arbitrary executing mechanism. The only specific feature of the normal form is that it models a cyclic mechanism which executes one action at a time, but it leaves open the choice of components of this mechanism (for example, the number and structure of registers) and the choice of a particular instruction set. The reduction theorems are proved for this general form, and therefore are independent of a particular target architecture. These theorems can then be instantiated to serve as compilation rules for specific machines, as the need arises.

- Each feature of the language is dealt with by a separate reduction theorem, which is the basis for the modularity of the approach. This gives some hope that additional features can be handled in complete isolation from the features already implemented. This is successfully achieved when the new features do not invalidate the algebraic laws assumed of the old features; but even when they do, the hope is that these interactions will be localised and only the proofs which rely on the invalidated laws will need to be revised.

- The mechanisation of the approach is relatively easy as a collection of algebraic structures in a term rewriting system such as OBJ3 [33]. The reduction theorems are mechanically checked and used themselves as rewrite rules to carry out compilation automatically, serving as a compiler prototype.

Although this approach to compilation comprises all these advantages, there are some pragmatic implications of some design decisions which can be contested by practical compiler writers, as discussed below.

- Defining the semantics of the target machine by a normal form written in the reasoning language allows great simplification of design and proofs (as claimed above and will be evident throughout this book). However, this decision may be considered controversial. The normal form as used in this approach is a *definition* of the behaviour of the target machine. In the view suggested by Hoare [49] it should be the task of the hardware designer to produce an interpreter which correctly specifies the behaviour of the target machine. In practice, however, compilers are designed for machines which already exist. Therefore it is likely that the compiler designer will end up writing this interpreter (or normal form). Thus discrepancies may arise between the normal form and the behaviour of the real machine. Although we do not address this problem here, a possible way of increasing confidence in the interpreter definition is to prove it to be equivalent to an independent (say, operational) description of the target machine.

- As explained above, we carry out compilation by a series of refinement steps. This means that the target code is no longer guaranteed to behave exactly the same as the source code; the target code is allowed to be more deterministic. This possible inequality of the semantics of source and target programs prevents one from constructing a debugger, since there might be no direct correspondence between the operators in the source and in the target program. This indeed imposes a practical limitation if the compiler is to be used in an informal program development environment. Nevertheless, as our main concern is correctness it is more likely that compilers designed using this approach will be components of rigorous development environments. In this context, our view is that the source program acts as a specification of its implementation expressed in the target language, and therefore we accept this implementation to be more deterministic. If an error is found during the execution of a target program, it is not the source code itself that should be debugged: either the original source program already included the error (in which case its development or derivation should be checked) or it was introduced during the translation (in which case the compiler design should be verified).

- We address only the code generation phase of a compiler. Although we recognise the importance of ensuring the correctness of the entire development process, parsing and semantic analysis are not dealt with. Optimisation is briefly considered in the final chapter as a topic for future research.

1.2. The Reasoning Language

The source programming language (a subset of the reasoning language) can be regarded as an extension of Dijkstra's guarded command language [21] with procedures and general recursion. Another difference is that our source language includes nondeterminism as an operator on its own right, and not confined to the body of a conditional or an iteration (as in Dijkstra's language). We also use a rather unconventional notation (following [55]) but one which allows us to describe the relationships (algebraic laws) between the language operators in a very concise way.

The operators of the source programming language are listed in Fig. 1.2. We use x to stand for an arbitrary program variable, e for an expression, b for a boolean expression, p and q for programs, and X for a program identifier.

skip	do nothing
$x := e$	assignment
$p;\ q$	sequential composition
$p \sqcap q$	nondeterminism (demonic)
$p \lhd b \rhd q$	conditional: if b then p else q
$b * p$	iteration: while b do p
dec $x \bullet p$	(static) declaration of variable x for use in p
proc $X \mathrel{\widehat{=}} p \bullet q$	procedure X with body p and scope q
$\mu\ X \bullet p$	recursive program X with body p

Fig. 1.2. The Source Language

Informally, the source language operators behave as follows.

- The program skip starts, produces no state change and terminates successfully.

- The assignment $x := e$ starts with the evaluation of e; its value is then assigned to x. For simplicity, we assume that the evaluation of an expression always delivers a value, so that the assignment will always terminate.

- The program $p;\ q$ denotes the usual sequential composition of programs p and q. If the execution of p terminates successfully then the execution of q follows that of p.

- The program $p \sqcap q$ behaves either like p or like q. This kind of nondeterministic choice is called *demonic* because if p or q *may* fail[1], so may $p \sqcap q$ and, at least in

---

[1]We consider that a program fails if it *diverges* (or aborts); see explanation of the operator $\bot$ below.

principle, this is as bad as the situation where $p \sqcap q$ *always* fails, because one can never rely on it (since the choice is totally arbitrary). This will be contrasted below with the choice known as *angelic*. For further reading on choice operators see, for example, [55, 7].

- The conditional $p \lhd b \rhd q$ starts with the evaluation of b; if b holds, the conditional behaves like p, otherwise it behaves like q.

- The iteration $b * p$ also starts with the evaluation of b; if it holds, p is executed and this is followed by the execution of the whole iteration again. If b does not hold, the iteration behaves like **skip**. Although iteration is a special case of recursion, it is convenient to name it using an independent notation.

- The notation **dec** $x \bullet p$ declares the variable x for use in the program p (the scope of the declaration). We do not enforce that a variable be declared before it is used. Undeclared (or global) variables can be considered as playing the role of input and output commands: the initial values of these variables are taken as the input to the program and their final values as the output produced by the program. A final remark is that we have taken the simplified view of not dealing with type information.

- The notation **proc** $X \mathrel{\hat{=}} p \bullet q$ introduces a non-recursive procedure with name X and body p. The program q following the symbol $\bullet$ is the scope of the procedure. Occurrences of X in q are interpreted as call commands. We separate procedures from recursion as an attempt to subordinate complexity.

- The recursive program $\mu\, X \bullet p$ has name X and body p; occurrences of X in p are interpreted as recursive calls.

It is worth observing that the source language allows arbitrary nesting of variable and procedure declarations, as well as recursive definitions. In Chapter 4, we deal with the compilation of a simplified version of the language, not including procedures or recursion. These are treated in Chapter 5, together with the issue of parametrisation.

For the purpose of generality, it is convenient to avoid defining a syntax for expressions; we use **uop** and **bop** as operators of the source language to stand for arbitrary unary and binary operators, respectively. We will also assume that the target machine has instructions which directly implement these operators.

The source language is embedded in a specification space including the constructions presented in Fig. 1.3. Again, x stands for an arbitrary program variable, b for an expression and p and q for programs (or specifications). An informal explanation of these operators is given below.

- Abort ($\perp$) has the most undefined behaviour possible: it may fail to terminate or it may terminate with any result whatsoever. Following Hoare [48, 81], we identify abort with all programs that might diverge before doing any action visible to its environment. The motivation for this decision is that, in principle,

$\bot$	abort
$\top$	miracle
$p \sqcup q$	nondeterminism (angelic)
$b_\bot$	assertion: if b then skip else $\bot$
$b^\top$	assumption: if b then skip else $\top$
$b \rightarrow p$	guarded command: if b then p else $\top$
$x :\in b$	generalised assignment: assign a value to x which makes b true; if not possible, $x :\in b$ behaves like $\top$
var x	declaration of variable x with undetermined (dynamic) scope
end x	end the previous (dynamic) scope of x introduced by a var x

Fig. 1.3. The Specification Space

a program which is continuously allowed to diverge can be considered a programming error, since one can never rely on it. The algebraic laws in Chapter 3 state that most of the operators of the reasoning language are *strict*: they yield abort when any of their arguments is abort. It should be mentioned, nevertheless, that the identification of abort with all programs that might diverge is controversial. For example, in CCS [63] distinctions can be drawn between divergent processes. Another observation is that we could have regarded abort as a construction of the source language, since it is equivalent, for example, to the divergent program true * skip (which is itself equivalent to the recursive program $\mu X \bullet X$). The reason why we have not included abort in the source language is that the programmer will never write $\bot$ intentionally; rather, it usually arises as a consequence of undesirable computations such as a non-terminating recursion.

- Miracle ($\top$) is the other extreme: it has the most possible defined behaviour and can serve any purpose. But it is only a theoretical concept which turns out to be useful for reasoning. Clearly, $\top$ is *infeasible* in that it cannot be implemented; otherwise we would not need to write programs—$\top$ would do anything for us.

- The program $p \sqcup q$ behaves either like p or like q. But unlike $\sqcap$ this choice is so-called *angelic* in that the most suitable program for a given situation is the one that is chosen. Therefore $p \sqcup q$ fails only when both p and q fail.

- The intended use of the construction $b_\bot$ is to model an *assertion*. It behaves like skip if b holds at the point where the assertion is placed; otherwise it fails, behaving like abort.

- Similarly, we use $b^\top$ to model an *assumption*. It can be regarded as a miraculous test: it leaves the state unchanged (behaving like skip) if b holds; otherwise it behaves like miracle.

- The notation $b \to p$ stands for a guarded command. If the condition b holds, the whole command behaves like p; otherwise it behaves like miracle. This suggests that a guard has the same effect as an assumption of the given condition.

- The program $x :\in b$ is a generalised or nondeterministic assignment. Its effect is to assign to x an arbitrary value which makes the condition b hold. We postulate that when such a value does not exist the assignment behaves like miracle. Therefore the nondeterminism in this case can be regarded as angelic. The main reason for this design decision is that we use nondeterministic assignments to abstract from the way control state is encoded in the target machine. In this case, the condition b describes the set of the next possible states and x represents the machine components (for example, registers); see Section 4.1 for more details. If there is no state satisfying b, the machine behaves like $\top$ which, as explained above, can serve any purpose whatsoever. The intended aim is to save the compiler designer from dealing with states not satisfying b. An alternative choice would be to consider that the assignment fails (behaving like $\bot$) when there is no value which makes b hold; the choice in this case would be demonic. Although this latter interpretation of a nondeterministic assignment would not be convenient for our purposes, there are applications where both interpretations are useful, as discussed in Section 2.6.

- There may seem to be unnecessary redundancy concerning the notation for variable declarations. The operator **dec** is the usual construct available in most programming languages for introducing local variables with a lexical (or static) scope semantics. For reasoning purposes which will be explained later, it is useful to have independent constructs to introduce a variable and to end its scope. Operationally, one can think of **var** x as pushing the current value of x into an implicit stack, and assigning to x an arbitrary value; **end** x pops the stack and assigns the popped value to x. If the stack was empty, this value is arbitrary. So **var** x introduces x with a dynamic scope semantics. This scope extends up to the next **end** x is executed or up to the end of the static scope of x, whichever happens first.

Furthermore, while the source language allows only single assignments, the specification language allows multiple assignments of the form

$$x_1, \ldots, x_n := e_1, \ldots, e_n$$

Of course, multiple assignment is implementable and could, alternatively, be considered a source language operator. But in the context of this book it is used only for reasoning.

Although some of the above constructs are not strictly necessary, as they can be defined in terms of others, each one represents a helpful concept both for specification and for reasoning.

The semantics of the specification (reasoning) language is given by algebraic laws. Most of these laws are expressed as equations of the form $p = q$. Informally, this means that p and q have the same behaviour: for an arbitrary initial state s, p terminates if and only if q does, and the final state produced by p starting in s is the same as the one produced by q. The programs p and q may possibly consume different amount of resources (for example, memory) and run at different speeds; what the equation really means is that an external observer (that is not able to see the internal states) cannot distinguish between them. Therefore we can replace p with q (and vice versa) in any context.

It is also possible to attach a boolean condition to a law, meaning that the law is guaranteed to hold only if the condition evaluates to true. Furthermore, the laws can be inequations (rather than equations). These use the refinement relation informally described previously in this chapter. For the purpose of illustration, a few algebraic laws are given below. They describe the fact that $\sqsubseteq$ is a lattice ordering[2]. For all programs p, q and r we have:

$$p \sqsubseteq \top \qquad\qquad \text{(miracle is the top of the lattice)}$$

$$\bot \sqsubseteq p \qquad\qquad \text{(abort is the bottom)}$$

$$(r \sqsubseteq p \wedge r \sqsubseteq q) \equiv r \sqsubseteq (p \sqcap q) \qquad\qquad \text{($\sqcap$ is the greatest lower bound)}$$

$$(p \sqsubseteq r) \wedge (q \sqsubseteq r) \equiv (p \sqcup q) \sqsubseteq r \qquad\qquad \text{($\sqcup$ is the least upper bound)}$$

An additional (and extremely important) fact about the refinement relation is that all the operators of the reasoning language are *monotonic* with respect to it. This means that if q refines p, then the replacement of p with q in any context leads to a refinement of the entire context. More formally, for an arbitrary context F:

$$p \sqsubseteq q \;\Rightarrow\; F(p) \sqsubseteq F(q)$$

1.3. The Approach through Examples

In this section we give an overview of the approach to compilation based on two simple examples. But first we need to define the machine used as the target of our compiler. The target machine is very simple, consisting of four components:

P	a sequential register (program counter)
A	a general purpose register
M	a store for variables (RAM)
m	a store for instructions (ROM)

As discussed previously, an essential feature of this approach to compilation is the embedding of the target language within the reasoning language. We represent the machine components as program variables and design the instructions as assignments that update the machine state. The instructions of our simple machine are defined

---

[2]A brief overview of the lattice theory relevant to us is presented in the next chapter.

by

$$
\begin{aligned}
\mathsf{load}(n) &\stackrel{def}{=} \mathsf{A},\mathsf{P} := \mathsf{M}[n],\mathsf{P}+1, \\
\mathsf{store}(n) &\stackrel{def}{=} \mathsf{M},\mathsf{P} := (\mathsf{M} \oplus \{n \mapsto \mathsf{A}\}),\mathsf{P}+1 \\
\mathsf{bop\text{--}A}(n) &\stackrel{def}{=} \mathsf{A},\mathsf{P} := (\mathsf{A}\,\mathsf{bop}\,\mathsf{M}[n]),\mathsf{P}+1 \\
\mathsf{uop\text{--}A} &\stackrel{def}{=} \mathsf{A},\mathsf{P} := (\mathsf{uop}\,\mathsf{A}),\mathsf{P}+1 \\
\mathsf{jump}(k) &\stackrel{def}{=} \mathsf{P} := k \\
\mathsf{cjump}(k) &\stackrel{def}{=} \mathsf{P} := (\mathsf{P}+1 \lhd \mathsf{A} \rhd k)
\end{aligned}
$$

where we use map overriding ($\oplus$) to update M at position n with the value of A. The more conventional notation is $\mathsf{M}[n] := \mathsf{A}$. We depart from the more usual notation because it is not suitable for reasoning since $\mathsf{M}[n]$ is not really a variable. In particular, we will need to define operators like non-freeness and substitution which regard two variables as distinct if they are syntactically different: but $\mathsf{M}[e]$ is the same as $\mathsf{M}[f]$ whenever e and f evaluate to the same value, even if e and f are syntactically distinct.

Recall that we do not deal with type information, but in this particular context we assume that P is an integer variable and that M is an array (or map) variable. Note that the instruction cjump jumps to address k if the condition is false; otherwise it continues execution in sequence. The conditional assignment which defines cjump is just an abbreviation of the conditional

$$(\mathsf{P} := \mathsf{P}+1) \lhd \mathsf{A} \rhd (\mathsf{P} := k)$$

It is worth emphasising that a similar strategy can be adopted to model the components and instructions of other target machines. For example, in [74] it is shown how to deal with the transputer.

The normal form describing the behaviour of our simple machine (executing a stored program) is an iterated execution of instructions taken from the store m at location P:

$$\mathsf{dec}\,\mathsf{P},\mathsf{A} \bullet \mathsf{P} := s;\ (s \le \mathsf{P} < f) * \mathsf{m}[\mathsf{P}];\ (P = f)_\perp$$

where s is the intended start address and f the finish address of the code to be executed. The obligation to start at the right instruction is expressed by the initial assignment $\mathsf{P} := s$, and the obligation to terminate at the right place (and not by a wild jump) is expressed by the final assertion $(P = f)_\perp$.

The design of a compiler in this approach is a constructive proof that every program, however deeply structured, can be improved by some program in this normal form[3]. The process is split into three main phases: concerns of control elimination are separated from those of expression simplification (or decomposition) and data refinement (the change of data representation).

---

[3]As mentioned previously, this is actually an abstract design of a code generator; in practice, there are other design aspects which we do not deal with here.

In order to illustrate these phases, and the compilation process in general, we give some examples in the remainder of this chapter. The main theorem which states the correctness of the compiler for this simple machine is presented at the very end of this chapter.

Example 1.1. (A simple assignment)
The first example is intentionally as simple as it can be, so that we are able to explain the entire process following all the steps. Consider the compilation of an assignment of the form

$$x := y$$

where both x and y are variables. One of the tasks involved in the translation process is the elimination of nested expressions. The expected outcome of this phase is a program in which each assignment will eventually give rise to one of the patterns used to define the machine instructions. Then, by definition, the actual instruction names can be introduced in place of these patterns. Note that the above assignment does not correspond to any of the machine instructions defined above: all the instructions are defined in terms of the machine registers.

Recalling that A represents the general purpose register of our simple machine, we can transform $x := y$ into

$$\text{dec } A \bullet A := y;\ x := A$$

where the first assignment will become a **load** and the second one a **store** instruction. It can be easily observed that the above two sequential assignments behave exactly the same as $x := y$. The fact that A is a local variable means that its scope ends after the two assignments are executed; therefore its final value cannot be observed after that point.

But the transformed program still operates on abstract global variables with symbolic names, whereas the target program operates only on the concrete store M. From the compiler's symbol table, say Ψ, an injection which maps each variable onto distinct memory addresses, we define a data refinement $\hat{\Psi}$ which maps each program variable x onto the corresponding machine location, so the value of x is held as $M[\Psi x]$[4]. The purpose of the data refinement $\hat{\Psi}$ is to substitute $M[\Psi x]$ for x throughout the program. When this data refinement is performed on our simple example program it becomes

$$\text{dec } A \bullet A := M[\Psi y];\ M := M \oplus \{\Psi x \mapsto A\}$$

The remaining task of the compiler is that of control elimination, reducing the nested control structure of the source program to a single flat iteration, like that of the target program. This is done by introducing a control state variable to schedule the selection

---

[4]Note that Ψx is the address of x in the memory M, whereas $M[\Psi x]$ represents the memory cell (location) which holds this value.

and sequencing of actions. In the case of our simple target machine, a single program pointer P indicates the location in memory of the next instruction[5]. The above then becomes

$$\mathsf{dec}\,\mathsf{P}, \mathsf{A} \bullet \mathsf{P} := s;$$
$$(s \leq \mathsf{P} < s + 2) * \left(\begin{array}{c} (\mathsf{P} = s) \to \mathsf{A}, \mathsf{P} := \mathsf{M}[\Psi y], \mathsf{P} + 1 \\ \square \quad (\mathsf{P} = s + 1) \to \mathsf{M}, \mathsf{P} := (\mathsf{M} \oplus \{\Psi x \mapsto \mathsf{A}\}), \mathsf{P} + 1 \end{array} \right);$$
$$(\mathsf{P} = s + 2)_{\perp}$$

where we use $\square$ as syntactic sugar for $\sqcap$ when the choice is deterministic. The initial assignment $\mathsf{P} := s$ ensures that the assignment with guard $(\mathsf{P} = s)$ will be executed first; as this increments P, the assignment with guard $(\mathsf{P} = s + 1)$ is executed next. This also increments P, falsifying the condition of the iteration and satisfying the final assertion.

Note that the guarded assignments correspond precisely to the patterns used to define the **load** and **store** instructions, respectively. Performing this simple syntactic substitution gives

$$\mathsf{dec}\,\mathsf{P}, \mathsf{A} \bullet \mathsf{P} := s;$$
$$(s \leq \mathsf{P} < s + 2) * \left(\begin{array}{c} (\mathsf{P} = s) \to \mathsf{load}(\Psi y) \\ \square \quad (\mathsf{P} = s + 1) \to \mathsf{store}(\Psi x) \end{array} \right);$$
$$(\mathsf{P} = s + 2)_{\perp}$$

The above expresses the fact that these instructions must be loaded into the memory m at positions s and $s + 1$, completing the overall process. Note that the product of the compilation process is just a program in the same language (the normal form) from which we can easily capture the sequence of generated instructions of the target machine.   ◇

Example 1.2. (A simple conditional)
Consider the following conditional which assigns x or y to z depending on whether some relation (**bop**) holds or not between x and y:

$$(z := x) \lhd x \ \mathsf{bop} \ y \rhd (z := y)$$

One possible instance of this conditional is a maximum-finding program in which case **bop** would be $\leq$; but we prefer sticking to the notation of the source language where **bop** stands for an arbitrary binary operator.

---

[5]Other alternatives of encoding control states are, for example, a stack of program pointers or a set of pointers (for multiprocessing).

The normal form of this conditional is

$\text{dec } \mathsf{P}, \mathsf{A} \bullet \mathsf{P} := s;$

$$(s \leq \mathsf{P} < s+8) * \begin{pmatrix} & (\mathsf{P} = s) \rightarrow \text{load}(\Psi x) \\ \Box & (\mathsf{P} = s+1) \rightarrow \text{bop} - \mathsf{A}(\Psi y) \\ \Box & (\mathsf{P} = s+2) \rightarrow \text{cjump}(s+6) \\ \Box & (\mathsf{P} = s+3) \rightarrow \text{load}(\Psi x) \\ \Box & (\mathsf{P} = s+4) \rightarrow \text{store}(\Psi z) \\ \Box & (\mathsf{P} = s+5) \rightarrow \text{jump}(s+8) \\ \Box & (\mathsf{P} = s+6) \rightarrow \text{load}(\Psi y) \\ \Box & (\mathsf{P} = s+7) \rightarrow \text{store}(\Psi z) \end{pmatrix};$$

$(\mathsf{P} = s+8)_{\perp}$

After the first two instructions are executed, the general purpose register A holds the value of x bop y. If this value is false[6], then a jump occurs and the two final instructions are executed (in which case the value of y is assigned to z). Otherwise execution continues with the instruction at address $s+3$ (in which case the value of x is assigned to z). ◇

1.4. The Formal Characterisation of Correctness

The reduction theorems which justify the entire compilation process have all been proved correct from the basic algebraic laws of the language. Below we anticipate the main theorem which states the correctness of the process.

Theorem 1.1. (Compilation Process)
Let p be an arbitrary source program. Given a constant s, and a symbol table Ψ which maps each global variable of p to the address of the memory M allocated to hold its value, there is a constant f and a sequence of machine instructions held in m between locations s and f such that

$$\dot{\Psi}_w(p) \sqsubseteq \text{dec } \mathsf{P}, \mathsf{A} \bullet \mathsf{P} := s; \ (s \leq \mathsf{P} < f) * \mathsf{m}[\mathsf{P}]; \ (\mathsf{P} = f)_{\perp}$$

where $\dot{\Psi}$ is a function (built from the symbol table Ψ) which performs the necessary change of data representation: from the abstract data space of the source program to the concrete state of the machine represented by the memory M. ◇

Note that $\dot{\Psi}$ plays an essential role in the correctness statement above: it would not make any sense to compare the source program p with its normal form directly, since they operate on different data spaces. While p operates on the program variables $x, y, \ldots z$, its normal form operates on the concrete store M. Further explanation and a proof of this theorem is given in Chapter 4.

---

[6]In practice it is usually necessary to define an encoding for boolean expressions; for example, false could be represented by 0 and true by 1.

CHAPTER 2

BACKGROUND

> The beauty of lattice theory derives in part from the ex-
> treme simplicity of its basic concepts: (partial) ordering,
> least upper and greatest lower bounds.
>
> — G. Birkhoff

The purpose of this chapter is to briefly describe a theoretical basis for the kind of refinement algebra we will be using. Based on the work of Morris [69] and Back and von Wright [5] we show that a specification language (as introduced in the previous chapter) forms a complete distributive lattice where, following Dijkstra [21], specifications are viewed as monotonic predicate transformers. We give examples of refinement calculi based on these ideas and address the problem of data refinement. Finally, we link our approach to compilation to the more general task of deriving programs from specifications.

The main importance of this chapter is that it presents a mathematical model in which the operators of the reasoning language can be defined and their algebraic laws can be verified; illustration of how to prove the validity of the laws is given in Section 3.20. In spite of playing such an important role, both this chapter and Section 3.20 can be safely skipped by those readers more concerned with the application of this approach to compilation than with its theoretical foundations.

The first section reviews the concepts of partial orders and complete distributive lattices, and a simple boolean lattice is presented as an example. The next section describes the predicate lattice as functions from (program) states to booleans; this is constructed by pointwise extension from the boolean lattice. Further pointwise extension is used to construct the lattice of predicate transformers described in Section 2.3; these are functions from predicates to predicates. In Section 2.4 we review some properties of predicate transformers (known as *healthiness conditions*) and explain that some of them are dropped as a consequence of adding non-implementable features to the language. Some refinement calculi based on the predicate transformer model are considered in Section 2.5, and some approaches to data refinement in Section 2.6. The final section relates all these to our work.

2.1. Partial Orders and Lattices

A *partial order* is a pair $(S, \sqsubseteq)$ where S is a set and $\sqsubseteq$ is a binary relation (the *partial ordering*) on S satisfying the following axioms, for all $x, y, z \in S$:

$x \sqsubseteq x$	reflexivity
$(x \sqsubseteq y) \wedge (y \sqsubseteq z) \Rightarrow (x \sqsubseteq z)$	transitivity
$(x \sqsubseteq y) \wedge (y \sqsubseteq x) \Rightarrow (x = y)$	antisymmetry

$(S, \sqsubseteq)$ is called a *total order* if, in addition to the above, each pair of elements in S are comparable: $(x \sqsubseteq y) \vee (y \sqsubseteq x)$. Following usual practice we will abbreviate $(S, \sqsubseteq)$ to S; the context will make it clear whether we are regarding S as a set or as a partial order.

Given a subset T of S, we say that $x \in S$ is an *upper bound* for T if $y \sqsubseteq x$ for all $y \in T$; x is the *least upper bound* of T if it is both an upper bound for T and whenever y is another upper bound for T then $x \sqsubseteq y$. Similarly, x is a *lower bound* for T if $x \sqsubseteq y$ for all $y \in T$; x is the *greatest lower bound* of T if it is both a lower bound for T and whenever y is another lower bound for T then $y \sqsubseteq x$. An element $\perp$ is a *least element* or *bottom* of S if $\perp \sqsubseteq x$ for all $x \in S$; $\top$ is a *greatest element* or *top* of S if $x \sqsubseteq \top$ for all $x \in S$.

Given sets S and T with T partially ordered by $\sqsubseteq_T$, the set $S \rightarrow T$ of functions from S to T is partially ordered by $\sqsubseteq$ defined by

$$f \sqsubseteq g \stackrel{def}{=} f(x) \sqsubseteq_T g(x) \quad \text{for all } x \in S$$

Additionally, if S is partially ordered by $\sqsubseteq_S$, then $f : S \rightarrow T$ is said to be *monotonic* if

$$x \sqsubseteq_S y \ \Rightarrow \ f(x) \sqsubseteq_T f(y) \quad \text{for all } x, y \in S$$

We denote by $[S \rightarrow T]$ the set of monotonic functions from S to T. If S is *discrete* (that is, $x \sqsubseteq_S y$ holds if and only if $x = y$) then $S \rightarrow T$ and $[S \rightarrow T]$ are identical.

A *complete lattice* is a partially ordered set containing greatest lower bounds (*meets*) and least upper bounds (*joins*) for all its subsets. A consequence is that every complete lattice has a bottom and a top element. Two additional well-known properties of complete lattices are given below; more details about lattice theory can be found, for example, in [10, 18].

- Any finite totally ordered set is a complete lattice.

- If S is a partially ordered set and T is a complete lattice, then $[S \rightarrow T]$ is a complete lattice.

A simple example of a complete lattice is the boolean set $\{true, false\}$ when ordered by the implication relation. The least upper bound $\vee$ and the greatest lower bound $\wedge$ have their usual interpretations as disjunction and conjunction, respectively.

The bottom element is *false* and the top element is *true*. This is actually a complete *distributive* lattice, since it satisfies, for all elements a, b and c:

$$a \wedge (b \vee c) = (a \wedge b) \vee (a \wedge c)$$
$$a \vee (b \wedge c) = (a \vee b) \wedge (a \vee c)$$

One can prove that the above two properties are actually equivalent in lattice theory [18]. The lattice under consideration has yet another property: it is a *boolean* lattice, since it has a *complement* (negation). In the next section we will refer to this lattice as *Bool*.

2.2. The Lattice of Predicates

Programs usually operate on a state space formed from a set of variables. We use *State* to stand for the set of all possible states partially ordered by the equality relation; therefore, it is a discrete partial order. In practice we need a way to describe particular sets of states; for example, to specify the set of initial states of a program, as well as the set of its final states. This can be described by boolean-valued functions (or predicates) on the state space.

As *State* is a partial order and *Bool* is a complete lattice, $[State \rightarrow Bool]$ is also a complete lattice. Furthermore, as *State* is discrete, $[State \rightarrow Bool]$ and $State \rightarrow Bool$ are identical. We will refer to it as the *Predicate* lattice. The least upper bound $a \vee b$ is the disjunction of the predicates a and b, and the greatest lower bound $a \wedge b$ is their conjunction. The bottom element false describes the empty set of states and the top element true describes the set of all possible states. These operations are defined by

$$(a \vee b) \stackrel{def}{=} \lambda x \bullet a(x) \vee b(x)$$
$$(a \wedge b) \stackrel{def}{=} \lambda x \bullet a(x) \wedge b(x)$$
$$\text{true} \stackrel{def}{=} \lambda x \bullet true$$
$$\text{false} \stackrel{def}{=} \lambda x \bullet false$$

where we use the notation $\lambda x \bullet t$ to stand for a lambda abstraction (anonymous function) with parameter x and body t. In the above definitions, x ranges over *State*. The lattice ordering is the implication on predicates, which is defined by pointwise extension in the usual way:

$$a \Rightarrow b \stackrel{def}{=} \forall x \bullet a(x) \Rightarrow b(x)$$

We use the notation $\forall x \mid p \bullet q$ (read as: for all x, if p then q) to stand for universal quantification in the predicate calculus. In particular, p can be omitted when it is equivalent to *true*, as in the above definition.

2.3. The Lattice of Predicate Transformers

The lattice presented next provides a theoretical basis for Dijkstra's view of programs as predicate transformers (functions from predicates to predicates) [21]. The usual notation

$$wp(p, a) = c$$

means that if program p is executed in an initial state satisfying its *weakest precondition* c, it will eventually terminate in a state satisfying the postcondition a. Furthermore, as the name suggests, the weakest precondition c describes the largest possible set of initial states which ensures that execution of p will terminate in a state satisfying a. It should be clear that the focus is on *total* rather than on *partial* correctness in the style of Hoare Logic. This means that the aim is not only to satisfy a on the eventual termination of p, but also to ensure that p will *always* terminate when executed in any state determined by c.

The predicate transformer lattice (*PredTran*) is the set of all monotonic functions from one predicate lattice to another: [*Predicate* → *Predicate*]. The result of applying program (predicate transformer) p to predicate a, denoted $p(a)$, is equivalent to Dijkstra's $wp(p, a)$. The ordering on predicate transformers is defined by pointwise extension from the ordering on predicates

$$p \sqsubseteq q \overset{def}{=} \forall a \bullet p(a) \Rightarrow q(a)$$

where the bounded variable a ranges over the set of predicates.

Clearly, *PredTran* is a complete lattice and, therefore, it contains arbitrary least upper bounds ($\sqcup$) and greatest lower bounds ($\sqcap$): $\sqcup$ is interpreted as angelic nondeterminism and $\sqcap$ as demonic nondeterminism. The top element is *miracle* ($\top$); it establishes every postcondition. The bottom element is *abort* ($\bot$), the predicate transformer that does not establish any postcondition. These are defined in the obvious way:

$$(p \sqcup q) \overset{def}{=} \lambda a \bullet p(a) \vee q(a)$$
$$(p \sqcap q) \overset{def}{=} \lambda a \bullet p(a) \wedge q(a)$$
$$\top \overset{def}{=} \lambda a \bullet \textsf{true}$$
$$\bot \overset{def}{=} \lambda a \bullet \textsf{false}$$

The usual program constructs can be defined as predicate transformers. As an example we define skip (the identity predicate transformer), assignment and sequential composition:

$$\textsf{skip} \overset{def}{=} \lambda a \bullet a$$
$$x := e \overset{def}{=} \lambda a \bullet a[x \leftarrow e]$$
$$p; q \overset{def}{=} \lambda a \bullet p(q(a))$$

where $a[x \leftarrow e]$ denotes the result of substituting e for every occurrence of x in a.

2.4. Properties of Predicate Transformers

Dijkstra [21] has suggested five *healthiness conditions* that every construct of a programming language must satisfy. They are defined below (we assume implicit universal quantification over a and b standing for predicates, and over p standing for programs)

1. $p(\mathsf{false}) = \mathsf{false}$ law of the excluded miracle
2. If $a \Rightarrow b$ then $p(a) \Rightarrow p(b)$ monotonicity
3. $p(a) \wedge p(b) = p(a \wedge b)$ conjunctivity
4. $p(a) \vee p(b) = p(a \vee b)$ disjunctivity
5. $p(\exists i \mid i \geq 0 \bullet a_i) = \exists i : i \geq 0 : p(a_i)$ continuity
   for all sequences of predicates $a_0, a_1, \ldots$
   such that $a_i \Rightarrow a_{i+1}$ for all $i \geq 0$

The last property is equivalent to requiring that nondeterminism be bounded [23]. (The notation $\exists x \mid p \bullet q$ stands for an existential quantification, read as: there exists an x such that p and q hold.) The fourth property is satisfied only by *deterministic* programs. It is easy to exemplify failure of disjunctivity by taking suitable values for p, a and b:

$$p = (x := 2 \sqcap x := 3)$$
$$a = (x = 2)$$
$$b = (x = 3)$$

First let us calculate the value of $p(a)$:

$\quad p(a)$
$= \quad$ {Predicate transformer definition of $\sqcap$}
$\quad x := 2\ (x = 2) \quad \wedge \quad x := 3\ (x = 2)$
$= \quad$ {Predicate transformer definition of assignment}
$\quad \mathsf{true} \wedge \mathsf{false}$
$= \quad$ {$\mathsf{true} \wedge \mathsf{false} = \mathsf{false}$}
$\quad \mathsf{false}$

Similarly, one can show that $p(b) = \mathsf{false}$ and, consequently, that $p(a) \vee p(b) = \mathsf{false}$. It is also trivial to show that $p(a \vee b) = \mathsf{true}$. Therefore we conclude that the fourth property does not hold in general for nondeterministic programs; it actually holds as an implication

$$p(a) \vee p(b) \Rightarrow p(a \vee b)$$

The complete lattice *PredTran* includes predicate transformers useful for specification purposes; they are not implementable in general. Of the above properties, only monotonicity is satisfied by all the predicate transformers in *PredTran*: $\top$ trivially breaks the law of the excluded miracle; the fact that greatest lower bounds over arbitrary sets are allowed implies that the assumption of bounded nondeterminism (and therefore continuity) is not satisfied; and angelic nondeterminism violates the property of conjunctivity. Failure of conjunctivity can be illustrated by a similar example to that used to show failure of disjunctivity. For instance, let p, a and b be as follows:

$$p = (x := 2 \sqcup x := 3)$$
$$a = (x = 2)$$
$$b = (x = 3)$$

It is easy to show that, in this particular case, $p(a) \wedge p(b) = \mathsf{true}$ whereas $p(a \wedge b) = \mathsf{false}$; the proof is left as a simple exercise to the reader.

Of course, the healthiness conditions are still of fundamental importance; they are the criteria for distinguishing the implementable from the non-implementable in a general space of specifications.

2.5. Some Refinement Calculi

Back [3, 5], Morris [69] and Morgan [65, 66] have developed refinement calculi based on weakest preconditions. These calculi have the common purpose of formalising the well established *stepwise refinement* method for the systematic construction of programs from high-level specifications [90, 20].

As originally proposed, the stepwise refinement method is partly informal. Although specifications and programs are formal objects, the intermediate terms of a given derivation do not have a formal status. The essence of all the refinement calculi cited above is to extend a given procedural language (in particular, Dijkstra's guarded command language) with additional features for specification. For example, let $[a, c]$ be a specification construct used to describe a program that when executed in a state satisfying a, terminates in a state satisfying c. This can be viewed as a predicate transformer in just the same way as the other operators of the language. Its definition is given by

$$[a, c] \overset{def}{=} \lambda b \bullet a \wedge (c \Rightarrow b)$$

The extended language is thus a specification language and programs appear as a subclass of specifications. Programming is then viewed as constructing a sequence of specifications; the initial specification is in a high-level of abstraction (not usually implementable) and the final specification is an executable program. The derivation process is to gradually transform specifications into programs. The intermediate steps of the derivation will normally contain a mixture of specification and program constructs; but these are formal objects too, since specifications and programs are embedded in the same semantic framework.

Derivation requires the notion of a refinement relation between specifications. All the cited calculi use the same definition of the refinement relation which is precisely the ordering on the lattice of predicate transformers described above. Two mathematical properties of this ordering are of fundamental importance to model stepwise refinement. Monotonicity of the language operators with respect to this ordering is necessary to allow a given specification to be replaced by a refinement of it in an arbitrary context; this property is also known as *compositionality*. The other required property is transitivity: as the derivation process will normally entail a large number of steps, it is necessary to ensure that the final product (that is, the program) satisfies the original specification.

Rules for introducing programming constructs from given specifications are the additional tools required in the process. For example, the following rules illustrate the introduction of skip and sequential composition:

$$[a, c] \sqsubseteq \text{skip} \ \text{if} \ a \Rightarrow c$$
$$[a, c] \sqsubseteq [a, b]; \ [b, c]$$

There are also rules for manipulating specifications; for example, weakening the precondition of a given specification or strengthening its postcondition (or both) lead to a specification which refines the original one:

$$[a_1, c_1] \sqsubseteq [a_2, c_2] \ \text{if} \ a_1 \Rightarrow a_2 \wedge c_2 \Rightarrow c_1$$

Morris [69] was the first to give a lattice theoretic basis for a refinement calculus. He extended Dijkstra's guarded command language with predicate pairs (as illustrated above) and general recursion. Although he observed that the framework contains arbitrary least upper bounds and greatest lower bounds, these have not been incorporated into his specification language.

Back and von Wright [5] further explored the lattice approach and suggested a more powerful (infinitary) language which is complete in the sense that it can express every monotonic predicate transformer. The only constructors in their language are the lattice operators $\sqcap$ and $\sqcup$, together with functional composition (modelling sequential composition). From a very simple command language including these constructors, they define ordinary program constructs such as assignment, conditional and recursion. Inverses of programs are defined and used to formalise the notion of data refinement. This is further discussed in the next section.

Morgan's calculus [66] is perhaps the most appealing to practising programmers. His language includes procedures (possibly recursive and parametrised) and even modules. He defines a large number of refinement laws and illustrates their application in a wide range of derivations. The *specification statement*

$$x : [a, c]$$

is another distinctive feature of his work. Although it is similar to the notation used above, it includes the notion of a *frame*: x is a list of variables whose values may change. The frame reduces the number of possible refinements from a given specification, and is a way of making the designer's intention clearer. Furthermore, the above construct is very general and can be specialised for many useful purposes.

For example, our *generalised assignment* command can be regarded as a special case of it:

$$x :\in a \; = \; x : [\text{true}, a]$$

where the purpose is to establish a without changing any variables other than x. Another example is an *assumption* of a, meaning that a must be established without changing any variable:

$$a^\top \; = \; : [\text{true}, a]$$

In [66] this is called a *coercion*.

2.6. Data Refinement

In the previous section we discussed how an abstract specification is transformed into a program by progressively introducing control structures; this is known as *algorithmic* or *control* refinement. But this is only part of the process to obtain an implementation. Specifications are usually stated in terms of mathematical data types like sets and relations, and these are not normally available in procedural programming languages. Therefore the complementary step to *control* refinement is the transformation of the abstract types into concrete types such as arrays and records which can be efficiently implemented. This task is known as *data refinement*.

The idea of data refinement was first introduced by Hoare [47]. The basis of his approach is the use of an *abstraction function* to determine the abstract state that a given concrete state represents; in addition, the set of concrete states may be constrained by an *invariant* relation. Since then many approaches have been suggested which build on these ideas. The more recent approaches use a single relation to capture both the abstraction function and the invariant, thus relaxing the assumption that the abstract state is functionally dependent on the concrete state.

In connection with the refinement calculi considered in the previous section, two similar approaches have been suggested by Morris [71] and Morgan and Gardiner [67]. In both cases, data refinement is characterised as a special case of algorithmic refinement between *blocks*. A block of the form

$$\text{dec } x : Tx \bullet p$$

is used to represent the abstract program p operating on the variables x with type[1] Tx. Similarly,

$$\text{dec } x' : Tx' \bullet p'$$

represents the concrete program p' which operates on the variables x' with type Tx'. The data refinement is captured by the inequation

$$(\text{dec } x : Tx \bullet p) \sqsubseteq (\text{dec } x' : Tx' \bullet p')$$

---

[1] Recall that our language is untyped; types are considered here only for the purpose of the present discussion.

The general aim is to construct the concrete block by replacing the abstract local variables with the concrete ones, in such a way that the overall effect of the abstract block is preserved. In particular, p' is constructed with the same structure as p in the sense that each command in p' is the translation of a corresponding command in p, according to a uniform rule.

An essential ingredient to this strategy is an abstract invariant I which links the abstract variables x to the concrete variables x' This is called the *coupling invariant*. The need for this invariant is that a direct comparison of programs operating on different data spaces is not possible. For example, in the design of a compiler this invariant would establish the relationship between the data space of the source program and that of the target program. As exemplified in the previous chapter, the concrete representation of a variable y in the store M of our simple target machine is denoted by $\mathsf{M}[\Psi y]$, where Ψ is a symbol table which maps identifiers to their respective addresses in M. For a list of global variables $y_1, \ldots, y_n$ representing the state of the source program, the relevant coupling invariant would be

$$y_1 = \mathsf{M}[\Psi y_1] \wedge \ldots \wedge y_n = \mathsf{M}[\Psi y_n]$$

Additional examples of coupling invariants can be found, for example, in [66].

In this approach to data refinement, a new relation between programs is defined to express that program p' (operating on variables x') is a data refinement of program p (operating on variables x) under coupling invariant I. This is written $p \leq_{I,x,x'} p'$ and is formally defined by (considering programs as predicate transformers)

$$p \leq_{I,x,x'} p' \overset{def}{=} (\exists x \bullet I \wedge p(a)) \Rightarrow p'(\exists x \bullet I \wedge a) \quad \text{for all } a \text{ not containing } x'$$

Broadly, the antecedent requires that the initial values of the concrete variables couple to some set of abstract values for which the abstract program will succeed in establishing postcondition a; the consequent requires that the concrete program yields new concrete values that also couple to an acceptable abstract state.

To illustrate a simple example of data refinement, consider the coupling invariant given above which relates the data space of the source program to that of the target program. We can then show that the program

$$x := y$$

is data refined by the program

$$\mathsf{M} := \mathsf{M} \oplus \{\Psi x \mapsto \mathsf{M}[\Psi y]\}$$

Note that this captures the desired intention: the effect of the latter program is to update the memory M at position Ψx (the address of x) with $\mathsf{M}[\Psi y]$, the value stored in the memory cell with address Ψy (the address of y). More generally, we can prove that an arbitrary source program operating on the source variables is data refined by the corresponding target program which operates on M; see Rule 4.13 in Chapter 4.

This definition is chosen for two main reasons. The first is that it guarantees the characterisation of data refinement given above, that is

If $(p \leq_{I,x,x'} p')$ then $(\text{dec } x : Tx \bullet p) \sqsubseteq (\text{dec } x' : Tx' \bullet p')$

The second reason is that it distributes through the program constructors, thus allowing data refinement to be carried out piecewise. For example, the distribution through sequential composition is given by

If $(p \leq_{I,x,x'} p')$ and $(q \leq_{I,x,x'} q')$ then $(p;\ q) \leq_{I,x,x'} (p';\ q')$

Back and von Wright [5] suggest an approach which avoids the need to define a data refinement relation. They use the algorithmic refinement relation not only to characterise data refinement, but also to carry out the calculations. The basic idea is to introduce an *encoding program*, say ψ, which computes abstract states from concrete states and a *decoding program*, say ϕ, which computes concrete states from abstract states. Then, for a given abstract program p, the task is to find a concrete program p' such that

$$\psi;\ p;\ \phi \sqsubseteq p'$$

With the aid of specification features, it is possible to give very high-level definitions for ψ and ϕ. Using the same convention adopted above that x stands for the abstract variables, x' for the concrete variables and I for the coupling invariant, ψ is defined by

$$\psi \stackrel{def}{=} \text{var } x;\ x :\in^{\perp} I;\ \text{end } x'$$

It first introduces the abstract variables x and assigns them values such that the invariant is satisfied, and then removes the concrete variables from the data space. The use of $\perp$ as an annotation in the above generalised assignment command means that it aborts if I cannot be established. Similarly we have the definition of ϕ

$$\phi \stackrel{def}{=} \text{var } x';\ x' :\in^{\top} I;\ \text{end } x$$

which introduces the concrete variables x' and assigns them values such that the invariant is satisfied, and then removes the abstract variables from the data space. But in this case the generalised assignment command results in a miracle if I cannot be established. (The above two kinds of generalised assignment commands were introduced only for the purpose of the present discussion. Recall from the previous chapter that our language includes only the latter kind, and henceforth we will use the previous notation $x :\in b$, instead of $x :\in^{\top} b$.)

Note that having separate commands to introduce and end the scope of a variable is an essential feature to define the encoding and decoding programs: the first introduces x and ends the scope of x'; the second introduces x' and ends the scope of x.

In this approach, data refinement can also be performed piecewise, by proving distributivity properties such as

$$\psi; \ (p; \ q); \ \phi \sqsubseteq (\psi; \ p; \ \phi); \ (\psi; \ q; \ \phi)$$

which illustrates that both algorithmic and data refinement can be carried out within the framework of one common refinement relation.

2.7. Refinement and Compilation

As explained in the previous chapter, we regard compilation as a task of program refinement. In this sense, we can establish some connections between our view of compiler design and the more general task of deriving programs from specifications (henceforth we will refer to the latter simply as "derivation"). In both cases, a programming language is extended with specification features, so that a uniform framework is built and the interface between programs and specifications (when expressed by distinct formalisms) is avoided. In particular, our language is roughly the same as the one defined by Back and von Wright [5], except that we deal with procedures and parametrisation. The first three sections of this chapter briefly explained how the language can be embedded in a complete distributive lattice of predicate transformers.

In a derivation, the idea is to start with an arbitrary specification and end with a program formed solely from constructs which can be executed by computer. In our case, the initial object is an arbitrary source program and the final product is its normal form. But the tools used to achieve the goals in both cases are of identical nature: transformations leading to refinement in the sense already discussed.

Derivation entails two main tasks: control and data refinement. We also split the design of the compiler into these two main phases. However, while in a derivation control refinement is concerned with progressively introducing control structure in the specification, we do the reverse process; we reduce the nested control structure of a source program to the single flat iteration of the normal form program.

Regarding data refinement, the general idea is the same both in a derivation process and in designing a compiler: to replace abstract data types with concrete representations. In particular, we use the idea of encoding and decoding programs. As discussed in the previous section, this avoids the need to define a separate relation to carry out data refinement. In our case, an encoding program retrieves the abstract space of the source program from the concrete state representing the store of the machine. Conversely, a decoding program maps the abstract space to the concrete machine state. In the next chapter, the pair formed by an encoding and the respective decoding program is formally defined as a *simulation*. It satisfies the distributivity properties illustrated above, allowing data refinement to be carried out piecewise.

But, as should be expected, there are some differences between designing a compiler in this way and the more general task of deriving programs from specifications. For example, we are not interested in capturing requirements in general, and therefore our language includes no construct to serve this purpose. The closest to a specification statement we have in our language is the generalised assignment command. Our use of it is to abstract from the way control state is encoded in a particular target machine.

Another difference is that we are mostly concerned with program transformation. We need a wide range of laws relating the operators of the language. In particular, we follow the approach suggested by Hoare and others [55] where the semantics of a language is characterised by a set of equations and inequations (laws) relating the language operators. The same approach has been used to define an algebraic semantics for occam [81]. In our case, the set of laws must be complete in that it should allow us to reduce an arbitrary program to normal form. The framework we use is better characterised as a *refinement algebra* (rather than as a calculus).

CHAPTER 3

THE REASONING LANGUAGE

> If you are faced by a difficulty or a controversy in science,
> an ounce of algebra is worth a ton of verbal argument.
>
> — J.B.S. Haldane

Here we give meaning to our specification (reasoning) language in terms of equations and inequations (laws) relating the operators of the language. Following Hoare and others [55, 81], we present the laws as self-evident axioms, normally preceded by an informal (operational) justification. Moreover, it is not our aim to describe a complete set of laws in the logical sense, although they are complete in that they will allow us to reduce an arbitrary source program to a normal form.

Most of the algebraic laws are expressed as equations of the form $p = q$. Recalling from Section 1.2, this means that p and q have the same behaviour: the programs p and q may possibly consume different amount of resources (for example, memory) and run at different speeds, but regarding the task they perform it is impossible to distinguish between them. Therefore we can replace p with q (and vice versa) in any context. It is also possible to attach a boolean condition to a law, meaning that the law is guaranteed to hold only if the condition evaluates to **true**. Furthermore, the laws can be inequations (rather than equations) expressing refinement.

It is possible to select a small subset of our language and define the additional operators in terms of the more basic ones. This is shown in [53], where the only constructors are sequential composition, angelic nondeterminism ($\sqcup$) and demonic nondeterminism ($\sqcap$). The additional operators are defined in terms of these and the primitive commands. The laws of derived operators can then be proved from their definition and the laws of the basic operators.

This is not our concern here; our emphasis is on the algebraic laws which will be used in the process of designing a compiler. However, we do illustrate how a few operators can be defined from others. In particular, iteration is defined as a special case of recursion and all the laws about iteration are proved. They deserve such special attention because of their central role in the proofs of the normal form reduction theorems.

Another concern is the correctness of the laws of the basic operators. To achieve this we need to link the algebraic semantics of the language with a suitable mathematical model in which the basic operators can be defined and their laws verified. In the final section of this chapter, we further discuss this issue and argue that the existence of nontrivial models for the reasoning language shows that its algebraic laws are in some sense consistent.

As explained in Section 2.5, both the programming and the specification operators of the reasoning language have the same status in that they can be viewed as predicate transformers. In this uniform framework, there is no need to distinguish between programs and specifications. We will refer to both of them as "programs" Another remark is that programs have both a syntactic and a semantic existence. On one hand we perform syntactic operations on them, such as substitution. On the other hand, the algebraic laws relating language operators express semantic properties. Strictly, we should distinguish between these two natures of programs. But it is not convenient to do so and it will be clear from the context which view we are taking.

The first section gives notational conventions and introduces the concepts of substitution and free and bound identifiers. Each of the subsequent sections describes the laws of one or more language operators. The concepts of a refinement relation, approximate inverse (Galois connection) and simulation will be introduced when the need arises. The final section describes alternative ways in which the laws of the basic operators could be verified. As an example, we take the view of programs as predicate transformers (as discussed in the previous chapter) and illustrate how the laws can be proved.

3.1. Concepts and Notation

Name conventions

It is helpful to define some conventions as regards the names used to denote program terms:

$$X, Y, Z \quad \text{variables denoting programs}$$
$$p, q, r \quad \text{arbitrary but given programs}$$
$$x, y, z \quad \text{lists of variables}$$
$$a, b, c \quad \text{boolean expressions}$$
$$e, f, g \quad \text{lists of expressions}$$

We also use subscripts in addition to the above conventions. For example, $b_0, b_1, \ldots$ stand for boolean expressions (also referred to as conditions). We use comma for list concatenation: x, y stands for the concatenation of lists x and y. Further conventions are explained when necessary.

Precedence rules

In order to reduce the number of brackets around program terms, we define the following precedence rules. Operators with the same precedence appear on the same line. As usual, we will assume that brackets bind tighter than any operator. Procedures are dealt with in Chapter 5 and are assumed to have the same precedence as μ.

uop	unary operators	**binds tightest**
bop	binary operators	
,	list concatenation	
$:\in$ and $:=$	(generalised) assignment	
$\rightarrow$	guarded command	
$*$	iteration	
;	sequential composition	
⊔ and ⊓	nondeterminism (angelic and demonic)	
◁ ▷	conditional	
μ	recursion	
dec	block with local declarations	**binds loosest**

Free and bound identifiers

An occurrence of a variable x in a program p is *bound* (or *local*) if it is in the scope of a static declaration of x in p, and *free* (or *global*) otherwise. For example, x is bound in $\text{dec}\,x \bullet x := y$, but free in $x := y$. Notice that the commands for dynamic declaration are not *binders* for variables. For example, x is free in $\text{var}\,x$ as well as in $\text{end}\,x$. A list of variables is free in p if each variable in the list is free in p; similarly, a list of variables is bound in p if each variable in the list is bound in p.

In the case of program identifiers, we say that an occurrence of X is free in a program p if it is not in the scope of any recursive program (with name X) defined in p, and bound otherwise.

Substitution

For variables x and y,

$$p[x \leftarrow y]$$

denotes the result of substituting y for every free occurrence of x in p. It is possible for x to be in the scope of (static) declarations of variables with the same name as y. In this case, a systematic renaming of local variables of p occurs in order to avoid variable *capture*. This is usually referred to as *safe* substitution.

If x and y are (equal-length) lists of variables, the substitution is positional. In this case, no variable may appear more than once in the list x.

Similarly,

$$f[x \leftarrow e]$$

denotes the substitution of the list of expressions e for the (equal-length) list of variables x in the list of expressions f.

We also allow the substitution of programs for program identifiers:

$$p[X \leftarrow q]$$

This avoids capture of any free identifiers of q by renaming local declarations in p, as discussed above. For conciseness, we will sometimes avoid writing substitutions of the latter kind by making (free) occurrences of X explicit, as in $F(X)$. Then, the substitution of q for X in this case is written $F(q)$. In any case we assume that no capture of free identifiers occur.

Laws, definitions, lemmas, theorems and proofs

Each of the laws described in the following sections is given a number and a name suggestive of its use. The number is prefixed with the corresponding section number, in order to ease further references. The name normally mentions the operators related by the law. For example,

$\langle ; - \mathsf{skip} \text{ unit} \rangle$

is the name associated with the law which says that **skip** is the unit of sequential composition. Every reference to a law comprises both its name and its number. Each of the definitions, lemmas and theorems is also given a number and a name for further references.

Some of the laws could be alternatively described as lemmas or theorems, as they are provable from more basic ones. Most of the derived laws are presented with their proofs, but in any case we always make it clear whether a given law can be derived.

Our proofs are confined to reasoning with conditional (in)equations. We use the terms *LHS* and *RHS* to refer to the left- and the right-hand sides of an (in)equation. The proof strategy is to start with one of the sides and try to reach the other side by a series of algebraic transformations. Each step is annotated with one or more references to laws, definitions, lemmas or theorems.

Each proof is essentially a program transformation activity. We assume that the program being transformed is (syntactically) valid to start with. Then application of most of the laws will always produce valid programs. Nevertheless, some of the laws (for example, see laws 3.3.2, 3.14.4 and 3.15.1) contain free variables on their left-hand sides which do not appear on their right-hand sides. Therefore the reverse (right to left) application of these equations requires the user to provide an explicit instantiation (binding) of these free variables; in these circumstances, care must be taken in order to avoid transforming a valid program into one that is not even syntactically well-formed. One advantage of mechanising the transformations (as we do in Chapter 6) is that one can ensure that this problem will not arise. In our case this is actually simplified by the fact that we do not deal with context information like types. Even undeclared variables can be introduced during the transformations; these variables are considered to be global.

3.2. Skip, Abort and Miracle

The **skip** command has no effect and always terminates successfully.

The *abort* command, denoted by $\bot$, is the most unpredictable of all programs. It may fail to terminate or it may terminate with any result whatsoever. Thus $\bot$ represents the behaviour of a broken machine, or a program that has run wild. As explained in Section 1.2, we identify abort with all programs that might diverge before doing any action visible to its environment. The motivation for this choice is that, in principle, a program which is continuously allowed to diverge can be considered a programming error, since one can never rely on it. This is formalised in Section 3.6 where we state that every program is a refinement of $\bot$. For example, the replacement of $\bot$ with an assignment such as $x := 1$ is an improvement in the sense we have already discussed: while the behaviour of the former is totally arbitrary, the latter always terminates with an expected result.

The *miracle* command, denoted by $\top$, is the other extreme: it can be used to serve any purpose (more formally, it refines every program). But it is *infeasible* in that it cannot be implemented; otherwise we would not need to write programs—$\top$ would do anything for us. We use $\top$ as a theoretical concept which turns out to be useful for reasoning.

The laws governing these primitive commands are included in the remaining sections. This is because each of these laws normally expresses a unit or zero property of one language operator.

3.3. Sequential Composition

The program $p;\ q$ denotes the usual sequential composition of programs p and q. If the execution of p terminates successfully then the execution of q follows that of p.

Since the execution of skip always terminates and leaves everything unchanged, to precede or follow a program p by skip does not change the effect of p. In other words, skip is both the left and the right unit of sequential composition.

Law 3.3.1. $(\text{skip};\ p)\ =\ p\ =\ (p;\ \text{skip})$ $\langle;-\text{skip unit}\rangle$

To specify the execution of a program p after the termination of $\bot$ cannot redeem the situation, because $\bot$ cannot be relied on to terminate. More precisely, $\bot$ is a left zero of sequential composition.

Law 3.3.2. $\bot;\ p\ =\ \bot$ $\langle;-\bot \text{ left zero}\rangle$

To precede a program p by $\top$ results in a miracle; $\top$ is a left zero of sequential composition.

Law 3.3.3. $\top;\ p\ =\ \top$ $\langle;-\top \text{ left zero}\rangle$

Sequential composition is associative.

Law 3.3.4. $(p;\ q);\ r\ =\ p;\ (q;\ r)$ $\langle;\text{ assoc}\rangle$

3.4. Demonic Nondeterminism

The program $p \sqcap q$ denotes the demonic choice of programs p and q: either p or q is selected, the choice being totally arbitrary.

The abort command already allows completely arbitrary behaviour, so an offer of further choice makes no difference to it.

Law 3.4.1. $p \sqcap \bot = \bot$ ⟨$\sqcap - \bot$ zero⟩

On the other hand, the miracle command offers no choice at all.

Law 3.4.2. $p \sqcap \top = p$ ⟨$\sqcap - \top$ unit⟩

When the two alternatives are the same program, the choice becomes vacuous—$\sqcap$ is idempotent.

Law 3.4.3. $p \sqcap p = p$ ⟨$\sqcap$ idemp⟩

The order in which a choice is offered is immaterial—$\sqcap$ is symmetric.

Law 3.4.4. $p \sqcap q = q \sqcap p$ ⟨$\sqcap$ sym⟩

Demonic choice is associative.

Law 3.4.5. $(p \sqcap q) \sqcap r = p \sqcap (q \sqcap r)$ ⟨$\sqcap$ assoc⟩

3.5. Angelic Nondeterminism

The angelic choice of two programs p and q is denoted by $p \sqcup q$. Informally, it is a program that may act like p or q, whichever is more suitable in a given context.

As we have mentioned before, $\bot$ is totally unpredictable and therefore the least suitable program for all purposes.

Law 3.5.1. $\bot \sqcup p = p$ ⟨$\sqcup - \bot$ unit⟩

At the other extreme, $\top$ suits any situation.

Law 3.5.2. $\top \sqcup p = \top$ ⟨$\sqcup - \top$ zero⟩

Like $\sqcap$, angelic choice $\sqcup$ is idempotent, symmetric and associative.

Law 3.5.3. $p \sqcup p = p$ ⟨$\sqcup$ idemp⟩

Law 3.5.4. $p \sqcup q = q \sqcup p$ ⟨$\sqcup$ sym⟩

Law 3.5.5. $(p \sqcup q) \sqcup r = p \sqcup (q \sqcup r)$ ⟨$\sqcup$ assoc⟩

3.6. The Ordering Relation

Here we define the ordering relation $\sqsubseteq$ on programs: $p \sqsubseteq q$ holds whenever the program q is at least as deterministic as p or, alternatively, whenever q offers only a subset of the choices offered by p. In this case, q is at least as predictable as p. This coincides with the meaning we adopt for *refinement*. Thus $p \sqsubseteq q$ can be read as "p is refined by q" or "p is worse than q"

We define $\sqsubseteq$ in terms of $\sqcap$. Informally, if the demonic choice of p and q always yields p, one can be sure that p is worse than q in all situations.

Definition 3.1. (The ordering relation)

$$p \sqsubseteq q \overset{def}{=} (p \sqcap q) = p$$

$\diamond$

In the final section we prove that this ordering coincides with the ordering on the lattice of predicate transformers described in the previous chapter.

Alternatively, the ordering relation could have been defined in terms of $\sqcup$.

Law 3.6.1. $p \sqsubseteq q \equiv (p \sqcup q) = q$ $\langle \sqsubseteq - \sqcup \rangle$

From Definition 3.1 and the laws of $\sqcap$, we conclude that $\sqsubseteq$ is a partial ordering on programs:

Law 3.6.2. $p \sqsubseteq p$ $\langle \sqsubseteq \text{ reflexivity} \rangle$

Law 3.6.3. $(p \sqsubseteq q) \wedge (q \sqsubseteq p) \Rightarrow (p = q)$ $\langle \sqsubseteq \text{ antisymmetry} \rangle$

Law 3.6.4. $(p \sqsubseteq q) \wedge (q \sqsubseteq r) \Rightarrow (p \sqsubseteq r)$ $\langle \sqsubseteq \text{ transitivity} \rangle$

Moreover $\sqsubseteq$ is a lattice ordering. The bottom and top elements are $\bot$ and $\top$, respectively; the *meet (greatest lower bound)* and *join (least upper bound)* operators are $\sqcap$ and $\sqcup$, in this order. These are also consequences of the definition of $\sqsubseteq$ and the laws of $\sqcap$ and $\sqcup$.

Law 3.6.5. $\bot \sqsubseteq p$ $\langle \sqsubseteq - \bot \text{ bottom} \rangle$

Law 3.6.6. $p \sqsubseteq \top$ $\langle \sqsubseteq - \top \text{ top} \rangle$

Law 3.6.7. $(r \sqsubseteq p \wedge r \sqsubseteq q) \equiv r \sqsubseteq (p \sqcap q)$ $\langle \sqsubseteq - \sqcap \text{ glb} \rangle$

Law 3.6.8. $(p \sqsubseteq r) \wedge (q \sqsubseteq r) \equiv (p \sqcup q) \sqsubseteq r$ $\langle \sqsubseteq - \sqcup \text{ lub} \rangle$

In order to be able to use the algebraic laws to transform subcomponents of compound programs, it is crucial that $p \sqsubseteq q$ imply $F(p) \sqsubseteq F(q)$, for all *contexts* F (functions from programs to programs). This is equivalent to saying that F (and consequently, all the operators of our language) must be *monotonic* with respect to $\sqsubseteq$. For example:

Law 3.6.9. If $p \sqsubseteq q$ then
(1) $(p \sqcap r) \sqsubseteq (q \sqcap r)$ $\langle \sqcap \text{ monotonic} \rangle$
(2) $(r; p) \sqsubseteq (r; q)$ and $(p; r) \sqsubseteq (q; r)$ $\langle ; \text{ monotonic} \rangle$

We will not state monotonicity laws explicitly for the remaining operators of our language.

3.7. Unbounded Nondeterminism

Here we generalise the operators $\sqcap$ and $\sqcup$ to take an arbitrary set of programs, say $\mathcal{P}$, as argument. $\sqcup\,\mathcal{P}$ denotes the least upper bound of $\mathcal{P}$; its definition is given below.

Definition 3.2. (Least upper bound)

$$(\sqcup\,\mathcal{P} \sqsubseteq p) \;\equiv\; (\forall X \mid X \in \mathcal{P} \bullet X \sqsubseteq p)$$

$\diamond$

The above definition states that p refines the least upper bound of the set $\mathcal{P}$ if and only if, for all X in $\mathcal{P}$, p refines X.

The greatest lower bound of $\mathcal{P}$, denoted by $\sqcap\,\mathcal{P}$, is defined in a similar way.

Definition 3.3. (Greatest lower bound)

$$(p \sqsubseteq \sqcap\,\mathcal{P}) \;\equiv\; (\forall X \mid X \in \mathcal{P} \bullet p \sqsubseteq X)$$

$\diamond$

Let $\mathcal{U}$ be the set of all programs, and $\emptyset$ be the empty set. Then we have:

$$\sqcup\,\emptyset = \bot = \sqcap\,\mathcal{U}$$
$$\sqcap\,\emptyset = \top = \sqcup\,\mathcal{U}$$

From the above we can easily show that sequential composition does not distribute rightward through the least upper bound or the greatest lower bound in general, since we have:

$$\bot; \sqcap\,\emptyset = \bot \neq \sqcap\,\emptyset$$
$$\top; \sqcup\,\emptyset = \top \neq \sqcup\,\emptyset$$

The rightward distribution of sequential composition through these operators is used below to define Dijkstra's healthiness conditions. However, the leftward distribution is valid in general, and can be verified by considering programs as predicate transformers. In the following, the notation $\{X \mid b \bullet F(X)\}$ should be read as: the set of elements $F(X)$ for all X in the range specified by b.

Law 3.7.1.
(1) $\sqcup\,\mathcal{P}; \; p \;=\; \sqcup\{X \mid X \in \mathcal{P} \bullet (X; \, p)\}$ $\langle;-\sqcup \text{ left dist}\rangle$
(2) $\sqcap\,\mathcal{P}; \; p \;=\; \sqcap\{X \mid X \in \mathcal{P} \bullet (X; \, p)\}$ $\langle;-\sqcap \text{ left dist}\rangle$

It is also possible to verify that the lattice of programs (considered as predicate transformers) is distributive.

Law 3.7.2.
(1) $(\sqcup\,\mathcal{P}) \sqcap p \;=\; \sqcup\{X \mid X \in \mathcal{P} \bullet (X \sqcap p)\}$ $\langle\sqcap-\sqcup \text{ dist}\rangle$
(2) $(\sqcap\,\mathcal{P}) \sqcup p \;=\; \sqcap\{X \mid X \in \mathcal{P} \bullet (X \sqcup p)\}$ $\langle\sqcup-\sqcap \text{ dist}\rangle$

As discussed in the previous chapter, among all the predicate transformers Dijkstra singles out the implementable ones by certain healthiness conditions. Here we formulate these conditions as equations relating operators of our language.

1. $p; \perp = \perp$ p is non-miraculous
2. $p; \sqcap \mathcal{P} = \sqcap \{X \mid X \in \mathcal{P} \bullet (p; X)\}$ p is conjunctive
   for all (non-empty) sets of programs $\mathcal{P}$
3. $p; \sqcup \mathcal{P} = \sqcup \{X \mid X \in \mathcal{P} \bullet (p; X)\}$ p is disjunctive
   for all (non-empty) sets of programs $\mathcal{P}$
4. $p; \sqcup \{i \mid i \geq 0 \bullet q_i\} = \sqcup \{i \mid i \geq 0 \bullet p; q_i\}$ p is continuous
   provided $q_i \sqsubseteq q_{i+1}$ for all $i \geq 0$

We say that a program p is *universally* conjunctive if the second equation above holds for all sets of programs $\mathcal{P}$ (possibly empty). Similarly, if the third equation holds for all $\mathcal{P}$, we say that p is universally disjunctive.

3.8. Recursion

Let X stand for the name of the recursive program we wish to construct, and let $F(X)$ define the intended behaviour of the program, for a given context F. If F is defined solely in terms of the notations introduced already, it follows by structural induction that F is monotonic:

$$p \sqsubseteq q \Rightarrow F(p) \sqsubseteq F(q)$$

Actually, this will remain true for the commands which will be introduced later, since they are all monotonic.

The following two properties, due to Knaster-Tarski [85], say that $\mu X \bullet F(X)$ is a solution of the equation $X = F(X)$; furthermore, it is the least solution.

Law 3.8.1. $\mu X \bullet F(X) = F(\mu X \bullet F(X))$ $\langle \mu$ fixed point$\rangle$

Law 3.8.2. $F(Y) \sqsubseteq Y \Rightarrow \mu X \bullet F(X) \sqsubseteq Y$ $\langle \mu$ least fixed point$\rangle$

3.9. Approximate Inverses

Let F and G be functions on programs such that, for all programs X and Y

$$F(X) = Y \equiv X = G(Y)$$

Then G is the inverse of F, and vice-versa. Therefore $G(F(X)) = X = F(G(X))$, for all X. It is well-known, however, that a function has an inverse if and only if it is bijective. As the set of bijective functions is relatively small this makes the notion of inverse rather limited. The standard approach is to generalise the notion of inverse functions as follows.

Definition 3.4. (Approximate inverses)

Let F and F^{-1} be functions on programs such that, for all X and Y

$$F(X) \sqsubseteq Y \;\;\equiv\;\; X \sqsubseteq F^{-1}(Y)$$

Then we call F the *weakest inverse* of F^{-1}, and F^{-1} the *strongest inverse* of F. The pair (F, F^{-1}) is called a *Galois connection*. $\Diamond$

Weakest inverses have been used in [55, 52] for top-down design of programs. In particular, the left and right weakest inverses of sequential composition are defined together with a calculus of program development. Broadly, the aim is to decompose a task (specification) r into two subtasks p and q, such that

$$r \sqsubseteq p; q$$

The method described in [52] allows one to calculate the *weakest* specification that must be satisfied by one of the components p or q when the other one is known. For example, one can calculate the weakest specification of p from q and r. It is denoted by $q\backslash r$ and satisfies $r \sqsubseteq (q\backslash r); q$. This is called the *weakest prespecification*. Dually, r/p is the weakest specification of component q satisfying $r \sqsubseteq p; (r/p)$. It is named the *weakest postspecification*.

Strongest inverses of language constructs are less commonly used. This is perhaps a consequence of the fact that they exist only for operators which are *universally disjunctive* (see theorem below). Gardiner and Pandya [26] have suggested a method to reason about recursion based on the notion of strongest inverses, which they call *weak-op-inverses*. Below we list some of the properties of strongest inverses that are proved in the cited paper. A similar treatment is given in [53].

Before presenting the properties of strongest inverses we review two basic definitions. F is *universally conjunctive* if for all (possibly empty) sets $\mathcal{P}$

$$F(\sqcap \mathcal{P}) = \sqcap\{X \mid X \in \mathcal{P} \bullet F(X)\}$$

Similarly, F is *universally disjunctive* if for all (possibly empty) sets $\mathcal{P}$

$$F(\sqcup \mathcal{P}) = \sqcup\{X \mid X \in \mathcal{P} \bullet F(X)\}$$

Theorem 3.1. (Strongest inverses)

(**1**) If F^{-1} exists then both F and F^{-1} are monotonic.

(**2**) F^{-1} is unique if it exists.

(**3**) If F^{-1} exists then, for all programs X,

$$F(F^{-1}(X)) \sqsubseteq X \sqsubseteq F^{-1}(F(X))$$

(**4**) F^{-1} exists if and only if F is universally disjunctive; in this case it is defined by

$$F^{-1}(Y) \stackrel{def}{=} \sqcup\{X \mid F(X) \sqsubseteq Y \bullet X\}$$

(**5**) F^{-1} is universally conjunctive if it exists. $\Diamond$

The following lemma shows that sequential composition has a strongest inverse in its first argument. As noted in [26] this allows a concise proof (given later in this chapter) of an important property about composition of iteration commands.

Lemma 3.1. (Strongest inverse of ;)
Let

$$F(X) \stackrel{def}{=} (X; \; p)$$

Then F has a strongest inverse which we denote by

$$F^{-1}(X) \stackrel{def}{=} X \overset{\sqcup}{;} p$$

Furthermore, for all X,

$$(X \overset{\sqcup}{;} p); \; p \sqsubseteq p$$

Proof: From Law $\langle; -\sqcup$ left dist$\rangle$(3.7.1) it follows that F is disjunctive. Consequently, from Theorem 3.1(4), it has a strongest inverse. The inequation follows from Theorem 3.1(3). $\Diamond$

3.10. Simulation

In the previous section we discussed the inverse of functions on programs. Here we consider the inverse of programs themselves. An inverse of a program S is a program T that satisfies

$$S; \; T \; = \; \mathsf{skip} \; = \; T; \; S$$

That means that running S followed by T or T followed by S is the same as not running any program at all, since **skip** has no effect whatsoever.

Inversion of programs has been previously discussed by Dijkstra [22] and Gries [37]. A more formal approach to program inversion is given in [15], which defines proof rules for inverting programs written in Dijkstra's language. A common feature of these works is the use of the notion of *exact* inverse given above. As mentioned for functions, this notion of inverse is rather limited. Following a similar idea to that of the previous section, we adopt a weaker definition of program inversion.

Definition 3.5. (Simulation)
Let S and S^{-1} be programs such that

$$(S; \; S^{-1}) \sqsubseteq \mathsf{skip} \sqsubseteq (S^{-1}; \; S)$$

Then the pair (S, S^{-1}) is called a *simulation*, S^{-1} is the *strongest inverse* of S, whereas S is the *weakest inverse* of S^{-1}. $\Diamond$

A very simple example of a simulation is the pair $(\perp, \top)$ since

$$(\perp; \top) = \perp \sqsubseteq \text{skip} \sqsubseteq \top = (\top; \perp)$$

For further examples of simulation see Laws 3.11.10 and 3.19.6.

Simulations are useful for calculation in general. When carrying out program transformation, it is not rare to reach situations where a program followed by its inverse (that is, S; S^{-1} or S^{-1}; S) appears as a subterm of the program being transformed. Thus, from the definition of simulation, it is possible to eliminate subterms of the above form by replacing them with **skip** (of course, this is only valid for inequational reasoning). This will be illustrated in many of the proofs in the next two chapters where we give further examples of simulations.

But the most valuable use that has been made of the concept of simulation is for data refinement. This was discussed in some detail in the previous chapter where we introduced the concepts of *encoding* and *decoding* programs which form a simulation pair. The distributivity properties of simulations given below are particularly useful to prove the correctness of the change of data representation phase of the compilation process, where the abstract space of the source program is replaced by the concrete state of the target machine. The appropriate encoding and decoding programs will be defined when the need arises.

A detailed discussion on simulations can be found in [5] (where it is called *inverse commands*) and in [53]. Here we present some of the properties of simulation. As should be expected, these are similar to the ones given in the previous section.

Theorem 3.2. (Simulation)
Let S be a program. The following properties hold:
(1) S^{-1} is unique if it exists.
(2) S^{-1} exists if and only if S is universally disjunctive.
(3) S^{-1} is universally conjunctive if it exists.   ◇

We define the following abbreviations.

Definition 3.6. (Simulation functions)
Let (S, S^{-1}) be a simulation. We use S and S^{-1} themselves as functions defined by

$$S(X) \stackrel{def}{=} S; X; S^{-1}$$
$$S^{-1}(X) \stackrel{def}{=} S^{-1}; X; S$$

◇

The next theorem shows that the concepts of simulation and approximate inverse are closely related.

Theorem 3.3. (Lift of simulation)
Let S and S^{-1} be simulation functions as defined above. Then S^{-1} is the strongest inverse of S. Furthermore, from Theorem 3.1 (Strongest inverses) we have

$$S(S^{-1}(X)) \sqsubseteq X \sqsubseteq S^{-1}(S(X))$$

◇

The following theorem shows how simulation functions distribute through all the language operators introduced so far, with a possible improvement in the distributed result.

Theorem 3.4.   (Distributivity of simulation functions)
(1) $S(\bot) = \bot$
(2) $S(\top) \sqsubseteq \top$
(3) $S(\mathsf{skip}) \sqsubseteq \mathsf{skip}$
(4) $S(X;\ Y) \sqsubseteq S(X);\ S(Y)$
(5) $S(\sqcap \mathcal{P}) \sqsubseteq \sqcap \{X \mid X \in \mathcal{P} \bullet S(X)\}$
(6) $S(\sqcup \mathcal{P}) = \sqcup \{X \mid X \in \mathcal{P} \bullet S(X)\}$
(7) $S(\mu\ X \bullet F(X)) \sqsubseteq \mu\ X \bullet S(F(S^{-1}(X)))$ $\diamond$

3.11. Assumption and Assertion

The assumption of a condition b, designated as $b^{\top}$, can be regarded as a miraculous test: it leaves the state unchanged (behaving like **skip**) if b is **true**; otherwise it behaves like $\top$. The assertion of b, $b_{\bot}$, also behaves like **skip** when b is true; otherwise it fails, behaving like $\bot$.

We assume that the evaluation of an expression always delivers a result. Clearly, for boolean expressions this is either **true** or **false**. While this decision considerably simplifies our algebraic system, it is worth pointing out that there are no theoretical limitations which prevent one from dealing with undefined expressions. One solution to this problem is presented in [55], where the algebraic laws hold even in circumstances in which unsuccessful evaluation of an expression (for instance, division by zero) occurs.

The intended purpose of assumptions and assertions is to give *preconditions* and *postconditions*, respectively, the status of programs. For example,

$$a^{\top};\ p;\ b_{\bot}$$

is used to express the fact that the assumption of a is an obligation placed on the environment of the program p. If the environment fails to provide a state satisfying a, $a^{\top}$ behaves like a miracle; this saves the programmer from dealing with states not satisfying a, since no program can implement $\top$. On the other hand, an assertion is an obligation placed on the program itself. If p fails to make b true on its completion, it ends up behaving like abort.

The first three laws formally state that the assumption and the assertion of a true condition are equivalent to **skip**, that the assumption of a false condition leads to miracle and that the assertion of a false condition leads to abortion.

Law 3.11.1. $\mathsf{true}^{\top} = \mathsf{true}_{\bot} = \mathsf{skip}$ $\langle b^{\top}, b_{\bot}\ \text{true cond}\rangle$

Law 3.11.2. $\mathsf{false}^{\top} = \top$ $\langle b^{\top}\ \text{false cond}\rangle$

Law 3.11.3. $\mathsf{false}_{\bot} = \bot$ $\langle b_{\bot}\ \text{false cond}\rangle$

Two consecutive assumptions can be combined, giving rise to an assumption of the conjunction of the original conditions; this obviously means that if any of the conditions is not satisfied, the result will be miraculous. An analogous law holds for assertions.

Law 3.11.4. $(a^\top; \, b^\top) \; = \; (a \wedge b)^\top \; = \; (a^\top \sqcup b^\top)$ $\qquad\qquad$ ⟨$b^\top$ conjunction⟩

Law 3.11.5. $(a_\perp; \, b_\perp) \; = \; (a \wedge b)_\perp \; = \; (a_\perp \sqcap b_\perp)$ $\qquad\qquad$ ⟨$b_\perp$ conjunction⟩

The assumption of the disjunction of two conditions will behave like a miracle if and only if none of the conditions are satisfied. There is a similar law for assertions.

Law 3.11.6. $(a \vee b)^\top \; = \; (a^\top \sqcap b^\top)$ $\qquad\qquad$ ⟨$b^\top$ disjunction⟩

Law 3.11.7. $(a \vee b)_\perp \; = \; (a_\perp \sqcup b_\perp)$ $\qquad\qquad$ ⟨$b_\perp$ disjunction⟩

It does not matter if a choice is made before or after an assumption (or an assertion) is executed.

Law 3.11.8. $b^\top; \, (p \sqcap q) \; = \; (b^\top; \, p) \sqcap (b^\top; \, q)$ $\qquad\qquad$ ⟨$b^\top - \sqcap$ dist⟩

Law 3.11.9. $b_\perp; \, (p \sqcap q) \; = \; (b_\perp; \, p) \sqcap (b_\perp; \, q)$ $\qquad\qquad$ ⟨$b_\perp - \sqcap$ dist⟩

The next law states that $(b_\perp, \, b^\top)$ is a simulation.

Law 3.11.10. $(b_\perp; \, b^\top) \; = \; b_\perp \sqsubseteq \mathsf{skip} \sqsubseteq b^\top \; = \; (b^\top; \, b_\perp)$

$\qquad\qquad\qquad\qquad\qquad\qquad\qquad\qquad\qquad$ ⟨$b_\perp - b^\top$ simulation⟩

An assumption commutes with an arbitrary program p in the following sense. (A similar law holds for assertions, but we do not need it here.)

Law 3.11.11. If the free variables of b are not assigned by p
$(p; \, b^\top) \sqsubseteq (b^\top; \, p)$ $\qquad\qquad\qquad\qquad\qquad\qquad\qquad$ ⟨$b^\top; \, p$ commute⟩

The inequality occurs when b is false and p is $\perp$, in which case the left-hand side reduces to $\perp$ whereas the right-hand side reduces to $\top$.

3.12. Guarded Command

The standard notation $b \to p$ stands for a guarded command. If the guard b is true, the whole command behaves like p; otherwise it behaves like $\top$. This suggests that a guard has the same effect as an assumption of the given condition, which allows us to define a guarded command as follows.

Definition 3.7. (Guarded command)

$$b \to p \; \overset{def}{=} \; b^\top; \, p$$

$\diamondsuit$

The laws of guarded commands can therefore be proved from the above definition and the laws of sequential composition and assumptions.

Law 3.12.1. $(\text{true} \to p) = p$ $\langle \to$ true guard$\rangle$

Law 3.12.2. $(\text{false} \to p) = \top$ $\langle \to$ false guard$\rangle$

Guards can be unnested by taking their conjunction.

Law 3.12.3. $a \to (b \to p) = (a \wedge b) \to p$ $\langle \to$ guard conjunction$\rangle$

Guards distribute over $\sqcap$.

Law 3.12.4. $b \to (p \sqcap q) = (b \to p) \sqcap (b \to q)$ $\langle$ guard $- \sqcap$ dist$\rangle$

The demonic choice of guarded commands can be written as a single guarded command by taking the disjunction of their guards. This is easily derived from the last two laws.

Law 3.12.5. $(a \to p \sqcap b \to q) = (a \vee b) \to (a \to p \sqcap b \to q)$

$\langle \to$ guard disjunction1$\rangle$

Proof:

$$
\begin{aligned}
&\quad RHS \\
&= \quad \{\langle \text{guard} - \sqcap \text{ dist}\rangle(3.12.4)\} \\
&\quad (a \vee b) \to (a \to p) \sqcap (a \vee b) \to (b \to q) \\
&= \quad \{\langle \to \text{ guard conjunction}\rangle(3.12.3)\} \\
&\quad LHS
\end{aligned}
$$

$\diamond$

When p and q above are the same program, we have:

Law 3.12.6. $(a \to p \sqcap b \to p) = (a \vee b) \to p$ $\langle \to$ guard disjunction2$\rangle$

Surprisingly, perhaps, this law is not a consequence of the previous one.

Sequential composition distributes leftward through guarded commands.

Law 3.12.7. $(b \to p); q = b \to (p; q)$ $\langle ; - \to$ left dist$\rangle$

3.13. Guarded Command Set

Our main use of guarded commands is to model the possible actions of a deterministic executing mechanism. The fact that the mechanism can perform one of n actions, according to its current state, can be modelled by a program fragment of the form

$$b_1 \to action_1 \sqcap \ldots \sqcap b_n \to action_n$$

provided $b_1, \ldots, b_n$ are pairwise disjoint. Instead of mentioning this disjointness condition explicitly, we will write the above as

$$b_1 \to action_1 \square \ldots \square b_n \to action_n$$

and will call it a guarded command set. Strictly, $\square$ is not a new operator of our language. It is just syntactic sugar to improve conciseness and readability. Any theorem that uses $\square$ can be readily restated in terms of $\sqcap$ with the associated disjointness conditions. As an example we have the following law.

If a guarded command set has the same guard as a command in this set, then the guarded set behaves the same as the command with this guard.

Law 3.13.1. $a \to (a \to p \square b \to q) = a \to p$ $\langle \square$ elim$\rangle$
Proof: The proof relies on the (implicit) assumption that a and b are disjoint (or $a \wedge b = \mathsf{false}$).

$$a \to (a \to p \sqcap b \to q)$$
$$= \quad \{\langle \text{guard} - \sqcap \text{ dist}\rangle(3.12.4)\}$$
$$a \to (a \to p) \sqcap a \to (b \to q)$$
$$= \quad \{\langle \to \text{ guard conjunction}\rangle(3.12.3) \text{ and } (a \wedge b = \mathsf{false})\}$$
$$a \to p \sqcap \mathsf{false} \to q$$
$$= \quad \{\langle \to \text{ false guard}\rangle(3.12.2) \text{ and } \langle \sqcap - \top \text{ unit}\rangle(3.4.2)\}$$
$$a \to p$$

$\diamondsuit$

Other laws and theorems involving $\square$ will be described as the need arises.

3.14. Conditional

A conditional command has the general syntax $p \vartriangleleft b \vartriangleright q$ which is a concise form of the more usual notation

if b then p else q

It can also be defined in terms of more basic operators.

Definition 3.8. (Conditional)

$$(p \lhd b \rhd q) \overset{def}{=} (b \to p \ \square \ \neg b \to q)$$

◇

The most basic property of a conditional is that its left branch is executed if the condition holds initially; otherwise its right branch is executed.

Law 3.14.1. $(a \wedge b)^\top; (p \lhd b \vee c \rhd q) = (a \wedge b)^\top; p$ ⟨◁ ▷ true cond⟩

Law 3.14.2. $(a \wedge \neg b)^\top; (p \lhd b \wedge c \rhd q) = (a \wedge \neg b)^\top; q$ ⟨◁ ▷ false cond⟩

The left branch of a conditional can always be preceded by an assumption of the condition. Similarly, to precede the right branch by an assumption of the negation of the condition has no effect.

Law 3.14.3. $(b^\top; p) \lhd b \rhd q = (p \lhd b \rhd q) = p \lhd b \rhd (\neg b^\top; q)$

⟨◁ ▷ void $b^\top$⟩

If the two branches are the same program, the conditional can be eliminated.

Law 3.14.4. $p \lhd b \rhd p = p$ ⟨◁ ▷ idemp⟩

Guard distributes through the conditional.

Law 3.14.5. $a \to (p \lhd b \rhd q) = (a \to p) \lhd b \rhd (a \to q)$ ⟨guard − ◁ ▷ dist⟩

Sequential composition distributes leftward through the conditional.

Law 3.14.6. $(p \lhd b \rhd q); r = (p; r) \lhd b \rhd (q; r)$ ⟨; − ◁ ▷ left dist⟩

The following two laws allow the elimination of nested conditionals in certain cases.

Law 3.14.7. $p \lhd b \rhd (p \lhd c \rhd q) = p \lhd b \vee c \rhd q$ ⟨◁ ▷ cond disjunction⟩

Law 3.14.8. $(p \lhd b \rhd q) \lhd c \rhd q = p \lhd b \wedge c \rhd q$ ⟨◁ ▷ cond conjunction⟩

We have considered assumptions and assertions as primitive commands and have defined guarded commands and the conditional in terms of them. The following equations show that an alternative could be to consider the conditional as a constructor and regard assumptions, assertions and guarded commands as special cases. These are not stated as laws because they are unnecessary in our proofs.

$$
\begin{aligned}
b_\perp &= \mathsf{skip} \lhd b \rhd \perp \\
b^\top &= \mathsf{skip} \lhd b \rhd \top \\
b \to p &= p \lhd b \rhd \top
\end{aligned}
$$

3.15. Assignment

The command $x := e$ stands for a multiple assignment where x is a list of distinct variables and e is an equal-length list of expressions. The components of e are evaluated and simultaneously assigned to the corresponding (same position) components of x. For example,

$$x, y := y, x$$

swaps the values of x and y.

Recall from Section 3.11 that we assume that the evaluation of an expression always delivers a result, so the assignment will always terminate. Furthermore, the validity of most of the laws relies on the fact that expression evaluation does not change the value of any variable; that is, no *side-effect* is allowed.

Obviously, the assignment of the value of a variable to itself does not change anything.

Law 3.15.1. $(x := x) = \text{skip}$ $\langle := \text{ skip} \rangle$

In fact, such a vacuous assignment can be added to any other assignment without changing its effect.

Law 3.15.2. $(x, y := e, y) = (x := e)$ $\langle := \text{ identity} \rangle$

The list of variables and expressions may be subjected to the same permutation without changing the effect of the assignment.

Law 3.15.3. $(x, y, z := e, f, g) = (y, x, z := f, e, g)$ $\langle := \text{ sym} \rangle$

The sequential composition of two assignments to the same variables is easily combined to a single assignment.

Law 3.15.4. $(x := e; \; x := f) = (x := f[x \leftarrow e])$ $\langle := \text{ combination} \rangle$

Recall that $f[x \leftarrow e]$ denotes the substitution of e for every free occurrence of x in f.

If the value of a variable is known, the occurrences of this variable in an expression can be replaced with that value.

Law 3.15.5. $(x = e) \to (y := f) = (x = e) \to (y := f[x \leftarrow e])$

$\langle := \text{ substitution} \rangle$

Assignment is universally conjunctive.

Law 3.15.6. $x := e; \; \sqcap \mathcal{P} = \sqcap \{X \mid X \in \mathcal{P} \bullet (x := e; \; X)\}$ $\langle := -\sqcap \text{ right dist} \rangle$

Assignment distributes rightward through a conditional, replacing occurrences of the assigned variables in the condition by the corresponding expressions.

Law 3.15.7. $x := e; \; (p \lhd b \rhd q) = (x := e; \; p) \lhd b[x \leftarrow e] \rhd (x := e; \; q)$

$\langle := - \lhd \rhd \text{ right dist} \rangle$

Similarly, assignment commutes with an assertion in the following sense.

Law 3.15.8. $(x := e; \; b_\perp) = (b[x \leftarrow e])_\perp; \; x := e$ $\langle := -b_\perp \text{ commutation} \rangle$

3.16. Generalised Assignment

The notation $x :\in b$ stands for a generalised or nondeterministic assignment command. Whenever possible, x is assigned an arbitrary value that makes the condition b hold; but if no such value exists, the assignment behaves like $\top$

Law 3.16.1. $(x :\in \mathsf{false}) = \top$ $\langle :\in \text{ false cond} \rangle$

On the other hand, a true condition imposes no constraints on the final value of x. In this case, the generalised assignment might even leave everything unchanged, behaving like skip.

Law 3.16.2. $(x :\in \mathsf{true}) \sqsubseteq \mathsf{skip}$ $\langle :\in \text{ true cond} \rangle$

To follow a generalised assignment by an assumption of the same condition has no effect: if the assignment establishes the condition, the assumption behaves like skip; otherwise, the assignment itself (and consequently, its composition with the assumption) behaves like $\top$.

Law 3.16.3. $x :\in b;\ b^{\top} = x :\in b$ $\langle :\in \text{ void } b^{\top} \rangle$

A similar law holds for assertions.

Law 3.16.4. $x :\in b;\ b_{\perp} = x :\in b$ $\langle :\in \text{ void } b_{\perp} \rangle$

A generalised assignment is refined by an assumption of the same condition. The reason is that the final values of the variables of the assignment might be arbitrary, whereas the assumption does not change the value of any variable. Actually, an assumption can be regarded as a generalised assignment to an empty list of variables.

Law 3.16.5. $(x :\in b) \sqsubseteq b^{\top}$ $\langle :\in \text{ refined by } b^{\top} \rangle$

Generalised assignment distributes rightward through the conditional, provided the following condition is observed.

Law 3.16.6. If x does not occur in b
$x :\in a;\ (p \lhd b \rhd q) = (x :\in a;\ p) \lhd b \rhd (x :\in a;\ q)$ $\langle :\in - \lhd \rhd \text{ right dist} \rangle$

In general, an assignment cannot be expressed in terms of a generalised assignment only. For example, there is no generalised assignment that corresponds to the assignment $x := x + 1$. The reason is that we have not introduced notation to allow the condition of a generalised assignment of the form $x :\in b$ to refer back to the initial value of x. But $x := e$ can always be written as a generalised assignment whenever the expression e does not mention x.

Law 3.16.7. If e does not mention x
$x :\in (x = e) = x := e$ $\langle :\in - := \text{ conversion} \rangle$

If x and y are to be assigned arbitrary values (in sequence) to make a given condition hold, we can reduce the nondeterminism by ensuring that the same (arbitrary) value is assigned to both x and y.

Law 3.16.8.   If b does not mention y

$$(x :\in b;\ y :\in b[x \leftarrow y]) \sqsubseteq (x :\in b;\ y := x) \qquad\qquad \langle :\in \text{ refined by } := \rangle$$

We can commute the order of execution of an assignment and an arbitrary program p, provided no interference occurs with the global variables.

Law 3.16.9.   If no free variables of b nor x are assigned by p

$$(p;\ x :\in b) \sqsubseteq (x :\in b;\ p) \qquad\qquad \langle x :\in b;\ p \text{ commute} \rangle$$

The inequality occurs when p is $\perp$ and the assignment results in $\top$.

3.17. Iteration

We use $b * p$ to denote the iteration command. It is a concise form of the more conventional syntax

   while b do p

Iteration can be defined as a special case of recursion.

Definition 3.9.   (Iteration)

$$b * p \stackrel{def}{=} \mu X \bullet ((p;\ X) \triangleleft b \triangleright \mathsf{skip})$$

$\diamond$

As iteration is a derived operator in our language, we are able to prove (rather than just postulate) some of its properties. This illustrates the modularity provided by the algebraic laws in developing more elaborate transformation strategies from the basic ones. These strategies are largely used in the next two chapters, substantially simplifying the proofs of normal form reduction.

If the condition b does not hold initially, the iteration $b * p$ behaves like skip; otherwise it behaves like p followed by the whole iteration.

Law 3.17.1. $(a \wedge \neg b)^\top;\ b * p\ =\ (a \wedge \neg b)^\top \qquad\qquad \langle * \text{ elim} \rangle$
Proof:

$\qquad$ *LHS*

$=$ $\quad$ {Definition 3.9(Iteration) and $\langle \mu$ fixed point$\rangle$(3.8.1)}
$\qquad$ $(a \wedge \neg b)^\top;\ ((p;\ b * p) \triangleleft b \triangleright \mathsf{skip})$
$=$ $\quad$ {$\langle \triangleleft \triangleright$ false cond$\rangle$(3.14.2) and $\langle ; -\mathsf{skip}$ unit$\rangle$(3.3.1)}
$\qquad$ *RHS*

$\diamond$

Law 3.17.2. $a^\top; (a \vee b) * p = a^\top; p; (a \vee b) * p$ $\langle * \text{ unfold}\rangle$
Proof:

> LHS
> $=$ {Definition 3.9(Iteration) and $\langle\mu$ fixed point$\rangle$(3.8.1)}
> $a^\top; ((p; (a \vee b) * p) \triangleleft (a \vee b) \triangleright \mathsf{skip})$
> $=$ {$\langle\triangleleft \triangleright$ true cond$\rangle$(3.14.1)}
> RHS

$\diamond$

A recurrent step in our proofs is to unfold an iteration and simplify the unfolded body when this is a guarded command set.

Law 3.17.3.   Let $R = (a \to p \,\square\, b \to q)$. Then
$a^\top; (a \vee b) * R = a^\top; p; (a \vee b) * R$ $\langle * - \square \text{ unfold}\rangle$
Proof: From $\langle * \text{ unfold}\rangle$(3.17.2) and $\langle\square \text{ elim}\rangle$(3.13.1). $\diamond$

A guarded command set within an iteration can be eliminated if the condition of the iteration allows only one of the guards to hold.

Law 3.17.4.   Let $R = (a \to p \,\square\, b \to q)$. Then $a * R = a * p$ $\langle * - \square \text{ elim}\rangle$
Proof:

> LHS
> $=$ {Definition 3.9(Iteration) and $\langle\triangleleft \triangleright$ void $b^\top\rangle$(3.14.3)}
> $\mu X \bullet ((a^\top; R; X) \triangleleft a \triangleright \mathsf{skip})$
> $=$ {$\langle\square \text{ elim}\rangle$(3.13.1)}
> $\mu X \bullet ((a^\top; p; X) \triangleleft a \triangleright \mathsf{skip})$
> $=$ {$\langle\triangleleft \triangleright$ void $b^\top\rangle$(3.14.3) and Definition 3.9(Iteration)}
> RHS

$\diamond$

The following allows the replacement of a guarded command inside an iteration.

Law 3.17.5.   Let $R = (a \to p \,\square\, b \to q)$. If $r; (a \vee b) * R \sqsubseteq p; (a \vee b) * R$, then
$(a \vee b) * (a \to r \,\square\, b \to q) \sqsubseteq (a \vee b) * R$ $\langle * \text{ replace guarded command}\rangle$
Proof:

> RHS
> $=$ {Definition 3.9(Iteration) and $\langle\mu$ fixed point$\rangle$(3.8.1)}
> $(R; RHS) \triangleleft a \vee b \triangleright \mathsf{skip}$

$=$ {⟨; −⊓ left dist⟩(3.7.1)}

   $(a → (p; RHS) □ b → (q; RHS)) ◁ a ∨ b ▷ \mathsf{skip}$

$⊒$ {Assumption}

   $(a → (r; RHS) □ b → (q; RHS)) ◁ a ∨ b ▷ \mathsf{skip}$

$=$ {⟨; −⊓ left dist⟩(3.7.1)}

   $((a → r □ b → q); RHS) ◁ a ∨ b ▷ \mathsf{skip}$

The final result follows from ⟨μ least fixed point⟩(3.8.2).   ◇

The following law establishes the connection between tail-recursion and iteration. Its proof illustrates the use of approximate inverses of programming constructs.

Law 3.17.6. $(b * p); q = \mu X \bullet ((p; X) ◁ b ▷ q)$ ⟨$* − \mu$ tail recursion⟩
Proof: $(LHS ⊒ RHS)$:

{Definition 3.9(Iteration) and ⟨μ fixed point⟩(3.8.1)}

$LHS = ((p; b * p) ◁ b ▷ \mathsf{skip}); q$

$≡$ {⟨; − ◁ ▷ left dist⟩(3.14.6) and ⟨; −skip unit⟩(3.3.1)}

$LHS = (p; LHS) ◁ b ▷ q$

$⇒$ {⟨μ least fixed point⟩(3.8.2)}

$LHS ⊒ RHS$

$(RHS ⊒ LHS)$:

{⟨μ fixed point⟩(3.8.1)}

$RHS = (p; RHS) ◁ b ▷ q$

$⇒$ {From Lemma 3.1(Strongest inverse of ;) we have $(RHS \overset{\cup}{;} q); q ⊑ RHS$}

$RHS ⊒ (p; (RHS \overset{\cup}{;} q); q) ◁ b ▷ q$

$≡$ {⟨; − ◁ ▷ left dist⟩(3.14.6) and ⟨; −skip unit⟩(3.3.1)}

$RHS ⊒ ((p; (RHS \overset{\cup}{;} q)) ◁ b ▷ \mathsf{skip}); q$

$≡$ {Definition 3.4(Approximate inverses)}

$(RHS \overset{\cup}{;} q) ⊒ (p; (RHS \overset{\cup}{;} q)) ◁ b ▷ \mathsf{skip}$

$⇒$ {⟨μ least fixed point⟩(3.8.1) and Definition 3.9(Iteration)}

$(RHS \overset{\cup}{;} q) ⊒ b * p$

$≡$ {Definition 3.4(Approximate inverses)}

$RHS ⊒ LHS$

                                                                    ◇

The following law is surprisingly important, mainly in proving the correctness of the normal form reduction of sequential composition. Its proof without assuming continuity of the language operators is originally due to Gardiner and Pandya [26].

Law 3.17.7. $(b * p); (b \vee c) * p = (b \vee c) * p$ ⟨∗ sequence⟩
Proof: $(RHS \sqsupseteq LHS)$:

$\qquad$ {⟨◁ ▷ idemp⟩(3.14.4)}
$\qquad RHS = RHS \triangleleft b \triangleright RHS$
$\equiv$ {Definition 3.9(Iteration) and (μ fixed point)(3.8.1)}
$\qquad RHS = ((p; RHS) \triangleleft b \vee c \triangleright \mathsf{skip}) \triangleleft b \triangleright ((b \vee c) * p)$
$\equiv$ {⟨◁ ▷ void $b^\top$⟩(3.14.3) and ⟨∗ elim⟩(3.17.1)}
$\qquad RHS = ((p; RHS) \triangleleft b \vee c \triangleright (b \vee c) * p) \triangleleft b \triangleright ((b \vee c) * p)$
$\equiv$ {⟨◁ ▷ cond conjunction⟩(3.14.8)}
$\qquad RHS = (p; RHS) \triangleleft b \triangleright ((b \vee c) * p)$
$\Rightarrow$ {⟨μ least fixed point⟩(3.8.2)}
$\qquad RHS \sqsupseteq \mu X \bullet (p; X) \triangleleft b \triangleright ((b \vee c) * p)$
$\equiv$ {⟨∗ $- \mu$ tail recursion⟩(3.17.6)}
$\qquad RHS \sqsupseteq (b * p); ((b \vee c) * p)$
$\equiv$ $RHS \sqsupseteq LHS$

$(LHS \sqsupseteq RHS)$:

$\qquad$ {Definition 3.9(Iteration) and (μ fixed point)(3.8.1)}
$\qquad LHS = ((q; (b * p)) \triangleleft b \triangleright \mathsf{skip}); (b \vee c) * p$
$\equiv$ {⟨; $- $ ◁ ▷ left dist⟩(3.14.6) and ⟨; $-\mathsf{skip}$ unit⟩(3.3.1)}
$\qquad LHS = (p; LHS) \triangleleft b \triangleright RHS$
$\equiv$ {⟨μ fixed point⟩(3.8.1)}
$\qquad LHS = (p; LHS) \triangleleft b \triangleright ((p; RHS) \triangleleft b \vee c \triangleright \mathsf{skip})$
$\Rightarrow$ {⟨◁ ▷ cond disjunction⟩(3.14.7) and $LHS \sqsubseteq RHS$}
$\qquad LHS \sqsupseteq (p; LHS) \triangleleft b \vee c \triangleright \mathsf{skip}$
$\Rightarrow$ {Definition 3.9(Iteration) and ⟨μ least fixed point⟩(3.8.2)}
$\qquad LHS \sqsupseteq RHS$

$\qquad\qquad\qquad\qquad\qquad\qquad\qquad\qquad\qquad\qquad\qquad\qquad\qquad\qquad$ ◇

3.18. Static Declaration

The notation dec $x \bullet p$ declares the list of distinct variables x for use in the program p (the scope of the declaration). Local blocks of this form may appear anywhere a program is expected.

It does not matter whether variables are declared in one list or singly.

Law 3.18.1. If x and y have no variables in common
dec $x \bullet$ (dec $y \bullet p$) = dec $x, y \bullet p$ (dec assoc)

Nor does it matter in which order they are declared.

Law 3.18.2. $\dec x \bullet (\dec y \bullet p) = \dec y \bullet (\dec x \bullet p)$ ⟨dec sym⟩

If a declared variable is never used, its declaration has no effect.

Law 3.18.3.   If x is not free in p
$$\dec x \bullet p = p$$ ⟨dec elim⟩

One can change the name of a bound variable, provided the new name is not used for a free variable.

Law 3.18.4.   If y is not free in p, then
$$\dec x \bullet p = \dec y \bullet p[x \leftarrow y]$$ ⟨dec rename⟩

The value of a declared variable is totally arbitrary. Therefore initialisation of a variable may reduce nondeterminism.

Law 3.18.5.
(1) $\dec x \bullet p \sqsubseteq \dec x \bullet x := e;\ p$ ⟨dec− := initial value⟩
(2) $\dec x \bullet p \sqsubseteq \dec x \bullet x :\in b;\ p$ ⟨dec− :∈ initial value⟩

An assignment to a variable just before the end of its scope is irrelevant. But a generalised assignment cannot be completely ignored, since it may result in a miracle.

Law 3.18.6.
(1) $\dec x \bullet p = \dec x \bullet p;\ x := e$ ⟨dec− := final value⟩
(2) $\dec x \bullet p \sqsubseteq \dec x \bullet p;\ x :\in b$ ⟨dec− :∈ final value⟩

The scope of a variable may be increased without effect, provided that it does not interfere with the other variables with the same name. Thus each of the programming constructs has a distribution law with declaration. For example, if one of the arguments of the sequential composition operator declares the variable x then the scope of the declaration can be extended with the other component, provided there is no capture of free variables.

Law 3.18.7.   If x is not free in q
(1) $(\dec x \bullet p);\ q = \dec x \bullet p;\ q$ ⟨;−dec left dist⟩
(2) $q;\ (\dec x \bullet p) = \dec x \bullet q;\ p$ ⟨;−dec right dist⟩

When both arguments declare the same variable, the two declarations can be replaced with a single one.

Law 3.18.8. $(\dec x \bullet p);\ (\dec x \bullet q) \sqsubseteq \dec x \bullet p;\ q$ ⟨dec−; dist⟩

But note that this may reduce nondeterminism. Consider the case where q is $y := x$. Then the final value of y on the left-hand side of the above inequation would be totally arbitrary. On the right-hand side, however, it may be the case that x was assigned a value in p; thus the final value of y would be that of x. In all cases, the right-hand side is at least as deterministic as the left-hand side.

If each component of a guarded command set or conditional declares the variable x then the declaration may be moved outside the constructor, provided that x does not occur in the guards or in the condition.

Law 3.18.9. If x does not occur in a or b
$$a \to (\text{dec } x \bullet p) \; \Box \; b \to (\text{dec } x \bullet q) \; = \; \text{dec } x \bullet a \to p \; \Box \; b \to q \qquad \langle \text{dec} - \Box \text{ dist} \rangle$$

Law 3.18.10. If x does not occur in b
$$(\text{dec } x \bullet p) \lhd b \rhd (\text{dec } x \bullet q) \; = \; \text{dec } x \bullet p \lhd b \rhd q \qquad \langle \text{dec} - \lhd \; \rhd \text{ dist} \rangle$$

Note that it is possible to deal with cases where x is only declared in one of the branches (and is not free in the other one) by using Law 3.18.3.

Declaration can also be moved outside an iteration, possibly reducing nondeterminism. As shown below, this law can be derived from more basic ones.

Law 3.18.11. If x does not occur in b
$$b * (\text{dec } x \bullet p) \; \sqsubseteq \; \text{dec } x \bullet b * p \qquad \langle \text{dec} - * \text{ dist} \rangle$$
Proof:

$$\begin{aligned}
& \{\text{Definition 3.9(Iteration) and } \langle \mu \text{ fixed point}\rangle(3.8.1)\} \\
& RHS \; = \; \text{dec } x \bullet (p; \; b * p) \lhd b \rhd \text{skip} \\
\equiv \; & \{\langle \text{dec} - \lhd \; \rhd \text{ dist}\rangle(3.18.10) \text{ and } \langle \text{dec elim}\rangle(3.18.3)\} \\
& RHS \; = \; (\text{dec } x \bullet p; \; b * p) \lhd b \rhd \text{skip} \\
\Rightarrow \; & \{\langle \text{dec}-; \text{ dist}\rangle(3.18.8)\} \\
& RHS \sqsupseteq ((\text{dec } x \bullet p); \; RHS) \lhd b \rhd \text{skip} \\
\Rightarrow \; & \{\text{Definition 3.9(Iteration) and } \langle \mu \text{ least fixed point}\rangle(3.8.2)\} \\
& RHS \sqsupseteq LHS
\end{aligned}$$

$$\diamondsuit$$

3.19. Dynamic Declaration

The command **var** x introduces a dynamic scope of x which extends up to

- the end of the static scope of x or

- the execution of the command **end** x

whichever comes first.

An operational argument may help to clarify how the two kinds of declaration relate to each other. The general idea is to associate an unbounded stack with each variable. One can think of a static declaration of x as introducing a new variable (which is assigned an arbitrary value) with its (implicit) unbounded stack which is initially empty. Rather than creating a new variable, the commands for dynamic declaration operate on this stack. The effect of **var** x is to push the current value of x onto the stack, assigning to x an arbitrary value; **end** x pops the stack and assigns the popped value to x. If the stack was empty, this value is arbitrary.

As our language does not enforce variable declaration (see Chapter 1) we must consider what is the view of an undeclared variable in this scenario. The operational interpretation in this case is that an unbounded (and initially empty) stack is automatically associated with the undeclared variable, when this variable is first used. The effect of var and end concerning this stack is the same as discussed above.

Recall from Section 2.6 that having separate commands to introduce and end the scope of a variable is an essential feature to define the encoding and decoding programs used in our approach to data refinement: the encoding program introduces the abstract state and ends the scope of the concrete state, whereas the decoding program introduces the concrete state and ends the scope of the abstract state.

The commands var and end obey laws similar to those of dec. Nevertheless, one immediate difference is that renaming is not valid in general for dynamic declarations (only when static and dynamic declarations have the same effect, as explained later in this section).

Both var and end are associative in the sense described below.

Law 3.19.1. If x and y have no variables in common
(1) $(\text{var } x;\ \text{var } y)\ =\ \text{var } x, y$ $\langle\text{var assoc}\rangle$
(2) $(\text{end } x;\ \text{end } y)\ =\ \text{end } x, y$ $\langle\text{end assoc}\rangle$

The (dynamic) scope of a variable may be increased without effect, provided that this does not interfere with other free variables.

Law 3.19.2. If x is not free in p
(1) $p;\ \text{var } x\ =\ \text{var } x;\ p$ $\langle\text{var change scope}\rangle$
(2) $\text{end } x;\ p\ =\ p;\ \text{end } x$ $\langle\text{end change scope}\rangle$

Both var and end distribute rightward through the conditional, as long as no interference occurs with the condition.

Law 3.19.3. If b does not mention x
(1) $(\text{var } x;\ p) \lhd b \rhd (\text{var } x;\ q)\ =\ \text{var } x;\ (p \lhd b \rhd q)$ $\langle\text{var} - \lhd \rhd \text{ right dist}\rangle$
(2) $(\text{end } x;\ p) \lhd b \rhd (\text{end } x;\ q)\ =\ \text{end } x;\ (p \lhd b \rhd q)$ $\langle\text{end} - \lhd \rhd \text{ right dist}\rangle$

As explained above var x assigns an arbitrary value to x. The nondeterminism can be reduced by initialisation of x.

Law 3.19.4.
(1) $\text{var } x \sqsubseteq (\text{var } x;\ x := e)$ $\langle\text{var} - := \text{ initial value}\rangle$
(2) $\text{var } x \sqsubseteq (\text{var } x;\ x :\in b)$ $\langle\text{var} - :\in \text{ initial value}\rangle$

An assignment to a variable just before the end of its scope is irrelevant. But a generalised assignment cannot be completely ignored, as it may result in a miracle.

Law 3.19.5.
(1) $\text{end } x\ =\ (x := e;\ \text{end } x)$ $\langle\text{end} - := \text{ final value}\rangle$
(2) $\text{end } x \sqsubseteq (x :\in b;\ \text{end } x)$ $\langle\text{end} - :\in \text{ final value}\rangle$

The next two laws are essential for reasoning about data refinement. They are precisely the ones that assign the dynamic declaration semantics to var and end. The first law says that end x followed by var x leaves all variables but x unchanged; var x followed by end x has no effect (even on x). Therefore the pair (end x, var x) is a simulation.

Law 3.19.6.   (end x; var x) $\sqsubseteq$ skip $=$ (var x; end x)   ⟨end − var simulation⟩

The second law postulates that the sequential composition of end x with var x has no effect whenever it is followed by an assignment to x that does not rely on the previous value of x.

Law 3.19.7.   (end x; var x; $x :\in b$) $=$ $x :\in b$ ⟨end − var skip⟩

Observe that this law holds even when x occurs in b because an occurrence of x in b does not refer to the previous value of x; rather, it is a requirement for the current value of x. Also note that the syntax of static declaration (dec) promptly disallows the above two laws, since there is no separate construct to end the scope of a variable.

The following laws relate the two kinds of declaration. They formalise the intuitive meaning given in the beginning of this section.

If the first command in the scope of a static declaration of x is var x or end x, this command has no effect.

Law 3.19.8.
(1) dec $x \bullet$ var x; p $=$ dec $x \bullet p$ ⟨var elim1⟩
(2) dec $x \bullet$ end x; p $=$ dec $x \bullet p$ ⟨end elim1⟩

First we give an operational justification of (1). Recall that a static declaration of x creates an implicit stack which is originally empty. Then the effect of var x on the left-hand side of (1) is to push the current value of x (which is arbitrary) onto this stack, and to assign an arbitrary value to x. But the value of x was already arbitrary; thus the assignment has no effect. Furthermore, the effect of pushing an arbitrary value onto the empty stack is also immaterial. The only command that may access this value is a subsequent end x which would assign an arbitrary value to x if the stack was empty anyway. The justification of (2) is simpler. As the stack associated with x is initially empty, the effect of end x is to assign an arbitrary value to x; but the value of x was already arbitrary.

As we said before, the dynamic scope of a variable x cannot extend further than its static scope. Therefore starting or ending a dynamic scope of x just before the end of its static scope is irrelevant.

Law 3.19.9.
(1) dec $x \bullet p$; var x $=$ dec $x \bullet p$ ⟨var elim2⟩
(2) dec $x \bullet p$; end x $=$ dec $x \bullet p$ ⟨end elim2⟩

In some cases, there is no need to distinguish between a static and a dynamic scope of a given variable. So we must examine when the two kinds of declaration have the same effect.

As already discussed, having separate constructs to introduce and end the (dynamic) scope of a variable allows more flexibility than with a single construct. This fact has been well illustrated by the simulation concept introduced above; it would not have been possible to express this notion in our language if we had allowed only static declarations.

Therefore, a static declaration cannot, in general, replace a dynamic declaration. However, under certain conditions this can be achieved. One immediate requirement is that each var x in a program has a corresponding, statically determined, end x, so that we can replace *blocks* of the form

   var x; q; end x

with

   dec $x \bullet q$

This requirement is captured by the following definition.

Definition 3.10. (Block-structure)
A program p is *block-structured* with respect to a variable x if it is built according to the following two rules:

  1. all the programs that do not contain the commands var x or end x are block-structured with respect to x;

  2. if p is block-structured with respect to x, so is
     var x; p; end x.   ◇

While the above condition is clearly necessary to allow the replacement of a dynamic by a static declaration of x, it is not sufficient. The reason is that a static declaration is governed by static scope rules, whereas a dynamic declaration is governed by dynamic scope rules [1], as illustrated by the following example.

Suppose that the program identifier X is bound to the program text $x := y$. Now consider the following program (assuming that x, y and z are distinct variables)

   var y; $y := z$; X; end y

where the above occurrence of X stands for a call of the program bound to it: $x := y$. Dynamic scope rules determine that the occurrence of y in the program (identified by) X is bound to the above (dynamic) declaration of y. Therefore one can easily conclude that the effect of the above program is to assign z to x.

Now let us consider what is the effect of the program

   dec $y \bullet y := z$; X

In this case, because the declaration of y is static, any call command in the scope of this declaration is governed by static scope rules. This means that the occurrence of y

in the program X is bound to the declaration of y whose scope includes the definition
of X, and not to the above declaration whose scope includes a call of X. Therefore
the y introduced in the above declaration is a different variable from the occurrence
of y in X; they just happen to have the same name. Renaming the local declaration
of y above (recall that renaming in general is allowed only for static declarations),
say with a fresh variable w, does not change the behaviour of the above program; this
leads to

> dec $w \bullet w := z;\ X$

which can itself be easily transformed (using simple laws of declaration) into

> $x := y$

As a result we observe that static and dynamic declarations of the same variable in
this case have distinct effects. This happens only in the presence of call commands
since these are governed by different scope rules, depending on whether static or
dynamic declarations are introduced.

   To capture the precise context where one cannot distinguish between a static and
a dynamic declaration of a given variable, we need the following concept.

Definition 3.11.   (Contiguous scope)
We say that a variable x has a *contiguous* scope in a program p if

- p contains no free program identifiers (standing for call commands) or

- if the program identifier X is free in p, then the variable x must not be free in
  (the program defining) X.   ◇

Note that in the situation exemplified above by the program

> dec $y;\ y := z;\ X$

the variable y does not have a contiguous scope, since there is a free program identifier
X in which y is free (recall that X is bound to the program $x := y$).

   We finally present the law which precisely relates the two forms of variable declaration.

Law 3.19.10.   If p is block-structured with respect to x, and x has a contiguous
scope in p, then
dec $x \bullet p$ = var $x;\ p;$ end x (dec $-$ (var, end) conversion)

We can ensure that programs will always have contiguous scope (with respect to any
local variable) by requiring that nested declarations always use distinct names for
variables (which are also distinct from the names used for global variables). When
applying the above law we will assume that the condition of contiguous scope is always
satisfied.

For example, as explained above, the scope of y in

> dec y; $y := z$; X

is not contiguous, but renaming allows us to transform this program into (assuming that w is a fresh variable)

> dec w; $w := z$; X

which clearly satisfies the contiguous scope condition concerning w, since w does not appear in the program ($x := y$) bound to X. Now we can deduce that the above is equivalent to

> var w; $w := z$; X; end w

which is itself equivalent to $x := y$, as expected.

From Law 3.19.10, we derive the following law about introduction of local declarations.

Law 3.19.11. If p is block-structured with respect to x, and x has a contiguous scope in p, then
$$x :\in b;\ p;\ x :\in c\ =\ (\text{dec}\,x \bullet x :\in b;\ p);\ x :\in c \qquad\qquad \langle\text{dec introduction}\rangle$$

Proof:

$$
\begin{aligned}
&\quad LHS \\
=&\ \{\langle\text{end} - \text{var skip}\rangle(3.19.7)\} \\
&\quad \text{end } x;\ \text{var } x;\ x :\in b;\ p;\ \text{end } x;\ \text{var } x;\ x :\in c \\
=&\ \{\langle\text{dec} - (\text{var}, \text{end})\ \text{conversion}\rangle(3.19.10)\} \\
&\quad \text{end } x;\ (\text{dec}\,x \bullet x :\in b;\ p);\ \text{var } x;\ x :\in c \\
=&\ \{\langle\text{end change scope}\rangle(3.19.2)\} \\
&\quad (\text{dec}\,x \bullet x :\in b;\ p);\ \text{end } x;\ \text{var } x;\ x :\in c \\
=&\ \{\langle\text{end} - \text{var skip}\rangle(3.19.7)\} \\
&\quad RHS
\end{aligned}
$$

$\Diamond$

The above two laws will be used in the next chapters to perform transformations on source programs. These are always block-structured, since var and end are not part of our source language. We have explained how to ensure that programs always have contiguous scope (with respect to any local variable). Therefore these laws will be applied assuming that these conditions are always satisfied.

3.20. The Correctness of the Basic Laws

In a purely algebraic view, the laws of a given language are an algebraic semantics for this language. There is no place for the task of verifying the validity of the more basic laws; they are axioms which express the relationship between the operators of the language. However, the method of postulating is questioned by those who follow a model-oriented approach, especially when the set of axioms is relatively large, as it is here. Postulating an inconsistent set of laws could be a disaster: it would allow one to prove invalid results, like the correctness of an inaccurate compiler.

The way to avoid this danger is to link the algebraic semantics of the language with a (non-trivial) mathematical model in which the laws can be proved. For example, Hoare and He [52] provide a relational model for programs where the correctness of the laws could be established by appealing to the calculus of relations [84]. Another model that has gained widespread acceptance is the predicate transformer model of Dijskstra [21], which was briefly discussed in the previous chapter. In this case, the semantics of each language construct (that is, its *weakest precondition*) is given, and the laws are verified by appealing to the predicate calculus.

It is also possible to link the algebraic semantics of the language to a more concrete (operational) model. This allows to check for feasibility (implementability) of the language operators. But in our case this is not possible, as our reasoning language includes non-implementable operators.

Once the laws have been proved, in whatever model, they should serve as tools for carrying out program transformation. The mathematical definitions that allow their verification are normally more complex, and therefore not appealing to practical use. This separation of concerns is well described in [50], which explores the role of algebra and models in the construction of theories relevant to computing.

But even after the model has served its intended purpose, additional results of practical interest can be achieved. For example, from the experience in the application of basic algebraic laws of programming to solve a given task, one discovers more elaborate transformation strategies that allow more concise and elegant proofs. This was illustrated in the section on iteration, where all the laws were derived from more basic ones.

The existence of these nontrivial models for the reasoning language shows that its algebraic laws are in some sense consistent. In the remainder of this section we use the predicate transformer model to illustrate how the basic laws of our language can be verified. For additional examples we refer the reader to [5] where it is also shown how this style of proof can be mechanised.

Predicate Transformers

We deal only with a few language operators. Their definitions as predicate transformers were given in the previous chapter, but are repeated here for convenience. In the following, a ranges over the set of predicates, p and q stand for arbitrary programs, and $\mathcal{P}$ for an arbitrary set of programs.

$$\text{skip} \stackrel{def}{=} \lambda a \bullet a$$
$$\bot \stackrel{def}{=} \lambda a \bullet \text{false}$$
$$\top \stackrel{def}{=} \lambda a \bullet \text{true}$$
$$\bigsqcup \mathcal{P} \stackrel{def}{=} \lambda a \bullet (\exists X \mid X \in \mathcal{P} \bullet X(a))$$
$$\bigsqcap \mathcal{P} \stackrel{def}{=} \lambda a \bullet (\forall X \mid X \in \mathcal{P} \bullet X(a))$$
$$p;\ q \stackrel{def}{=} \lambda a \bullet p(q(a))$$

The binary versions of $\bigsqcup$ and $\bigsqcap$ are defined as special cases of the above definitions:

$$p \sqcup q \stackrel{def}{=} \lambda a \bullet p(a) \vee q(a)$$
$$p \sqcap q \stackrel{def}{=} \lambda a \bullet p(a) \wedge q(a)$$

The definition of the remaining operators can be found, for example, in [5]. From the above definitions we can prove the laws of the corresponding operators. For example, from the definition of $\sqsubseteq$ we can derive its characterisation in terms of weakest preconditions:

$$p \sqsubseteq q$$
$\equiv$ {Definition 3.1(The ordering Relation)}
$$(p \sqcap q) = p$$
$\equiv$ {Definition of $\sqcap$}
$$(\lambda a \bullet p(a) \wedge q(a)) = p$$
$\equiv$ {The axiom of extensionality}
$$\forall a \bullet (p(a) \wedge q(a) \Leftrightarrow p(a))$$
$\equiv$ {Predicate calculus}
$$\forall a \bullet (p(a) \Rightarrow q(a))$$

which corresponds precisely to the definition of refinement adopted in all approaches to the refinement calculus based on weakest preconditions, as discussed in the previous chapter. As another example, we verify Law $\langle \sqcup - \sqcap \text{ dist} \rangle (3.7.2)$.

$$(\bigsqcup \mathcal{P}) \sqcap p$$
$=$ {Definition of $\sqcap$}
$$\lambda a \bullet (\bigsqcup \mathcal{P})(a) \wedge p(a)$$
$=$ {Definition of $\sqcup$}
$$\lambda a \bullet (\exists X \mid X \in \mathcal{P} \bullet X(a)) \wedge p(a)$$
$=$ {Assuming that X is not free in p}
$$\lambda a \bullet (\exists X \mid X \in \mathcal{P} \bullet (X(a) \wedge p(a)))$$

$\quad = \quad \{\text{Definition of } \sqcap\}$

$\qquad \lambda\, a \bullet (\exists\, X \mid X \in \mathcal{P} \bullet (X \sqcap p)(a))$

$\quad = \quad \{\text{Set theory}\}$

$\qquad \lambda\, a \bullet (\exists\, X \mid X \in \{X \mid X \in \mathcal{P} \bullet (X \sqcap p)\} \bullet X(a))$

$\quad = \quad \{\text{Definition of } \bigsqcup\}$

$\qquad \bigsqcup \{X \mid X \in \mathcal{P} \bullet (X \sqcap p)\}$

CHAPTER 4

A SIMPLE COMPILER

> Setting up equations is like translating from one language into another.
>
> — G. Polya

In the first two sections of this chapter we describe the *normal form* as a model of an arbitrary executing mechanism. The normal form theorems of Section 4.2 are concerned with control elimination: the reduction of the nested control structure of the source program to a single flat iteration. These theorems are largely independent of a particular target machine.

In the subsequent sections, we design and prove the correctness of a compiler for a subset of our source language, not including procedures or recursion (which are dealt with in the next chapter). The constructions considered here are skip, assignment, sequential composition, demonic nondeterminism, conditional, iteration and local declarations.

As described earlier, we split the compilation process into three main phases: simplification of expressions, control elimination and data refinement (the conversion from the abstract space of the source program to the concrete state of the target machine). The control elimination phase in particular is directly achieved by instantiating the generic theorems of Section 4.2.

Each of these generic transformations has the status of a theorem. The more specific transformations (presented in Sections 4.4, 4.5 and 4.6) which illustrate the compilation process for a specific target machine have the status of a *rule*. Each rule expresses a transformation which brings the source program closer to a normal form with the same structure as the specific target machine. The final section shows that, taken collectively, these rules can be used to carry out the compilation task.

It is important to emphasise the different roles played by the algebraic laws described in the previous chapter and these reduction rules: the laws express general properties of the language operators, whereas the rules serve the special purpose of transforming an arbitrary program to a normal form. The laws are necessary to prove the rules, and these (not the laws) are used to carry out compilation.

4.1. The Normal Form

A program of the form

$$\text{dec } v \bullet v :\in a; \ b * p; \ c_\perp$$

can be interpreted as a very general model of a machine executing a stored program in the following way:

- The list of variables v represents the machine components (for example, registers). They are introduced as local variables since they have no counterpart at the source level; therefore their final values are irrelevant.

- a is an assumption about the initial state. If it is impossible to make a true by assigning to v, the machine behaves miraculously; this saves the compiler designer from dealing with states not satisfying a. Observe that the use of the nondeterministic assignment $v :\in a$ to initialise the machine allows us to abstract from the way control state is encoded.

- p is the stored program; it is executed until the condition b becomes false. Usually, p will be a guarded command set of the form

$$b_1 \rightarrow p_1 \ \Box \ldots \Box \ b_n \rightarrow p_n$$

  Whenever the machine is in state b_i the *action* (or *instruction*) p_i is executed. In this case, the condition b is given by

$$b_1 \vee \ldots \vee b_n$$

- c is an assertion about the final state of the machine; if execution of the stored program does not assert c, the machine ends up behaving like abort.

Notice that, upon termination of the iteration $b * p$, b is false and we have

$$b * p; \ c_\perp \ = \ b * p; \ (\neg b)_\perp; \ c_\perp \ = \ b * p; \ (\neg b \wedge c)_\perp$$

Thus, there is no loss of generality in assuming that $c = (\neg b \wedge c)$, and consequently that $(b \wedge c) = \mathsf{false}$. The normal form theorems will rely on the assumption that b and c are disjoint.

A normal form program will be abbreviated as follows.

Definition 4.1. (Normal form)

$$v : [a, \ b \rightarrow p, \ c] \ \stackrel{def}{=} \ \mathsf{dec} \ v \bullet v :\in a; \ b * p; \ c_\perp, \quad \text{where } (b \wedge c) = \mathsf{false}.$$

◇

For convenience. we will sometimes use the form

$$v : [a, \ (b_1 \rightarrow p_1 \ \Box \ldots \Box \ b_n \rightarrow p_n), \ c]$$

as an abbreviation of

$$v : [a, \ (b_1 \vee \ldots \vee b_n) \rightarrow (b_1 \rightarrow p_1 \ \Box \ldots \Box \ b_n \rightarrow p_n), \ c]$$

4.2. Normal Form Reduction

To reduce an arbitrary program to normal form, it is sufficient to show how each primitive command can be written in normal form, and how each operator of the language (when applied to operands in normal form) yields a result expressible in normal form. The following reductions involve no change of data representation. Therefore we can directly compare the source constructs with the associated normal form programs.

Some of the theorems in this section state very simple results (some are just corollaries of algebraic laws or lemmas), but they have this status because each one shows how a given operator of the source language can be reduced to normal form. These theorems can be regarded as expressing generic transformations in that they are independent of the target machine. In Section 4.5 we show how they can be instantiated to give rise to compilation rules for a specific machine.

If the initial state coincides with the final state, the machine does not perform any action. In more concrete terms, the empty code is a possible implementation of skip.

Theorem 4.1. (Skip)

$$\mathsf{skip} \sqsubseteq v : [a, b \to p, a]$$

Proof:

$$
\begin{aligned}
& RHS \\
=\ & \{(\ast\ \mathsf{elim})(3.17.1),\ \text{remember}\ a \wedge b = \mathsf{false}\} \\
& \mathsf{dec}\ v \bullet v :\in a;\ a_\perp \\
=\ & \{(:\in\ \mathsf{void}\ a_\perp)(3.16.4)\ \text{and}\ (;-\mathsf{skip}\ \mathsf{unit})(3.3.1)\} \\
& \mathsf{dec}\ v \bullet v :\in a;\ \mathsf{skip} \\
\sqsupseteq\ & \{(\mathsf{dec}-\ :\in\ \mathsf{initial}\ \mathsf{value})(3.18.5)\ \text{and}\ (\mathsf{dec}\ \mathsf{elim})(3.18.3)\} \\
& LHS
\end{aligned}
$$

$\diamond$

The following lemma shows how a primitive command can be written in normal form. Actually, the lemma is valid for all programs p, but we will not make use of it for non-primitive constructs because we follow an innermost (*bottom-up*) reduction strategy.

Lemma 4.1. (Primitive commands)
If v is not free in p then

$$p \sqsubseteq v : [a, a \to (p;\ v :\in c),\ c]$$

Proof:

RHS

$=$ $\{\langle * \text{ unfold}\rangle(3.17.2) \text{ and } \langle * \text{ elim}\rangle(3.17.1)\}$

dec $v \bullet v :\in a; \; p; \; v :\in c; \; c_\perp$

$\sqsupseteq$ $\{\langle\text{dec} - \; :\in \text{ initial value}\rangle(3.18.5) \text{ and } \langle:\in \text{ void } c_\perp\rangle(3.16.4)\}$

dec $v \bullet p; \; v :\in c$

$\sqsupseteq$ $\{\langle\text{dec} - \; :\in \text{ final value}\rangle(3.18.6) \text{ and } \langle\text{dec elim}\rangle(3.18.3)\}$

LHS

$\diamond$

The following normal form representations of **skip** and assignment are instantiations of the above lemma. The one of **skip** is further simplified by the fact that it is an identity of sequential composition. The operational interpretation is that **skip** can be implemented by a jump.

Theorem 4.2. (Skip)

$$\text{skip} \sqsubseteq v : [a, (a \rightarrow v :\in c), c]$$

$\diamond$

Theorem 4.3. (Assignment)

$$x := e \sqsubseteq v : [a, a \rightarrow (x := e; \; v :\in c), c]$$

$\diamond$

The reduction of sequential composition assumes that both arguments are already in normal form, and that the final state of the left argument coincides with the initial state of the right argument. The guarded command set of the resulting normal form combines the original guarded commands. First we consider the particular case where the guarded command set of the right argument includes that of the left argument.

Lemma 4.2. (Sequential composition)

$$v \; [a, b_1 \rightarrow p, c_0]; \; v : \left[c_0, \left(\square \begin{array}{c} b_1 \rightarrow p \\ b_2 \rightarrow q \end{array} \right), c\right] \sqsubseteq v : \left[a, \left(\square \begin{array}{c} b_1 \rightarrow p \\ b_2 \rightarrow q \end{array} \right), c\right]$$

Proof:
Let $R = (b_1 \rightarrow p \; \square \; b_2 \rightarrow q)$.

LHS

$\sqsubseteq$ $\{\langle\text{dec} - ; \text{ dist}\rangle(3.18.8)\}$

dec $v \bullet v :\in a; \; b_1 * p; \; c_{0\perp}; \; v :\in c_0; \; (b_1 \vee b_2) * R; \; c_\perp$

$\sqsubseteq$ $\{\langle v :\in c_0$ refined by $c_0{}^{\mathsf{T}}\rangle(3.19.6)$ and $\langle c_{0\perp} - c_0{}^{\mathsf{T}}$ simulation$\rangle(3.11.10)\}$

dec $v \bullet v :\in a;\ b_1 * p;\ (b_1 \vee b_2) * R;\ c_\perp$

$=$ $\{\langle * - \square$ elim$\rangle(3.17.4)\}$

dec $v \bullet v :\in a;\ b_1 * R;\ (b_1 \vee b_2) * R;\ c_\perp$

$=$ $\{\langle *$ sequence$\rangle(3.17.7)\}$

RHS

$\diamond$

Now we show that the guarded command set of a normal form program can be reduced by eliminating arbitrary guarded commands; the program obtained is worse than the original one. Put the other way round: extending the guarded command set by introducing new guarded commands leads to refinement.

Lemma 4.3.   (Eliminate guarded command)

$$v : [a, \left(\begin{matrix} & b_1 \to p \\ \square & b_2 \to q \end{matrix}\right), c] \sqsupseteq v : [a, b_1 \to p, c]$$

Proof:

Let $R = (b_1 \to p \ \square \ b_2 \to q)$

$\qquad$ *LHS*

$\quad \sqsupseteq$ $\{$Lemma 4.2(Sequential composition)$\}$

$\qquad v : [a, b_1 \to p, c];\ v : [c, R, c]$

$\quad \sqsupseteq$ $\{$Theorem 4.1(Skip) and $\langle ; -$skip unit$\rangle(3.3.1)\}$

$\qquad$ *RHS*

$\diamond$

The reduction of sequential composition is proved directly from the above two lemmas. These lemmas will be of more general utility.

Theorem 4.4.   (Sequential composition)

$$v : [a, b_1 \to p, c_0];\ v : [c_0, b_2 \to q, c] \sqsubseteq v : [a, \left(\begin{matrix} & b_1 \to p \\ \square & b_2 \to q \end{matrix}\right), c]$$

Proof:

$\qquad$ *RHS*

$\quad \sqsupseteq$ $\{$Lemma 4.2(Sequential composition)$\}$

$\qquad v : [a, b_1 \to p, c_0];\ v : [c_0, \left(\begin{matrix} & b_1 \to p \\ \square & b_2 \to q \end{matrix}\right), c]$

$\quad \sqsupseteq$ $\{$Lemma 4.3(Eliminate guarded command)$\}$

$\qquad$ *LHS*

$\diamond$

The following lemma shows how to eliminate a conditional command when its branches are normal form programs with identical components, except for the initial state. The first action to be executed in the resulting normal form program determines which of the original initial states should be activated.

Lemma 4.4.   (Conditional)
If v is not free in b then

$$v : [a_1, R, c] \triangleleft b \triangleright v : [a_2, R, c] \sqsubseteq v : [a, R, c]$$

where $R = \begin{pmatrix} & a \to (v :\in a_1 \triangleleft b \triangleright v :\in a_2) \\ \Box & b_1 \to p \end{pmatrix}$

Proof:

$\quad$ *RHS*

$=$ $\{\langle * - \Box \text{ unfold}\rangle(3.17.3)\}$

$\quad$ $\text{dec } v \bullet v :\in a; \ (v :\in a_1 \triangleleft b \triangleright v :\in a_2); \ (a \lor b_1) * R; \ c_\perp$

$=$ $\{\langle ; - \triangleleft \triangleright \text{ left dist}\rangle(3.14.6)\}$

$\quad$ $\text{dec } v \bullet v :\in a; \ (v :\in a_1; \ (a \lor b_1) * R; \ c_\perp) \triangleleft b \triangleright (v :\in a_2; \ (a \lor b_1) * R; \ c_\perp)$

$=$ $\{\langle :\in - \triangleleft \triangleright \text{ right dist}\rangle(3.16.6) \text{ and } \langle \text{dec} - \triangleleft \triangleright \text{ dist}\rangle(3.18.10)\}$

$\quad$ $(\text{dec } v \bullet v :\in a; \ v :\in a_1; \ (a \lor b_1) * R; \ c_\perp) \triangleleft b \triangleright$

$\quad$ $(\text{dec } v \bullet v :\in a; \ v :\in a_2; \ (a \lor b_1) * R; \ c_\perp)$

$\sqsupseteq$ $\{\langle \text{dec} - :\in \text{ initial value}\rangle(3.18.5)\}$

$\quad$ *LHS*

$\diamond$

The above lemma is useful for intermediate calculations. It is used in the proof of the normal form reduction of conditional and iteration commands.

Theorem 4.5.   (Conditional)
If v does not occur in b then

$$v : [a_1, b_1 \to p, c_1] \triangleleft b \triangleright v : [a_2, b_2 \to q, c] \sqsubseteq v : [a, R, c]$$

where $R = \begin{pmatrix} & a \to (v :\in a_1 \triangleleft b \triangleright v :\in a_2) \\ \Box & b_1 \to p \ \Box \ c_1 \to v :\in c \\ \Box & b_2 \to q \end{pmatrix}$

Proof:

$\quad$ *RHS*

$\sqsupseteq$ $\{\text{Lemma 4.4(Conditional)}\}$

$\quad$ $v : [a_1, R, c] \triangleleft b \triangleright v : [a_2, R, c]$

$\sqsupseteq$ {Lemmas 4.2(Sequential composition) and
  4.3(Eliminate guarded command)}
  $(v : [a_1, b_1 \rightarrow p, c_1]; \; v : [c_1, c_1 \rightarrow v :\in c, c]) \lhd b \rhd v : [a_2, b_2 \rightarrow q, c]$

$\sqsupseteq$ {Theorem 4.2(Skip) and $(; -\text{skip unit})(3.3.1)$}
  LHS

$\diamond$

The next lemma establishes a simple fact: if the unique effect of the first guarded command to be executed is to make a certain expression **true**, we may substitute the expression for the initial state of the normal form program.

Lemma 4.5. (Void initial state)

$$v : \left[c_0, \left(\begin{array}{cc} c_0 \rightarrow v :\in a \\ \Box \quad b \rightarrow p \end{array} \right), c \right] \sqsupseteq v : \left[a, \left(\begin{array}{cc} c_0 \rightarrow v :\in a \\ \Box \quad b \rightarrow p \end{array} \right), c \right]$$

Proof:

$\quad$ *LHS*

$=$ {$(* - \Box \text{ unfold})(3.17.3)$}

$\quad$ $\text{dec } v \bullet v :\in c_0; \; v :\in a; \; (c_0 \lor b) * \left(\begin{array}{cc} c_0 \rightarrow v :\in a \\ \Box \quad b \rightarrow p \end{array} \right); \; c_\perp$

$\sqsupseteq$ {$(\text{dec}- :\in \text{ initial value})(3.18.5)$}

$\quad$ *RHS*

$\diamond$

In order to reduce an iteration command, we assume that its body is in normal form. Let a_0 and c_0 be the initial and final states of this normal form program. The normal form of the whole iteration behaves as follows. The first action to be executed is a conditional command which tests if the condition of the iteration holds, in which case a_0 is activated; otherwise, the program reaches its final state. When c_0 is activated, the guard of the first action is activated so that the conditional command is executed again.

Theorem 4.6. (Iteration)
If v does not occur in b then

$$b * v : [a_0, b_1 \rightarrow p, c_0] \sqsubseteq v : [a, R, c]$$

where $R = \left(\begin{array}{cc} a \rightarrow (v :\in a_0 \lhd b \rhd v :\in c) \\ \Box \quad c_0 \rightarrow v :\in a \\ \Box \quad b_1 \rightarrow p \end{array} \right)$

Proof:

RHS

$\sqsupseteq$ {Lemma 4.4(Conditional)}

$\quad v : [a_0,\ R,\ c] \lhd b \rhd v : [c,\ R,\ c]$

$\sqsupseteq$ {Lemma 4.2(Sequential composition) and Theorem 4.1(Skip)}

$\quad v : [a_0,\ b_1 \to p,\ c_0];\ \ v : [c_0,\ R,\ c] \lhd b \rhd \text{skip}$

$\sqsupseteq$ {Lemma 4.5(Void initial state)}

$\quad (v : [a_0,\ b_1 \to p,\ c_0];\ RHS) \lhd b \rhd \text{skip}$

The final result follows from the above and $\langle \mu$ least fixed point$\rangle$(3.8.2). $\diamondsuit$

The demonic nondeterministic choice $\sqcap$ of two programs can be implemented by either of them. We can actually eliminate the choice at the source level, and avoid compiling one of the components.

Theorem 4.7. (Nondeterminism)

(**1**) $(p \sqcap q) \sqsubseteq p$

(**2**) $(p \sqcap q) \sqsubseteq q$

Proof: From $\langle \sqsubseteq - \sqcap$ glb$\rangle$(3.6.7). $\diamondsuit$

4.3. The Target Machine

The compiler we design in the next three sections produces code for a simple target machine which consists of four components:

P	a sequential register (program counter)
A	a general purpose register
M	a store for variables (RAM)
m	a store for instructions (ROM)

The idea is to regard the machine components as program variables and design the instructions as assignments that update the machine state.

P and A will be represented by single variables. Although we do not deal with types explicitly, P will be assigned integer expressions, standing for locations in ROM. A will be treated as an ordinary source variable; it will play an important role in the decomposition of expressions, which is the subject of the next section. M will be modelled as a map (finite function) from addresses of locations in RAM to expressions denoting the corresponding values, and m as a map from addresses of locations in ROM to instructions.

In order to model M and m, we need to extend our language to allow map variables. We use the following operators on maps:

$\{x \mapsto e\}$	Singleton map
$m_1 \cup m_2$	union
$m_1 \oplus m_2$	overriding
$m[x]$	application

Perhaps the least familiar of these operators is overriding: $m_1 \oplus m_2$ contains all the pairs in m_2 plus each pair in m_1 whose domain element is not in the domain of m_2. For example,

$$\{x \mapsto e, y \mapsto f\} \oplus \{y \mapsto g, z \mapsto h\} \;=\; \{x \mapsto e, y \mapsto g, z \mapsto h\}$$

Furthermore, we use the following abbreviations:

$$\{x_1, \ldots, x_n \mapsto e_1, \ldots, e_n\} \stackrel{def}{=} \{x_1 \mapsto e_1\} \cup \ldots \cup \{x_n \mapsto e_n\}$$
$$m[x_1, \ldots, x_n] \stackrel{def}{=} m[x_1], \ldots, m[x_n]$$

In the first case we assume that no variable appears more than once in the list $x_1, \ldots, x_n$.

One of the greatest advantages of algebra is abstraction. All the laws of our language are unaffected by this extension. In particular, the laws of assignment and declaration can be readily used to manipulate map variables and expressions, and no additional laws turn out to be necessary. For example, we can combine the two assignments

$$m := m \oplus \{x \mapsto e\}; \; m := m \oplus \{y \mapsto f\}$$

by using Law $\langle := \text{ combination}\rangle(3.15.4)$, resulting in

$$m := m \oplus \{x \mapsto e\} \oplus \{y \mapsto f\}$$

Similarly,

$$m := m \oplus \{x \mapsto e\}; \; \text{end } m$$

is equivalent to (from Law $\langle \text{end}- := \text{ final value}\rangle(3.19.5)$)

$$\text{end } m$$

The instructions of our simple machine are defined below. We assume that n stands for an address in RAM and k for an address in ROM.

$$
\begin{aligned}
\text{load}(n) \quad &\stackrel{def}{=} \quad A, P := M[n], P + 1 \\
\text{store}(n) \quad &\stackrel{def}{=} \quad M, P := (M \oplus \{n \mapsto A\}), P + 1 \\
\text{bop--A}(n) \quad &\stackrel{def}{=} \quad A, P := (A \text{ bop } M[n]), P + 1 \\
\text{uop--A} \quad &\stackrel{def}{=} \quad A, P := (\text{uop } A), P + 1 \\
\text{jump}(k) \quad &\stackrel{def}{=} \quad P := k \\
\text{cjump}(k) \quad &\stackrel{def}{=} \quad P := (P + 1 \lhd A \rhd k)
\end{aligned}
$$

where

$$x := (e_1 \lhd b \rhd e_2) \stackrel{def}{=} (x := e_1) \lhd b \rhd (x := e_2)$$

and, as before, bop and uop stand for arbitrary binary and unary operators, respectively.

The normal form describing the behaviour of this machine is an iterated execution of instructions taken from the store m at location P:

$$\text{dec P, A} \bullet \text{P} := s; \; (s \leq \text{P} < f) * \text{m[P]}; \; (\text{P} = f)_\perp$$

where s is the intended start address of code and f the finish address. The aim of the following sections is to show how an arbitrary source program can be reduced to this form.

4.4. Simplification of Expressions

One of the tasks involved in the translation process is the elimination of nested expressions. The outcome of this phase is a program where each assignment is *simple* (see definition below). Furthermore, all the local variables are expanded to widest scope, so that they can be implemented as global variables. Of course, this is valid only in the absence of recursion, and it requires that all local variables have distinct names, which must also be different from the names used for global variables.

Definition 4.2. (Simple assignment)
An assignment is simple if it has one of the forms

      A := x
      x := A
      A := A bop x
      A := uop A

where x is a source variable.   ◇

These patterns are closely related to the ones used to define the instructions. For example, the first one will eventually turn into a load instruction: the variable P will appear as a result of the control elimination phase, and x will be replaced by its memory location as a result of the change of data representation.

In the remainder of this section we will show how to simplify expressions by using the register variable A and new local variables. We assume that x is a single variable and e a single expression, rather than arbitrary lists.

The first rule transforms an assignment into a block that introduces A as a local variable.

Rule 4.1. (Introduce A)
If A does not occur in $x := e$

      $(x := e) \;=\; \text{dec A} \bullet \text{A} := e; \; x := \text{A}$

Proof: From the laws to combine assignment and eliminate local variables.   ◇

Note that the assignment $x := \mathsf{A}$ is already simple. By transforming all the assignments in this way, we need only simplify expressions assigned to A.

The next rule deals with unary operators.

Rule 4.2. (Unary operator)

$$(\mathsf{A} := \mathsf{uop}\ e) \;=\; (\mathsf{A} := e;\ \mathsf{A} := \mathsf{uop}\ A)$$

Proof: From the law to combine assignments.   ◇

Observe that the second assignment on the right-hand side of the above equation is simple.

To deal with binary operators we need to introduce a fresh local variable t. It plays the role of a temporary variable that holds the value of a subexpression.

Rule 4.3. (Binary operator)
If neither A nor t occur in e or f

$$(\mathsf{A} := e\ \mathsf{bop}\ f) \;=\; \mathsf{dec}\ t \bullet \mathsf{A} := f;\ t := \mathsf{A};\ \mathsf{A} := e;\ \mathsf{A} := \mathsf{A}\ \mathsf{bop}\ t$$

Proof:

$$RHS$$
$$= \quad \{ \langle := \text{ combination} \rangle (3.15.4) \text{ and } \langle := \text{ identity} \rangle (3.15.2) \}$$
$$\mathsf{dec}\ t \bullet \mathsf{A} := f;\ t := f;\ \mathsf{A} := e\ \mathsf{bop}\ t$$
$$= \quad \{ \langle := \text{ combination} \rangle (3.15.4) \text{ and } \langle := \text{ identity} \rangle (3.15.2) \}$$
$$\mathsf{dec}\ t \bullet \mathsf{A} := f;\ \mathsf{A} := e\ \mathsf{bop}\ f;\ t := f$$
$$= \quad \{ \langle := \text{ combination} \rangle (3.15.4), \langle \mathsf{dec} - := \text{ final value} \rangle (3.18.6) \text{ and}$$
$$\langle \mathsf{dec}\ \text{elim} \rangle (3.18.3) \}$$
$$LHS$$

     ◇

Again, the only expressions that may still need to be simplified (e and f) are both assigned to the variable A. An exhaustive application of the above rules will simplify arbitrarily nested expressions, turning every assignment into a simple one.

When the expression f above is a variable, it is unnecessary to create a temporary variable to hold its value. The following is an optimisation of the previous rule for this particular case.

Rule 4.4. (Binary operator — optimisation)
If A does not occur in e or x

$$(\mathsf{A} := e\ \mathsf{bop}\ x) \;=\; (\mathsf{A} := e;\ \mathsf{A} := \mathsf{A}\ \mathsf{bop}\ x)$$

Proof: From the law to combine assignments.   ◇

The boolean expressions appearing in iteration and conditional commands may also be arbitrarily nested, and therefore need to be simplified.

Rule 4.5.   (Condition of iteration)
If neither A nor v occur in b

$$b * (\text{dec } v, \text{A} \bullet p) \sqsubseteq \text{dec } v, \text{A} \bullet \text{A} := b; \text{ A} * (p; \text{ A} := b)$$

Proof:

> $\qquad$ *RHS*
>
> $=\quad$ {$\langle \mu$ fixed point$\rangle(3.8.1)$}
>
> $\qquad$ dec $v, \text{A} \bullet \text{A} := b; ((p; \text{ A} := b; \text{ A} * (p; \text{ A} := b)) \lhd \text{A} \rhd \text{skip})$
>
> $=\quad$ {$\langle := - \lhd \rhd$ right dist$\rangle(3.15.7)$, $\langle$dec $- \lhd \rhd$ dist$\rangle(3.18.10)$ and
>
> $\qquad$ $\langle$dec elim$\rangle(3.18.3)$}
>
> $\qquad$ $(\text{dec } v, \text{A} \bullet \text{A} := b; \ p; \text{ A} := b; \text{ A} * (p; \text{ A} := b)) \lhd b \rhd \text{skip}$
>
> $\sqsupseteq\quad$ {$\langle$dec$-;$ dist$\rangle(3.18.8)$ and $\langle$dec$- :=$ initial value$\rangle(3.18.5)$}
>
> $\qquad$ $((\text{dec } v, \text{A} \bullet p); \ RHS) \lhd b \rhd \text{skip}$

The result follows from $\langle \mu$ least fixed point$\rangle(3.8.2)$. $\qquad\qquad\qquad\qquad\qquad\qquad\Diamond$

The local variable A on the left-hand side of the above inequation is a result of the simplification of assignments in p. Likewise, v may be an arbitrary list of temporary variables created to simplify boolean operators or originally introduced by the programmer. By moving these declarations out of the body of the iteration, we avoid nested declarations of the variable A. The expression b can now be simplified using the previous theorems.

In a similar way, we can simplify the boolean expressions of conditional statements.

Rule 4.6.   (Condition of conditional)
If neither v nor A occur in b

$$(\text{dec } v, \text{A} \bullet p) \lhd b \rhd (\text{dec } v, \text{A} \bullet q) \sqsubseteq \text{dec } v, \text{A} \bullet \text{A} := b; \ (p \lhd \text{A} \rhd q)$$

Proof: Similar to the proof of Rule 4.5. $\qquad\qquad\qquad\qquad\qquad\qquad\qquad\qquad\Diamond$

The following theorem summarises the outcome of this phase of compilation. It is regarded as a theorem rather than as a rule because it is not used to carry out compilation; it establishes that the rules described above (together with a few algebraic laws) are sufficient to eliminate nested expressions in an arbitrary source program.

Theorem 4.8.   (Expression simplification)
For an arbitrary source program p, there is a program q such that

$$p \sqsubseteq \text{dec } v, \text{A} \bullet q$$

where q contains no local declarations, all assignments in q are simple and the only boolean condition in q is the variable A.

Proof: By structural induction using rules 4.1–4.6, together with the following laws:

- $\langle ; -\mathsf{dec}\ \mathsf{dist} \rangle (3.18.7, 3.18.8)$
  This is used to increase the scope of the local variables as much as possible.

- $\langle \mathsf{dec}\ \mathsf{assoc} \rangle (3.18.1)$ and $\langle \mathsf{dec}\ \mathsf{rename} \rangle (3.18.4)$
  The former is used to eliminate nested declarations that may have been intro-
  duced by the programmer or resulted from the simplification of boolean operators; the latter is used to rename nested occurrences of variables which were
  declared with the same name, so that the nesting can be eliminated.

- $\langle \mathsf{dec}\ \mathsf{elim} \rangle (3.18.3)$
  Rule 4.6 assumes that the local variables of the two branches of a conditional
  are the same. The above law can be used to introduce void declarations (local
  variables declared but not used) to ensure that this assumption will be satisfied.

$\diamond$

The following example illustrates how the rules presented in this section can be
used effectively to carry out the simplification of expressions.

Example 4.1. (Expression simplification)
Consider the assignment

$$x := y \,\mathsf{bop}\, (\mathsf{uop}\ z)$$

As explained in the beginning of this section, Rule 4.1 is always the first one to be
applied, since it introduces the register variable A in terms of which the subsequent
rules are expressed. This results in

$$\mathsf{dec}\ \mathsf{A} \bullet \mathsf{A} := y \,\mathsf{bop}\, (\mathsf{uop}\ z);\ x := \mathsf{A}$$

In the next step we use Rule 4.3 to deal with the top (binary) operator which appears
in the expression assigned to A:

$$\mathsf{dec}\ \mathsf{A} \bullet (\mathsf{dec}\ t \bullet \mathsf{A} := (\mathsf{uop}\ z);\ t := \mathsf{A};\ \mathsf{A} := y;\ \mathsf{A} := \mathsf{A} \,\mathsf{bop}\, t);\ x := \mathsf{A}$$

Then we apply Rule 4.2 to simplify the first assignment above.

$$\mathsf{dec}\ \mathsf{A} \bullet (\mathsf{dec}\ t \bullet \mathsf{A} := z;\ \mathsf{A} := (\mathsf{uop}\ \mathsf{A});\ t := \mathsf{A};\ \mathsf{A} := y;\ \mathsf{A} := \mathsf{A} \,\mathsf{bop}\, t);\ x := \mathsf{A}$$

Now all the assignments are simple (see Definition 4.2). To reach the final format
stated by Theorem 4.8, the only remaining step is to extend the scope of the inner
block which declares the local variable t; as a result we end up with a single block
which declares the two local variables A and t. This is achieved using Laws 3.18.1
and 3.18.7:

$$\mathsf{dec}\ \mathsf{A}, t \bullet \mathsf{A} := z;\ \mathsf{A} := (\mathsf{uop}\ \mathsf{A});\ t := \mathsf{A};\ \mathsf{A} := y;\ \mathsf{A} := \mathsf{A} \,\mathsf{bop}\, t;\ x := \mathsf{A}$$

4.5. Control Elimination

Recall that the machine considered here is equipped with the program counter P which is used for scheduling the selection and sequencing of instructions. This can be simulated by regarding P as a variable in the following way:

- Selection is achieved by representing the stored program as a set of guarded commands, each one of the form

  $$(P = k) \to q$$

  meaning that q (standing for some machine instruction) will be executed when P has value k.

- Sequencing is modelled by incrementing P

  $$P := P + 1$$

- A jump to an instruction at memory location k is achieved by the assignment

  $$P := k$$

Clearly, the initial value of P must be the address of the location of the first instruction to be executed. These conventions are our basis to transform the nested control structure of the source program into a single flat iteration which models the execution of a stored program.

The outcome of this section is a *simple* normal form program.

Definition 4.3. (Simple normal form)
We say that a normal form program is *simple* if it has the form

$$P : [(P = s), b \to p, (P = f)]$$

where p is a set of guarded commands of the form

$$\square_{s \leq k < f}(P = k) \to x_k, P := e_k, d_k$$

and b is the disjunction of the guards $(P = k)$, for all k such that $s \leq k < f$. Furthermore, the assignment $x_k, P := e_k, d_k$ follows one of the patterns used to define the machine instructions, except that the source variables may not yet have been replaced by their corresponding memory locations (this is addressed in the next section). ◇

Reduction to this simple normal form can be achieved by instantiating the normal form theorems of Section 4.2, taking into account the particular encoding of control state of our simple machine. In the following we abbreviate

$$P : [(P = s), b \to p, (P = f)]$$

to

$$P : [s, b \to p, f]$$

The purpose of the first implementation of skip is to generate empty code: false → skip is equivalent to ⊤ which is the identity of □.

Rule 4.7. (Skip)

$$\text{skip} \sqsubseteq \text{P} : [s, \text{false} \rightarrow \text{skip}, s]$$

$\Diamond$

Rule 4.8. (Skip)

$$\text{skip} \sqsubseteq \text{P} : [s, (\text{P} = s \rightarrow \text{P} := s + 1), s + 1]$$

$\Diamond$

Rule 4.9. (Assignment)

$$(x := e) \sqsubseteq \text{P} : [s, (\text{P} = s \rightarrow (x, \text{P} := e, \text{P} + 1)), s + 1]$$

$\Diamond$

Rule 4.10. (Sequential composition)

$$(\text{P} : [s, b_1 \rightarrow p, f_0]); \ (\text{P} : [f_0, b_2 \rightarrow q, f]) \sqsubseteq \text{P} : [s, \left(\begin{array}{c} b_1 \rightarrow p \\ \Box \quad b_2 \rightarrow q \end{array} \right), f]$$

$\Diamond$

Rule 4.11. (Conditional)

$$(\text{P} : [s + 1, b_1 \rightarrow p, f_0]) \lhd \text{A} \rhd (\text{P} : [f_0 + 1, b_2 \rightarrow q, f]) \sqsubseteq \text{P} : [s, R, f]$$

$$\text{where } R = \left(\begin{array}{c} \text{P} = s \rightarrow \text{P} := (\text{P} + 1 \lhd \text{A} \rhd f_0 + 1) \\ \Box \quad b_1 \rightarrow p \ \Box \ \text{P} = f_0 \rightarrow \text{P} := f \\ \Box \quad b_2 \rightarrow q \end{array} \right)$$

$\Diamond$

Rule 4.12. (Iteration)

$$\text{A} * (\text{P} : [s + 1, b \rightarrow p, f_0]) \sqsubseteq \text{P} : [s, R, f_0 + 1]$$

$$\text{where } R = \left(\begin{array}{c} \text{P} = s \rightarrow \text{P} := (\text{P} + 1 \lhd \text{A} \rhd f_0 + 1) \\ \Box \quad b \rightarrow p \ \Box \ \text{P} = f_0 \rightarrow \text{P} := s \end{array} \right)$$

$\Diamond$

It is worth observing that the above rules assume the allocation of contiguous addresses for the stored program. For example, the rule for sequential composition assumes that the finish address of the normal form program on the left coincides with the start address of the normal form program on the right.

Strictly, the above rules cannot be justified only from the reduction theorems of Section 4.2. Some additional (although trivial) transformations are required. As an example, we present the proof of Rule 4.9.

$$\mathsf{P} : [s, (\mathsf{P} = s \to (x, \mathsf{P} := e, \mathsf{P} + 1)), s + 1]$$
$$= \quad \{\langle := \text{ substitution}\rangle(3.15.5)\}$$
$$\mathsf{P} : [s, (\mathsf{P} = s \to (x, \mathsf{P} := e, s + 1)), s + 1]$$
$$= \quad \{\langle := \text{ combination}\rangle(3.15.4) \text{ and } \langle := \text{ identity}\rangle(3.15.2)\}$$
$$\mathsf{P} : [s, (\mathsf{P} = s \to (x := e; \ \mathsf{P} := s + 1)), s + 1]$$
$$= \quad \{\langle :\in - := \text{ conversion}\rangle(3.16.7)\}$$
$$\mathsf{P} : [s, (\mathsf{P} = s \to (x := e; \ \mathsf{P} :\in (\mathsf{P} = s + 1))), s + 1]$$
$$\sqsupseteq \quad \{\text{Theorem } 4.3(\text{Assignment})\}$$
$$x := e$$

The additional transformations required to prove the other theorems are similar.

The next theorem summarises the outcome of this phase of compilation.

Theorem 4.9.   (Control elimination)
Consider a program of the form

$$\text{dec } v, \mathsf{A} \bullet q$$

where q contains no local declaration, all assignments in q are simple and the only boolean condition in q is the variable A. Then there is a *simple* normal form program such that

$$\text{dec } v, \mathsf{A} \bullet q \sqsubseteq v, \mathsf{A}, \mathsf{P} : [(\mathsf{P} = s), b \to r, (\mathsf{P} = f)]$$

Proof: By structural induction using rules 4.7–4.12, we transform q into

$$\mathsf{P} : [(\mathsf{P} = s), b \to r, (\mathsf{P} = f)]$$

The final result follows from (dec assoc)(3.18.1).   ◇

The following example illustrates how the rules presented in this section can be used to perform control elimination.

Example 4.2.   (Control elimination)
In Example 4.1, we started with the assignment $x := y \text{ bop } (\text{uop } z)$ and, as a result of expression simplification, this was transformed into

$$\text{dec } \mathsf{A}, t \bullet \mathsf{A} := z; \ \mathsf{A} := (\text{uop } \mathsf{A}); \ t := \mathsf{A}; \ \mathsf{A} := y; \ \mathsf{A} := \mathsf{A} \text{ bop } t; \ x := \mathsf{A}$$

which we take as a starting point to illustrate control elimination.

Observe that the compilation rule for assignment (Rule 4.9) is immediately applicable to each of the above assignments; the order in which each one is reduced to normal form is irrelevant. Let us consider the leftmost assignment $A := z$. For a given location s in ROM, the reduction of this assignment results in

$$P : [s, (P = s \rightarrow (A, P := z, P + 1)), s + 1]$$

The remaining assignments are transformed in a similar way. In other to combine these normal forms we use the reduction rule for sequential composition (Rule 4.10). But this rule requires that the finish address of its left argument coincide with the start address of its right argument. For example, if the rule for sequential composition is to be applicable, the normal form of the assignment $A := (uop\, A)$ must be

$$P : [s + 1, (P = s + 1 \rightarrow (A, P := (uop\, A), P + 1)), s + 2]$$

Then the combination of the above two normal forms gives

$$P \cdot [s, \left(\begin{array}{l} P = s \rightarrow (A, P := z, P + 1) \\ \Box\, P = s + 1 \rightarrow (A, P := (uop\, A), P + 1) \end{array} \right), s + 2]$$

A strategy to ensure that the addresses allocated for the machine instructions are distinct and contiguous is discussed in Section 6.5 which deals with the issue of compiler prototyping.

The step by step reduction of the other assignment statements of our example should be obvious and is left as an exercise to the reader. The final result is given by the normal form program

$$A, t, P : [s, \left(\begin{array}{l} P = s \rightarrow (A, P := z, P + 1) \\ \Box\, P = s + 1 \rightarrow (A, P := (uop\, A), P + 1) \\ \Box\, P = s + 2 \rightarrow (t, P := A, P + 1) \\ \Box\, P = s + 3 \rightarrow (A, P := y, P + 1) \\ \Box\, P = s + 4 \rightarrow (A, P := A\, bop\, t, P + 1) \\ \Box\, P = s + 5 \rightarrow (x, P := A, P + 1) \end{array} \right), s + 6]$$

Note that in addition to P, the variables A and t are also local to the above normal form program.   ◇

4.6. Data Refinement

The only task that remains to be addressed is the replacement of the abstract space of the source program (formed from the source variables) by the concrete state of the target machine, represented by the store M. As mentioned in Section 3.10, the idea is to define a simulation function and use its distributivity properties to perform this data refinement in a systematic way.

Suppose that Ψ is a symbol table which maps each global variable of the source program to the address of the storage M allocated to hold its value, so $M[\Psi x]^1$ is

---

[1] To improve readability we abbreviate the function application $\Psi[x]$ to Ψx.

the location holding the value of x. Clearly it is necessary to insist that Ψ is a total injection. Assuming that w is a list formed from the global variables (where each variable in the domain of Ψ occurs exactly once in w) we define the following *encoding* program.

Definition 4.4. (Encoding Program)

$$\hat{\Psi}_w \stackrel{def}{=} \mathsf{var}\, w;\ w := \mathsf{M}[\Psi w];\ \mathsf{end}\,\mathsf{M}$$

$\diamond$

It *retrieves* the abstract state from the concrete state by assigning to each source variable the value in the corresponding location (recall that we allow list application: for $w = x, \ldots, z$ the above assignment is equivalent to $x, \ldots, z := \mathsf{M}[\Psi x], \ldots, \mathsf{M}[\Psi z]$). Observe that once the abstract state (the data space of the source program) is initialised, the concrete (machine) state will play no further role and therefore its scope is ended

The following *decoding* program maps the abstract state to the concrete machine state. For the same reason explained above, once the machine state is initialised, the data space of the source program is ended.

Definition 4.5. (Decoding program)

$$\hat{\Psi}_w^{-1} \stackrel{def}{=} \mathsf{var}\, \mathsf{M};\ \mathsf{M} := \mathsf{M} \oplus \{\Psi w \mapsto w\};\ \mathsf{end}\, w$$

$\diamond$

Also recall that for $w = x, \ldots, z$ the above assignment corresponds to

$$\mathsf{M} := \mathsf{M} \oplus (\{\Psi x \mapsto x\} \cup \ldots \cup \{\Psi z \mapsto z\})$$

which updates the memory M at position Ψx with the value currently held by the variable x, and so on.

The first theorem formalises the obvious relationship between $\hat{\Psi}_w$ and $\hat{\Psi}_w^{-1}$

Theorem 4.10. $((\hat{\Psi}_w, \hat{\Psi}_w^{-1})$ simulation)
The pair of programs $(\hat{\Psi}_w, \hat{\Psi}_w^{-1})$ is a simulation.
Proof:

$\qquad \hat{\Psi}_w;\ \hat{\Psi}_w^{-1}$

$\quad \sqsubseteq \quad \{\text{Definitions of } \hat{\Psi}_w, \hat{\Psi}_w^{-1} \text{ and } \langle \mathsf{end} - \mathsf{var} \text{ simulation} \rangle (3.19.6)\}$

$\qquad \mathsf{var}\, w;\ w := \mathsf{M}[\Psi w];\ \mathsf{M} := \mathsf{M} \oplus \{\Psi w \mapsto w\};\ \mathsf{end}\, w$

$\quad = \quad \{\langle := \text{ combination}\rangle (3.15.4) \text{ and } \langle := \text{ identity}\rangle (3.15.2)\}$

$\qquad \mathsf{var}\, w;\ w, \mathsf{M} := \mathsf{M}[\Psi w], (\mathsf{M} \oplus \{\Psi w \mapsto \mathsf{M}[\Psi w]\});\ \mathsf{end}\, w$

$\quad = \quad \{\text{Property of maps } (\mathsf{M} = \mathsf{M} \oplus \{\Psi w \mapsto \mathsf{M}[\Psi w]\}) \text{ and}$

$\qquad\quad \langle := \text{ identity}\rangle (3.15.2)\}$

$\quad$ var w; $\;w := \mathsf{M}[\Psi w]$; end w

$=\;\;\{\langle\mathsf{end} - \mathsf{var}\ \mathsf{simulation}\rangle(3.19.6)\ \text{and}\ \langle\mathsf{end}-\mathsf{:=}\ \mathsf{final}\ \mathsf{value}(3.19.5)\rangle\}$

$\quad$ skip

$=\;\;\{\langle\mathsf{end} - \mathsf{var}\ \mathsf{simulation}\rangle(3.19.6)\ \text{and}\ \langle\mathsf{end}-\mathsf{:=}\ \mathsf{final}\ \mathsf{value}(3.19.5)\rangle\}$

$\quad$ var M; $\;\mathsf{M} := \mathsf{M} \oplus \{\Psi w \mapsto w\}$; end M

$=\;\;\{\langle\mathsf{:=}\ \mathsf{combination}\rangle(3.15.4)\ \text{and}\ \langle\mathsf{:=}\ \mathsf{identity}\rangle(3.15.2)\}$

$\quad$ var M; $\;\mathsf{M} := \mathsf{M} \oplus \{\Psi w \mapsto w\}$; $\;w := \mathsf{M}[\Psi w]$; end M

$=\;\;\{\langle\mathsf{end} - \mathsf{var}\ \mathsf{skip}\rangle(3.19.7)\}$

$\quad$ (var M; $\;\mathsf{M} := \mathsf{M} \oplus \{\Psi w \mapsto w\}$; end w); (var w; $\;w := \mathsf{M}[\Psi w]$; end M)

$=\;\;\{\text{Definitions of}\ \hat{\Psi}_w, \hat{\Psi}_w^{-1}\}$

$\quad \hat{\Psi}_w^{-1}; \;\hat{\Psi}_w$

$\hfill\Diamond$

Recall from Section 3.10 that we use the first component of a simulation as a function. For example, for a program p we have

$$\hat{\Psi}_w(p) \;=\; \hat{\Psi}_w;\ p;\ \hat{\Psi}_w^{-1}$$

Here we generalise this particular simulation function to take an expression as argument. The effect of applying $\hat{\Psi}_w$ to e is to replace free occurrences of w in e with the corresponding machine locations $\mathsf{M}[\Psi w]$.

Definition 4.6. (Simulation as substitution)

$$\hat{\Psi}_w(e) \;\overset{def}{=}\; e[w \leftarrow \mathsf{M}[\Psi w]]$$

$\hfill\Diamond$

In order to carry out the change of data representation in a systematic way, we need to prove the following distributivity properties.

Rule 4.13. (Piecewise data refinement)

(1) $\hat{\Psi}_w(\mathsf{skip}) \sqsubseteq \mathsf{skip}$

(2) $\hat{\Psi}_{x,w}(x := e) \sqsubseteq \mathsf{M} := \mathsf{M} \oplus \{\Psi x \mapsto \hat{\Psi}_{x,w}(e)\}$

(3) $\hat{\Psi}_w(x := e) \sqsubseteq x := \hat{\Psi}_w(e)\quad$ if x does not occur in w

(4) $\hat{\Psi}_w(p;\ q) \sqsubseteq \hat{\Psi}_w(p); \hat{\Psi}_w(q)$

(5) $\hat{\Psi}_w(p \triangleleft b \triangleright q) \sqsubseteq \hat{\Psi}_w(p) \triangleleft \hat{\Psi}_w(b) \triangleright \hat{\Psi}_w(q)$

(6) $\hat{\Psi}_w(b * p) \sqsubseteq \hat{\Psi}_w(b) * \hat{\Psi}_w(p)$

(7) $\hat{\Psi}_w(b_\perp) \sqsubseteq (\hat{\Psi}_w(b))_\perp$

(8) $\hat{\Psi}_w(b \rightarrow p) \sqsubseteq \hat{\Psi}_w(b) \rightarrow \hat{\Psi}_w(p)$

(9) $\hat{\Psi}_w(p \ \square\ q) \sqsubseteq \hat{\Psi}_w(p) \ \square\ \hat{\Psi}_w(q)$

Proof: (1), (4) and (9) follow directly from the fact that $\hat{\Psi}_w$ is a simulation function (see Theorem 3.4). Below we verify the others.

(2) $\hat{\Psi}_{x,w}(x := e)$

=   {Definition of $\hat{\Psi}_{x,w}$ and $\langle$end change scope$\rangle$(3.19.2)}

    var x, w; $x, w := M[\Psi x, w]$; $x := e$; end M; $\hat{\Psi}_{x,w}^{-1}$

=   {$\langle := $ combination$\rangle$(3.15.4), $\langle := $ identity$\rangle$(3.15.2) and Definition 4.6(Simulation as substitution)}

    var x, w; $x, w := \hat{\Psi}_{x,w}(e), M[\Psi w]$; end M; $\hat{\Psi}_{x,w}^{-1}$

$\sqsubseteq$ {Definition of $\hat{\Psi}_{x,w}^{-1}$ and $\langle$end − var simulation$\rangle$(3.19.6)}

    var x, w; $x, w := \hat{\Psi}_{x,w}(e), M[\Psi w]$; M $:= M \oplus \{\Psi x, w \mapsto x, w\}$; end x, w

=   {$\langle := $ combination$\rangle$(3.15.4), $\langle := $ identity$\rangle$(3.15.2) and $\langle$end change scope$\rangle$(3.19.2)}

    var x, w; $x, w := \hat{\Psi}_{x,w}(e), M[\Psi w]$; end x, w;

    M $:= M \oplus \{\Psi x \mapsto \hat{\Psi}_{x,w}(e)\}$

=   {$\langle$end− $:=$ final value$\rangle$(3.19.5) and $\langle$end − var simulation$\rangle$(3.19.6)}

    M $:= M \oplus \{\Psi x \mapsto \hat{\Psi}_{x,w}(e)\}$

(3)   Similar to (2).

(5) $\hat{\Psi}_w(p \lhd b \rhd q)$

=   {Definition of $\hat{\Psi}_w$ and $\langle$end − $\lhd \rhd$ right dist$\rangle$(3.19.3)}

    var w; $w := M[\Psi w]$; ((end M; $p) \lhd b \rhd ($end M; q)); $\hat{\Psi}_w^{-1}$

=   {$\langle := - \lhd \rhd$ right dist$\rangle$(3.15.7) and Definition 4.6(Simulation as substitution)}

    var w; (($w := M[\Psi w]$; end M; $p) \lhd \hat{\Psi}_w(b) \rhd (w := M[\Psi w]$; end M; q)); $\hat{\Psi}_w^{-1}$

=   {$\langle$var − $\lhd \rhd$ right dist$\rangle$(3.19.3) and $\langle ; - \lhd \rhd$ left dist$\rangle$(3.14.6)}

    $\hat{\Psi}_w(p) \lhd \hat{\Psi}_w(b) \rhd \hat{\Psi}_w(q)$

(6) $\hat{\Psi}_w(b * p)$

$\sqsubseteq$ {Theorem 3.4(Distributivity of simulation through) μ}

    $\mu X \bullet \hat{\Psi}_w((p; \hat{\Psi}_w^{-1}(X)) \lhd b \rhd \text{skip})$

$\sqsubseteq$ {(5) and (1)}

    $\mu X \bullet (\hat{\Psi}_w(p; \hat{\Psi}_w^{-1}(X)) \lhd \hat{\Psi}_w(b) \rhd \text{skip})$

$\sqsubseteq$ {(4) and Theorem 3.3(Lift of simulation)}

$$\hat{\Psi}_w(b) * \hat{\Psi}_w(p)$$

(7)   Similar to (5).

(8)   From (4), (7) and $(b \to p) = (b_\perp; p)$.

$\diamond$

The above rule deals with the global variables. But the local variables v (introduced either by the programmer or during the simplification of expressions) also require locations to hold their values during execution. For simplicity, we assume that all local variables are distinct, and that they are also different from the global variables. We extend the symbol table Ψ to cover all the local variables v:

$$\Phi \stackrel{def}{=} \Psi \cup \{v \mapsto n\}$$

where n is a list of addresses distinct from the ones already used by Ψ.

The next lemma states that the encoding program $\hat{\Psi}_w$ (when followed by a declaration of the local variables v) can be refined to an encoding program $\hat{\Phi}_{v,w}$ that deals with the global and the local variables.

Lemma 4.6. (Extending the encoding program)

$$\hat{\Psi}_w; \ \text{var} \ v \ \sqsubseteq \hat{\Phi}_{v,w}$$

Proof:

$\hat{\Psi}_w; \ \text{var} \ v$

$\sqsubseteq$ {$\langle$var change scope$\rangle$(3.19.2), $\langle$var assoc$\rangle$(3.19.1) and
    $\langle$var$- :=$ initial value$\rangle$(3.19.4)}

   var $v, w; \ v := \mathsf{M}[n]; \ w := \mathsf{M}[\Psi w]; \ \text{end} \ \mathsf{M}$

$=$ {$\langle := $ combination$\rangle$(3.15.4) and $\langle := $ identity$\rangle$(3.15.2)}

   var $v, w; \ v, w := \mathsf{M}[n, \Psi w]; \ \text{end} \ \mathsf{M}$

$=$ {Definition of Φ and $(\Phi v, \Phi w) = \Phi(v, w)$}

   var $v, w; \ v, w := \mathsf{M}[\Phi(v, w)]; \ \text{end} \ \mathsf{M}$

$=$ {Definition 4.4(Encoding program)}

   $\hat{\Phi}_{v,w}$

The decoding program can be extended in an analogous way.

Lemma 4.7. (Extending the decoding program)

$$\text{end} \ v; \ \hat{\Psi}_w^{-1} \ \sqsubseteq \hat{\Phi}_{v,w}^{-1}$$

Proof:

$$\text{end } v;\ \hat{\Psi}_w^{-1}$$

$\sqsubseteq$ {⟨end change scope⟩(3.19.2), ⟨end assoc⟩(3.19.1) and
⟨var− := initial value⟩(3.19.4)}

$$\text{var M};\ \text{M} := \text{M} \oplus \{n \mapsto v\};\ \text{M} := \text{M} \oplus \{\Psi w \mapsto w\};\ \text{end } v, w$$

$=$ {⟨:= combination⟩(3.15.4) and Definition of Φ}

$$\text{var M};\ \text{M} := \text{M} \oplus \{\Phi(v, w) \mapsto v, w\};\ \text{end } v, w$$

$=$ {Definition 4.5(Decoding program)}

$$\hat{\Phi}_{v,w}^{-1}$$

◇

Using the above two lemmas we show how to assign locations in the memory M
to hold the values of the local variables v.

Rule 4.14. (Allocating local variables)

$$\hat{\Psi}_w(\text{dec } v, \text{P}, \text{A} \bullet p) \sqsubseteq \text{dec P}, \text{A} \bullet \hat{\Phi}_{v,w}(p)$$

Proof:

$$\hat{\Psi}_w(\text{dec } v, \text{P}, \text{A} \bullet p)$$

$=$ {Definition 3.6(Simulation function)}

$$\hat{\Psi}_w;\ (\text{dec } v, \text{P}, \text{A} \bullet p);\ \hat{\Psi}_w^{-1}$$

$=$ {⟨dec assoc⟩(3.18.1) and ⟨dec − (var, end) conversion⟩(3.19.10)}

$$\hat{\Psi}_w;\ \text{var } v;\ (\text{dec P}, \text{A} \bullet p);\ \text{end } v;\ \hat{\Psi}_w^{-1}$$

$\sqsubseteq$ {Lemmas 4.6 and 4.7}

$$\hat{\Phi}_{v,w};\ (\text{dec P}, \text{A} \bullet p);\ \hat{\Phi}_{v,w}^{-1}$$

$=$ {⟨; −dec left dist⟩(3.18.7) and ⟨; −dec right dist⟩(3.18.7)}

$$\text{dec P}, \text{A} \bullet \hat{\Phi}_{v,w}(p)$$

◇

The next theorem summarises the outcome of this phase of compilation.

Theorem 4.11. (Data refinement)
Consider a program of the form

$$\text{dec } v, \text{A} \bullet q$$

where q contains no local declaration, all assignments in q are simple and the only
boolean condition in q is the variable A. Then there is a program r such that

$$\hat{\Psi}_w(\text{dec } v, \text{A} \bullet q) \sqsubseteq \text{dec A} \bullet r$$

where r preserves the control structure of q but operates exclusively on the concrete state represented by M.

Proof: Using Rule 4.14 (Allocating local variables), we transform

$$\hat{\Psi}_w(\text{dec } v, \text{A} \bullet q)$$

into

$$\text{dec A} \bullet \hat{\Phi}_{v,w}(q)$$

Then by structural induction using Rule 4.13 (Piecewise data refinement), we transform $\hat{\Phi}_{v,w}(q)$ into r. $\diamondsuit$

It is worth noting that this theorem does not prevent q from being a normal form program. This suggests that we can carry out data refinement either before or after control refinement. In the latter case, note that Rule 4.13 (in particular (7), (8) and (9)) covers the additional operators used to describe a normal form program.

With examples 4.1 and 4.2, we illustrated the simplification of expressions and control elimination, respectively. The next example shows how the rules presented in this section can be used to carry out the necessary change of data representation.

Example 4.3.   (Data refinement)
In Example 4.1, we started with the assignment $x := y \text{ bop } (\text{uop } z)$ and, as a result of expression simplification, this was transformed into

$$\text{dec A}, t \bullet \text{A} := z; \ \text{A} := (\text{uop A}); \ t := \text{A}; \ \text{A} := y; \ \text{A} := \text{A bop } t; \ x := \text{A}$$

The above was then used in Example 4.2 (to illustrate control elimination) and was further transformed into

$$\text{A}, t, \text{P} : [s, \begin{pmatrix} \text{P} = s \rightarrow (\text{A}, \text{P} := z, \text{P} + 1) \\ \Box \ \text{P} = s + 1 \rightarrow (\text{A}, \text{P} := (\text{uop A}), \text{P} + 1) \\ \Box \ \text{P} = s + 2 \rightarrow (t, \text{P} := \text{A}, \text{P} + 1) \\ \Box \ \text{P} = s + 3 \rightarrow (\text{A}, \text{P} := y, \text{P} + 1) \\ \Box \ \text{P} = s + 4 \rightarrow (\text{A}, \text{P} := \text{A bop } t, \text{P} + 1) \\ \Box \ \text{P} = s + 5 \rightarrow (x, \text{P} := \text{A}, \text{P} + 1) \end{pmatrix}, s + 6]$$

Observe that each of the guarded assignments is closely related to the definition of the behaviour of some machine instruction (see Section 4.3). In order for these assignments to match precisely the corresponding definitions, we need to replace the source variables of the above normal form program with the corresponding locations in the machine store M. As explained above, this is achieved by applying a simulation function constructed from the symbol table. The list w of global variables of our simple program is

$$w = x, y, z$$

and suppose that the symbol table is as follows

$$\Psi = \{x \mapsto 101, y \mapsto 102, z \mapsto 103\}$$

Now we can use the distributivity properties of the simulation function $\overset{\circ}{\Psi}_w$ (Rule 4.13) to carry out the relevant data refinement. But note that there is a local variable t which must also be replaced by its location in M. Therefore before applying Rule 4.13 we need to use Rule 4.14. Assuming that 104 is the address where t is held[2] the application of the above mentioned rules results in

$$A, P : [s, \left(\begin{array}{l} P = s \rightarrow (A, P := M[103], P + 1) \\ \Box \, P = s + 1 \rightarrow (A, P := (\text{uop A}), P + 1) \\ \Box \, P = s + 2 \rightarrow (M, P := (M \oplus \{104 \mapsto A\}), P + 1) \\ \Box \, P = s + 3 \rightarrow (A, P := M[102], P + 1) \\ \Box \, P = s + 4 \rightarrow (A, P := A \text{ bop } M[104], P + 1) \\ \Box \, P = s + 5 \rightarrow (M, P := (M \oplus \{101 \mapsto A\}), P + 1) \end{array} \right), s + 6]$$

A simple syntactic transformation of the patterns used to define the instructions into the corresponding instruction names finally gives

$$A, P : [s, \left(\begin{array}{l} P = s \rightarrow \text{load}(103) \\ \Box \, P = s + 1 \rightarrow \text{uop-A} \\ \Box \, P = s + 2 \rightarrow \text{store}(104) \\ \Box \, P = s + 3 \rightarrow \text{load}(102) \\ \Box \, P = s + 4 \rightarrow \text{bop-A}(104) \\ \Box \, P = s + 5 \rightarrow \text{store}(101) \end{array} \right), s + 6]$$

completing the compilation of our simple assignment command.   ◇

Further details about the compilation process in general are discussed in the next section.

4.7. The Compilation Process

In principle, there is no reason for imposing any order on the phases of compilation. But there are practical considerations which favour some permutations. In particular, we suggest that the simplification of expressions should be the first phase. Performing data refinement as a first step would not be appealing, because the simplification of expressions normally generates new local variables. Therefore a second phase of data refinement would be required to deal specifically with the local declarations.

We have also explored the possibility of carrying out control elimination as a first step. It turned out to be necessary to allocate relative addresses to commands of the source program, and (in the end of the process) to convert them into absolute

---

[2]In Chapter 6 we devise a strategy to generate addresses for the local variables which are guaranteed to be distinct from those used for the global variables.

addresses. The standard approach would be to model an address as a pair. For example, the normal form of an assignment statement $x := \text{uop } y$ (where x and y are single variables) would be

$$\mathsf{P} : [(k,0), \mathsf{P} = (k,0) \rightarrow (x := \text{uop } y; \ \mathsf{P} := (k+1,0)), (k+1,0)]$$

As a result of expression simplification, the above guarded command would be transformed into

$$\mathsf{P} = (k,0) \rightarrow ((\text{dec } \mathsf{A} \bullet \mathsf{A} := y; \ \mathsf{A} := \text{uop } \mathsf{A}; \ x := \mathsf{A}); \ \mathsf{P} := (k+1,0))$$

containing only simple assignments. In a similar way, all the other assignments and conditions of the source program would be simplified. However, we must eventually end with a simple normal form program, and there are two remaining tasks. One is to move the local declarations generated by this process out from the body of the loop; this is justified by the distribution laws of declaration with the other operators of our language. The other task is to split the above command into a series of guarded commands (one for each assignment) and model the sequencing by incrementing the second component of the pair representing a relative address:

$$\mathsf{P} = (k,0) \rightarrow \mathsf{A} := y; \ \mathsf{P} := (k,1) \ \square$$
$$\mathsf{P} = (k,1) \rightarrow \mathsf{A} := \text{uop } \mathsf{A}; \ \mathsf{P} := (k,2) \ \square$$
$$\mathsf{P} = (k,2) \rightarrow x := \mathsf{A}; \ \mathsf{P} := (k+1,0)$$

This is necessary to ensure that each instruction will be placed in a separate memory location. Assuming that the relative address $(k,0)$ will eventually turn into the absolute address j, the above becomes

$$\mathsf{P} = j \rightarrow \mathsf{A}, \mathsf{P} := y, (\mathsf{P}+1) \ \square$$
$$\mathsf{P} = (j+1) \rightarrow \mathsf{A}, \mathsf{P} := (\text{uop } \mathsf{A}), (\mathsf{P}+1) \ \square$$
$$\mathsf{P} = (j+2) \rightarrow x, \mathsf{P} := \mathsf{A}, (\mathsf{P}+1)$$

which is in the required form. While the conversion from relative to absolute addresses is in principle a simple process, there is the associated proof obligation to show that the iteration is not affected by this change of data representation. It seems sensible to avoided these complications by starting the compilation process with the simplification of expressions.

Once the expressions are simplified, the order in which data refinement and control elimination are carried out is irrelevant. Apart from these steps, in practice there are at least two additional phases (*linking* and *loading*) before the produced code can actually be executed. Linking is not considered here, since our concern in this work is with code generation for a given program unit. Loading is the placement of the generated code in the memory M, as explained in the proof of the following theorem which summarises the compilation process.

Theorem 4.12. (Compilation Process)
Let p be an arbitrary source program. Given a constant s, and a symbol table Ψ

which maps each global variable of p to the address of the memory M allocated to hold its value, there is a constant f and a sequence of machine instructions held in m between locations s and f such that

$$\hat{\Psi}_w(p) \sqsubseteq \text{dec } P, A \bullet P := s;\ (s \leq P < f) * m[P];\ (P = f)_\perp$$

Proof: From theorems 4.8 (Expression simplification), 4.9 (Control elimination) and 4.11 (Data refinement), $\hat{\Psi}_w(p)$ is transformed into

$$\text{dec } P, A \bullet P := s;\ (s \leq P < f) * p;\ (P = f)_\perp$$

where p is a guarded command set of the form

$$\square_{s \leq k < f} P = k \rightarrow q_k$$

and each q_k is an assignment which corresponds to one of the patterns used to define the machine instructions. This guarded command set is an abstract representation of the memory m, whose contents are affected by the compilation process as follows:

$$m[k] = q_k, \quad \text{for } s \leq k < f$$

and the value of m outside the range $s..(f-1)$ is arbitrary. This last step corresponds to the actual loading process. $\diamond$

Examples 4.1, 4.2 and 4.3 illustrated the overall process in a phase by phase fashion. A more detailed description of how the reduction theorems can be used as rewrite rules to carry out compilation is given in Chapter 6, which deals with the mechanisation of compilation and proofs.

CHAPTER 5

PROCEDURES, RECURSION AND PARAMETERS

> The main characteristic of intelligent thinking is that
> one is willing and able to study in depth an aspect of
> one's subject matter in isolation [...]
> Such separation, even if not perfectly possible, is yet the
> only available technique for effective ordering of one's
> thoughts.
>
> — E. W. Dijkstra

In this chapter we extend the source language with more elaborate notions: procedures, recursion and parameters. We show how each of these can be eliminated through reduction to normal form, but we leave open the choice of a target machine to implement them.

Most practical programming languages group these notions into a single construction which allows parametrised recursive procedures. Here we follow Hoare [46], Morgan [64] and Back [4], and treat them separately—both syntactically and semantically. Existing practice is in most cases realised by appropriate combinations of these features; nevertheless, the separation gives more freedom and elegance, and helps to simplify the overall task.

5.1. Notation

In order to prove the correctness of the elimination rule for recursion, we need to extend our language with sequence variables together with some familiar operations. By convention, a variable name decorated with ‾, such as $\bar{x}$, denotes a sequence variable. The following operators are assumed:

$\langle\rangle$ the empty sequence

$\langle x\rangle$ the singleton sequence with element x

$\bar{x} \frown \bar{y}$ the concatenation of $\bar{x}$ and $\bar{y}$

head $\bar{x}$ the leftmost element of $\bar{x}$

last $\bar{x}$ the rightmost element of $\bar{x}$

front $\bar{x}$ the sequence which results from removing the last element of $\bar{x}$

tail $\bar{x}$ the sequence which results from removing the head element of $\bar{x}$

$\#\bar{x}$ the number of elements of $\bar{x}$

89

The result of head, last, front and tail, when applied to empty sequences, is arbitrary. Some familiar laws of sequences are reviewed below.

Law 5.1.1.   ⟨laws of sequences⟩
(1) $\mathsf{head}(\langle x \rangle \frown \bar{x}) = x = \mathsf{last}(\bar{x} \frown \langle x \rangle)$
(2) $\mathsf{front}(\bar{x} \frown \langle x \rangle) = \bar{x} = \mathsf{tail}(\langle x \rangle \frown \bar{x})$
(3) If $\bar{x}$ is non-empty then
        $(\langle \mathsf{head}\ \bar{x} \rangle \frown \mathsf{tail}\ \bar{x}) = \bar{x} = (\mathsf{front}\ \bar{x} \frown \langle \mathsf{last}\ \bar{x} \rangle)$

Although the notion of sequences is necessary in the intermediate steps of our proof, the elimination rule for recursion mentions only patterns which can be implemented by stack operations. To emphasise this point we define the following:

Definition 5.1. (Stack operations)

$$\mathsf{push}(x, \bar{x}) \stackrel{def}{=} (\bar{x} := \langle x \rangle \frown \bar{x})$$
$$\mathsf{pop}(x, \bar{x}) \stackrel{def}{=} (x, \bar{x} := \mathsf{head}\ \bar{x}, \mathsf{tail}\ \bar{x})$$
$$\mathsf{empty}\ \bar{x} \stackrel{def}{=} (\bar{x} = \langle \rangle)$$

$$\diamond$$

For a list of variables $x = x_1, \ldots, x_n$ and a list of sequence variables $\bar{x} = \bar{x}_1, \ldots, \bar{x}_n$ we use the abbreviations

$$\mathsf{push}(x, \bar{x}) \stackrel{def}{=} \mathsf{push}(x_1, \bar{x}_1); \ldots; \mathsf{push}(x_n, \bar{x}_n)$$
$$\mathsf{pop}(x, \bar{x}) \stackrel{def}{=} \mathsf{pop}(x_1, \bar{x}_1); \ldots; \mathsf{pop}(x_n, \bar{x}_n)$$

From the laws of sequences, it follows that the pair $(\mathsf{pop}(x, \bar{x}), \mathsf{push}(x, \bar{x}))$ is a simulation.

Law 5.1.2. $\mathsf{pop}(x, \bar{x}); \mathsf{push}(x, \bar{x}) \sqsubseteq \mathsf{skip} = \mathsf{push}(x, \bar{x}); \mathsf{pop}(x, \bar{x})$
                                                    ⟨pop − push simulation⟩

The following law suggests that var and end operate on an implicit stack that can be made explicit by using push and pop.

Law 5.1.3. If $\bar{x}$ is not free in p or q, then
$\mathsf{dec}\ x \bullet p[X \leftarrow \mathsf{var}\ x; q; \mathsf{end}\ x] \sqsubseteq \mathsf{dec}\ x, \bar{x} \bullet p[X \leftarrow \mathsf{push}(x, \bar{x}); q; \mathsf{pop}(x, \bar{x})]$
                                                    ⟨(var, end) − (push, pop) conversion⟩

Recall that $p[X \leftarrow r]$ is the result of substituting r for every free occurrence of X in p, where capture of free identifiers of r is avoided by renaming local declarations in p. The inequality in the above law is a consequence of the fact that $\mathsf{push}(x, \bar{x})$ leaves x unchanged, while var x assigns an arbitrary value to x.

5.2. Procedures

We use the notation

$$\text{proc } X \,\hat{=}\, p \bullet q$$

to declare a non-recursive, parameterless procedure named X with body p. The program q following the symbol $\bullet$ is the scope of the procedure. Occurrences of X in q are interpreted as call commands. The semantics of a call is textual substitution, like the *copy rule* of Algol 60.

Definition 5.2. (Procedures)

$$(\text{proc } X \,\hat{=}\, p \bullet q) \stackrel{def}{=} q[X \leftarrow p]$$

$$\diamondsuit$$

Notice that the above definition could be used as a rewrite rule to eliminate procedures even prior to the reduction of the procedure body and scope to normal form; this technique is known as *macro-expansion*. But this may substantially increase the size of the target code if the scope of the procedure contains a large number of call statements. An alternative is to compile the procedure body and calls into separate segments of code so that, during execution of a procedure call, control passes back and forth between these segments in a manner that simulates the copy rule.

As usual, we assume that the components of the procedure construction (the body and the scope) are in normal form, as in

$$\text{proc } X \,\hat{=}\, v : [a_0, \, b_0 \to p, \, c_0] \bullet v : \left[a, \left(\begin{array}{l} b_1 \to (X; \;\; v :\in r_1) \\ \square \quad \dots \\ \square \quad b_n \to (X; \;\; v :\in r_n) \\ \square \quad b \to q \end{array} \right), \, c \right]$$

where the scope of the procedure may have an arbitrary number of call commands still to be eliminated; each r_i stands for the return address of the corresponding call. The guarded command $b \to q$ stands for the remaining part of the code which does not contain any calls of procedure X. By definition, the above is equivalent to the nested normal form

$$v : \left[a, \left(\begin{array}{l} b_1 \to (v : [a_0, \, b_0 \to p, \, c_0]; \;\; v :\in r_1) \\ \square \quad \dots \\ \square \quad b_n \to (v : [a_0, \, b_0 \to p, \, c_0]; \;\; v :\in r_n) \\ \square \quad b \to q \end{array} \right), \, c \right]$$

The reduction rule for procedures can be regarded as a special case of a theorem about removal of nested normal form. We adopt a standard strategy, keeping a single copy of the code of the procedure body. Whenever any of the conditions $b_1, \dots, b_n$ is true, the corresponding return address is saved in a fresh variable, say w, and the start address of the code of the procedure body is assigned to the control variables in the list v. On exit from the execution of the procedure body, the value of w is copied back into v. For this to be valid, it is necessary that each r_i is not changed by the procedure body (that is, no free variable in any r_i is assigned by the procedure body). But this is not a serious limitation, since in practice the free variables of r_i are the control variables v, and these are local to the normal form program which implements the procedure body. The following theorem formalises the overall strategy.

Theorem 5.1. (Nested normal form)
If w is not free on the left-hand side of the following inequation, and r_i is not changed by $v : [a_0, b_0 \rightarrow p, c_0]$, then

$$v : \left[a, \begin{pmatrix} & b_1 \rightarrow (v : [a_0, b_0 \rightarrow p, c_0]; \ v :\in r_1) \\ \square & \cdots \\ \square & b_n \rightarrow (v : [a_0, b_0 \rightarrow p, c_0]; \ v :\in r_n) \\ \square & b \rightarrow q \end{pmatrix}, c\right]$$

$$\sqsubseteq$$

$$v, w : [a, \ T, \ c]$$

$$\text{where } T = \begin{pmatrix} & b_1 \rightarrow (w :\in r_1[v \leftarrow w]; \ v :\in a_0) \\ \square & \cdots \\ \square & b_n \rightarrow (w :\in r_n[v \leftarrow w]; \ v :\in a_0) \\ \square & c_0 \rightarrow v := w \\ \square & b_0 \rightarrow p \ \square \ b \rightarrow q \end{pmatrix}$$

Proof: First we show how each copy of the procedure body can be recovered by performing symbolic execution on the right-hand side of the above inequation. Let r_i stand for any of the return addresses $r_1, \ldots, r_n$, and $d = (b_1 \vee \ldots \vee b_n \vee c_0 \vee b_0 \vee b)$.

(1) $w :\in r_i[v \leftarrow w]; \ v :\in a_0; \ d * T$

   $= \quad \{\langle * \text{ sequence}\rangle(3.17.7) \text{ and } \langle * - \square \text{ elim}\rangle(3.17.4)\}$

   $\quad w :\in r_i[v \leftarrow w]; \ v :\in a_0; \ b_0 * p; \ d * T$

   $\sqsupseteq \quad \{c_{0\perp} \sqsubseteq \text{skip and } \langle * - \square \text{ unfold}\rangle(3.17.3)\}$

   $\quad w :\in r_i[v \leftarrow w]; \ v :\in a_0; \ b_0 * p; \ c_{0\perp}; \ v := w; \ d * T$

   $= \quad \{\langle \text{dec introduction}\rangle(3.19.11) \text{ and Definition 4.1(Normal form)}\}$

   $\quad w :\in r_i[v \leftarrow w]; \ v : [a_0, b_0 \rightarrow p, c_0]; \ v := w; \ d * T$

   $\sqsupseteq \quad \{w :\in r_i[v \leftarrow w] \text{ commutes with } v : [a_0, b_0 \rightarrow p, c_0] \ (3.16.9)\}$

   $\quad v : [a_0, b_0 \rightarrow p, c_0]; \ w :\in r_i[v \leftarrow w]; \ v := w; \ d * T$

   $\sqsupseteq \quad \{\langle :\in \text{ refined by } :=\rangle(3.16.8)\}$

(2) $v : [a_0, b_0 \rightarrow p, c_0]; \ w :\in r_i[v \leftarrow w]; \ v :\in r_i; \ d * T$

Then we have:

RHS

$\sqsupseteq$ $\{(*$ replace guarded command$)(3.17.5)$ and $(1) \sqsupseteq (2)\}$

$$v, w : [a, \begin{pmatrix} b_1 \rightarrow (v : [a_0, \ b_0 \rightarrow p, \ c_0]; \ w :\in r_1[v \leftarrow w]; \ v :\in r_1) \\ \square \quad \dots \\ \square \quad b_n \rightarrow (v : [a_0, \ b_0 \rightarrow p, \ c_0]; \ w :\in r_n[v \leftarrow w]; \ v :\in r_n) \\ \square \quad c_0 \rightarrow v := w \\ \square \quad b_0 \rightarrow p \ \square \ b \rightarrow q \end{pmatrix}, c]$$

$\sqsupseteq$ $\{$Lemma $4.3($Eliminate guarded command$)\}$

$$v, w : [a, \begin{pmatrix} b_1 \rightarrow (v : [a_0, \ b_0 \rightarrow p, \ c_0]; \ w :\in r_1[v \leftarrow w]; \ v :\in r_1) \\ \square \quad \dots \\ \square \quad b_n \rightarrow (v : [a_0, \ b_0 \rightarrow p, \ c_0]; \ w :\in r_n[v \leftarrow w]; \ v :\in r_n) \\ \square \quad b \rightarrow q \end{pmatrix}, c]$$

$\sqsupseteq$ $\{\langle \text{dec} - * \text{ dist}\rangle(3.18.11)$ and $\langle \text{dec elim}\rangle(3.18.3)\}$

$$v : [a, \begin{pmatrix} b_1 \rightarrow (v : [a_0, \ b_0 \rightarrow p, \ c_0]; \ (\text{dec } w \bullet w :\in r_1[v \leftarrow w]); \\ \qquad v :\in r_1) \\ \square \quad \dots \\ \square \quad b_n \rightarrow (v : [a_0, \ b_0 \rightarrow p, \ c_0]; \ (\text{dec } w \bullet w :\in r_n[v \leftarrow w]); \\ \qquad v :\in r_n) \\ \square \quad b \rightarrow q \end{pmatrix}, c]$$

$\sqsupseteq$ $\{\langle \text{dec}- :\in \text{ final value}\rangle(3.18.6)$ and $\langle \text{dec elim}\rangle(3.18.3)\}$

LHS

$\diamond$

5.3. Recursion

We have already introduced the notation

$$\mu X \bullet p$$

which defines a recursive, parameterless program named X with body p. Unlike a procedure, a recursive program cannot be called from outside its body: only recursive calls are allowed. Occurrences of X in p are interpreted as recursive calls. The semantics of recursion is given by fixed point laws (see Section 3.8).

Before giving the reduction rule for recursive programs, we introduce some abbreviations which will help in structuring the proof. The left-hand side of the reduction rule is a recursive program of the form

$$LHS \ = \ \mu X \bullet v : [a_0, \begin{pmatrix} b \rightarrow (X; \ v :\in r) \\ \square \quad b_0 \rightarrow p \end{pmatrix}, c_0]$$

where its body is in normal form, except for the recursive calls. For conciseness, we assume that there is only one call to be eliminated (no free occurrence of X in p);

the theorem is easily generalised for an arbitrary number of calls, as in the case of procedures.

The recursive definition can be eliminated by reducing the above to

$$MID \;=\; v, \bar{v} : [a_0 \wedge \text{empty } \bar{v}, \; S, \; c_0 \wedge \text{empty } \bar{v}]$$

$$\text{where} \quad S \;=\; \begin{pmatrix} b \rightarrow (v :\in r; \; \text{push}(v, \bar{v}); \; v :\in a_0) \\ \square \quad (c_0 \wedge \neg\text{empty } \bar{v}) \rightarrow \text{pop}(v, \bar{v}) \\ \square \quad b_0 \rightarrow p \end{pmatrix}$$

As in the previous section, a call is implemented by saving the return address before control is transferred; this address is then used to resume control. In the case of procedures, a local variable was used for this purpose, but for recursive calls we need the notion of a stack. By assuming that the stack is empty initially, we can distinguish between the exit from a recursive call of the program and the end of its execution. In the former case, the condition c_0 is true, but the stack is not yet empty; then control is resumed by popping the stack and assigning the popped value to v. The exit condition of the entire program is $c_0 \wedge \text{empty } \bar{v}$.

Although our emphasis is on the control structure of the program, note that v may be an arbitrary list of variables, possibly including data variables declared by the programmer. The overall task is simplified by not distinguishing between these two kinds of variable.

An alternative implementation of *LHS* is given by the program:

$$RHS \;=\; v, \bar{v} : [a \wedge \text{empty } \bar{v}, \; T, \; c \wedge \text{empty } \bar{v}]$$

$$\text{where} \quad T \;=\; \begin{pmatrix} a \rightarrow (v :\in c; \; \text{push}(v, \bar{v}); \; v :\in a_0) \\ \square \quad b \rightarrow (v :\in r; \; \text{push}(v, \bar{v}); \; v :\in a_0) \\ \square \quad c_0 \rightarrow \text{pop}(v, \bar{v}) \\ \square \quad b_0 \rightarrow p \end{pmatrix}$$

Its first action is to push onto the stack a value which satisfies the condition c, an exit condition for the loop associated with the above normal form program. In this way we ensure that, whenever c_0 is true, the stack is non-empty, since the last value to be popped satisfies a termination condition of the loop. The advantage of this implementation is that it avoids the use of the condition $\neg\text{empty } \bar{v}$ as part of a guard. Therefore *RHS* is more suitable for a low-level implementation.

A convenient way to prove *LHS* $\sqsubseteq$ *RHS* is to show that *LHS* $\sqsubseteq$ *MID* and that *MID* $\sqsubseteq$ *RHS*. We use the following lemmas.

Lemma 5.1. (Symbolic execution of S) Let $d = (b \vee (c_0 \wedge \neg\text{empty } \bar{v}) \vee b_0)$.

$$b^{\top}; \; d * S \;\sqsupseteq\; (\text{empty } \bar{v})_{\perp}; \; MID; \; v :\in r; \; d * S$$

$\diamond$

Lemma 5.2. (Symbolic execution of T) Let $d = (a \lor b \lor c_0 \lor b_0)$.

$$a^\top;\ d * T \sqsupseteq (\text{empty } \bar{v})_\perp;\ MID;\ v :\in c;\ d * T$$

$\diamond$

The proof of Lemma 5.1 is given in Appendix B. The proof of Lemma 5.2 is similar. The reduction theorem for recursive programs can now be proved.

Theorem 5.2. (Recursion)
Let LHS, MID and RHS be as defined above. If X is not free in p, and $\bar{v}$ occurs only where explicitly shown, then $LHS \sqsubseteq RHS$.

Proof: *(LHS $\sqsubseteq$ MID):*

> MID
>
> $\sqsupseteq$ {(* replace guarded command)(3.17.5), and
>
> Lemma 5.1(Symbolic execution of S)}
>
> $v, \bar{v} : [(a_0 \land \text{empty } \bar{v}), \begin{pmatrix} b \to (\text{empty } \bar{v})_\perp;\ MID;\ v :\in r \\ \square\ (c_0 \land \neg\text{empty } \bar{v}) \to \text{pop}(v, \bar{v}) \\ \square\ b_0 \to p \end{pmatrix}, (c_0 \land \text{empty } \bar{v})]$
>
> $\sqsupseteq$ {Lemma 4.3(Eliminate guarded command)}
>
> $v, \bar{v} : [(a_0 \land \text{empty } \bar{v}), \begin{pmatrix} b \to (\text{empty } \bar{v})_\perp;\ MID;\ v :\in r \\ \square\ b_0 \to p \end{pmatrix}, (c_0 \land \text{empty } \bar{v})]$
>
> $\sqsupseteq$ {$\langle b_\perp - b^\top$ simulation$\rangle$(3.11.10)}
>
> $v, \bar{v} : [a_0, \begin{pmatrix} b \to (\text{empty } \bar{v})^\top;\ (\text{empty } \bar{v})_\perp;\ MID;\ v :\in r;\ (\text{empty } \bar{v})_\perp \\ \square\ b_0 \to p \end{pmatrix}, c_0]$
>
> $\sqsupseteq$ {$b^\top;\ b_\perp = b^\top$ and $\langle b^\top;\ p$ commute$\rangle$(3.11.11)}
>
> $v, \bar{v} : [a_0, \begin{pmatrix} b \to (MID;\ v :\in r;\ (\text{empty } \bar{v})^\top;\ (\text{empty } \bar{v})_\perp \\ \square\ b_0 \to p \end{pmatrix}, c_0]$
>
> $\sqsupseteq$ {$b^\top;\ b_\perp = b^\top \sqsupseteq$ skip and $\langle$dec elim$\rangle$(3.18.3)}
>
> $v : [a_0, \begin{pmatrix} b \to (MID;\ v :\in r) \\ \square\ b_0 \to p \end{pmatrix}, c_0]$

From the above and $\langle \mu$ least fixed point$\rangle$(3.8.2), it follows that $LHS \sqsubseteq MID$.

(MID $\sqsubseteq$ RHS):

> RHS
>
> $\sqsupseteq$ {(* replace guarded command)(3.17.5) and
>
> Lemma 5.2(Symbolic execution of T)}

$$v, \bar{v} : [(a \wedge \text{empty } \bar{v}), \begin{pmatrix} a \rightarrow (\text{empty } \bar{v})_\perp; \; MID; \; v :\in c \\ \square \;\; b \rightarrow (v :\in r; \; \text{push}(v, \bar{v}); \; v :\in a_0) \\ \square \;\; c_0 \rightarrow \text{pop}(v, \bar{v}) \\ \square \;\; b_0 \rightarrow p \end{pmatrix}, (c \wedge \text{empty } \bar{v})]$$

$\sqsupseteq$ {Lemma 4.3(Eliminate guarded command)}

$\quad v, \bar{v} : [(a \wedge \text{empty } \bar{v}), (a \rightarrow (\text{empty } \bar{v})_\perp; \; MID; \; v :\in c), (c \wedge \text{empty } \bar{v})]$

$\sqsupseteq$ {$\langle b_\perp - b^\top$ simulation$\rangle$(3.11.10)}

$\quad v, \bar{v} : [a, (a \rightarrow (\text{empty } \bar{v})^\top; \; (\text{empty } \bar{v})_\perp; \; MID; \; v :\in c; \; (\text{empty } \bar{v})_\perp), c]$

$\sqsupseteq$ {$b^\top; \, b_\perp \; = \; b^\top$ and $\langle b^\top; \, p$ commute$\rangle$(3.11.11)}

$\quad v, \bar{v} : [a, (a \rightarrow (MID; \; v :\in c; \; (\text{empty } \bar{v})^\top; \; (\text{empty } \bar{v})_\perp), c]$

$\sqsupseteq$ {$b^\top; \, b_\perp \; = \; b^\top \; \sqsupseteq$ skip and $\langle$dec elim$\rangle$(3.18.3)}

$\quad v : [a, (a \rightarrow (MID; \; v :\in c), c]$

$\sqsupseteq$ {Lemma 4.1(Primitive commands)}

$\quad MID$

$\diamond$

5.4. Parametrised Programs

Here we show that parametrisation can be treated in complete isolation from procedures. Let p be a program and x a variable. Then

$\quad par \; x \bullet p$

is a parametrised program, where par stands for some parameter transmission mechanism; here we will deal with value-result (**valres**), value (**val**), result (**res**) and name parameters. The latter kind is restricted so that the actual parameter must be a variable and no *aliasing* must occur; in this case we can prove that parametrisation by name and by value-result have the same effect. Although we do not address parametrisation by reference explicitly, it coincides with parametrisation by name when variables (rather than arbitrary expressions) are used as arguments.

We adopt the conventional notation of function application for the instantiation of a parametrised program. The effect of an instantiation varies according to the type of parametrisation. The definitions are given below. In all cases, z must be a fresh variable, occurring only where explicitly shown.

Definition 5.3. (Value-result parameters)

$\quad (\text{valres } x \bullet p)(y) \overset{def}{=} \text{dec } z \bullet z := y; \; p[x \leftarrow z]; \; y := z$

$\diamond$

Definition 5.4. (Value parameters)

$\quad (\text{val } x \bullet p)(e) \overset{def}{=} \text{dec } z \bullet z := e; \; p[x \leftarrow z]$

$\diamond$

Definition 5.5. (Result parameters)

$$(\text{res } x \bullet p)(y) \overset{def}{=} \text{dec } z \bullet p[x \leftarrow z]; \; y := z$$

$\diamondsuit$

Definition 5.6. (Name parameters)
If y is not free in p, then

$$(\text{name } x \bullet p)(y) \overset{def}{=} p[x \leftarrow y]$$

$\diamondsuit$

These definitions are reasonably standard. They appear, for example, in [4, 64, 70]. In [4] the notion of refinement is generalised for parametrised statements:

Let $P = par \; x \bullet p$ and $Q = par \; x \bullet q$. Then
$P \sqsubseteq Q \overset{def}{=} P(t) \sqsubseteq Q(t)$ for all valid arguments t.

Moreover, it is shown that the crucial property of monotonicity with respect to refinement is retained by the new constructs:

(1) $p \sqsubseteq q \Rightarrow par \; x \bullet p \sqsubseteq par \; x \bullet q$
(2) Let P and Q be parametrised programs. Then, for any valid argument t
$P \sqsubseteq Q \Rightarrow P(t) \sqsubseteq Q(t)$

For name parameters, this result is not true in general. The instantiation may lead to aliasing, in which case monotonicity is lost. This is why we need the condition attached to Definition 5.6.

Multiple parametrisation of a particular kind can be achieved by allowing programs to be parametrised by lists of variables. The corresponding instantiations are similarly extended to allow lists of arguments. In this case, the two lists must be of equal length and the association between parameters and arguments is positional. Notice that we do not need to change the previous definitions, as our language allows multiple declaration and multiple assignment, and we have already introduced the notation for multiple substitution. For example,

$$(\text{res } x_1, x_2 \bullet p)(y_1, y_2) \overset{def}{=} \text{dec } z_1, z_2 \bullet p[x_1, x_2 \leftarrow z_1, z_2]; \; y_1, y_2 := z_1, z_2$$

However, except for call by value, an extra restriction must be observed: the list of actuals must be disjoint. For example, in the above case this is necessary to ensure that the multiple assignment $y_1, y_2 := z_1, z_2$ is defined.

Multiple parametrisation of (possibly) different kinds can be achieved by combining the effects of the related definitions. In this case we use a semicolon to separate the parameter declarations. As an example we have

$$(\text{val } x_1; \; \text{res } x_2 \bullet p)(e, y) \overset{def}{=} \text{dec } z_1, z_2 \bullet z_1 := e; \; p[x_1, x_2 \leftarrow z_1, z_2]; \; y := z_2$$

In the remainder of this chapter we will confine our attention to single parametrisation, but the results can be easily extended to multiple parametrisation.

Definitions 5.3–5.6 above could be used directly as elimination rules for parameter passing. However, this would not allow sharing the code of a parametrised program when instantiated with distinct arguments. This is a consequence of the renaming of variables on the right-hand sides of these definitions.

It is possible to avoid the renaming by using the parameter variable x itself as a local variable on the right-hand sides of Definitions 5.3–5.6. This is formalised by Theorems 5.3–5.6 below. Note the restriction that x must not be free in the argument used to instantiate the parametrised program; otherwise the occurrences of x in the argument would be captured by the local declaration of x which is introduced in each case.

Theorem 5.3.   (Elimination of value-result parameters)
If x and y are distinct, then

$$(\mathsf{valres}\, x \bullet p)(y) \;=\; \mathsf{dec}\, x \bullet x := y;\; p;\; y := x$$

Proof: Direct from Definition 5.3 and Law $\langle\mathsf{dec}\ \mathsf{rename}\rangle(3.18.4)$.   ◇

Theorem 5.4.   (Elimination of value parameters)
If x does not occur in e, then

$$(\mathsf{val}\, x \bullet p)(e) \;=\; \mathsf{dec}\, x \bullet x := e;\; p$$

Proof: Direct from Definition 5.4 and Law $\langle\mathsf{dec}\ \mathsf{rename}\rangle(3.18.4)$.   ◇

Theorem 5.5.   (Elimination of result parameters)
If x and y are distinct, then

$$(\mathsf{res}\, x \bullet p)(y) \;=\; \mathsf{dec}\, x \bullet p;\; y := x$$

Proof: Direct from Definition 5.5 and Law $\langle\mathsf{dec}\ \mathsf{rename}\rangle(3.18.4)$.   ◇

A mechanism to implement name (or reference) parameters by allowing sharing of code requires an explicit account of variable addresses. As our strategy is to eliminate parameters at the source level (and hence before the allocation of addresses to variables) this mechanism does not fit within our strategy[1]. But the following theorem establishes that, in the absence of aliasing, parametrisation by name is identical to parametrisation by value-result.

Theorem 5.6.   (Equivalence of name and value-result parameters)
If x and y are distinct and y is not free in p then

$$(\mathsf{name}\, x \bullet p)(y) \;=\; (\mathsf{valres}\, x \bullet p)(y)$$

---

[1]An alternative would be to implement this mechanism in a later phase of compilation, after the change of data representation, but we have not explored this alternative.

Proof:

> *RHS*
> = {Theorem 5.3(Elimination of value – result parameters)}
>   dec $x \bullet x := y;\ p;\ y := x$
> = {⟨dec elim⟩(3.18.3), ⟨dec– := final value⟩(3.18.6) and
>   assuming that w is a fresh variable}
>   dec $w \bullet w := y;\ (\text{dec } x \bullet x := y;\ p;\ y := x);\ w := y$
> = {⟨:= combination⟩(3.15.4) and ⟨:= identity⟩(3.15.2)}
>   dec $w \bullet w := y;\ (\text{dec } x \bullet x := w;\ p;\ w := x);\ y := w$
> = {⟨dec rename⟩(3.18.4)}
>   dec $w \bullet w := y;\ (\text{dec } y \bullet y := w;\ p[x \leftarrow y];\ w := y);\ y := w$
> = {⟨dec introduction⟩(3.19.11) and ⟨:∈ – := conversion⟩(3.16.7)}
>   dec $w \bullet w := y;\ y := w;\ p[x \leftarrow y];\ w := y;\ y := w$
> = {⟨:= combination⟩(3.15.4) and ⟨:= identity⟩(3.15.2)}
>   dec $w \bullet w := y;\ p[x \leftarrow y];\ w := y$
> = {⟨dec elim⟩(3.18.3) and ⟨dec– := final value⟩(3.18.6)}
>   *LHS*

$\diamond$

It should be clear that the conditions on the above theorems impose no practical limitations; they can be automatically satisfied by using locally declared variables as arguments. For example,

> $(\text{valres } x \bullet p)(x)$

can be replaced with (assuming that z is a fresh variable)

> dec $z \bullet z := x;\ (\text{valres } x \bullet p)(z);\ x := z$

The validity of this transformation follows direct from Definition 5.3 (Value-result parameters) and some basic laws of declaration and assignment. Similar transformations can be carried out for the other parametrisation mechanisms.

5.5. Parametrised Procedures

As a consequence of the results in the previous section, we can treat a parametrised procedure in the same way as a parameterless one. The same notation is used

> proc $X \mathrel{\hat{=}} (par\ x \bullet p) \bullet q$

except that now the body is a parametrised program (by any of the mechanisms discussed above) and all occurrences of X in q are of the form $X(t)$, for some appropriate actual parameter t.

This allows the meaning of a parametrised procedure to be given by the copy rule, as before. Therefore the above is equivalent to

$$q[X \leftarrow (par\ x \bullet p)]$$

This textual substitution could be used to eliminate parametrised procedures by macro-expansion. Sharing the code of the procedure body can be achieved by transforming a parametrised procedure into a parameterless one, and then using the reduction theorem for parameterless procedures (Theorem 5.2).

Another source of optimisation is the sharing of local variables used to eliminate parametrisation. This is established by the following lemma.

Lemma 5.3. (Sharing of local variables)
If x is not free in p, then

$$p[X \leftarrow (dec\ x \bullet q)] \sqsubseteq dec\ x \bullet p[X \leftarrow q]$$

Proof: By structural induction, using the distribution laws of dec with the other program constructs.   ◇

Then we have the following elimination rule for parametrised procedures. (We use value-result parameters as illustration; the rules for the other parametrisation mechanisms are similar.)

Theorem 5.7. (Value-result parameters of procedures)
If x is not free in q, then

$$\mathsf{proc}\ X \mathrel{\widehat=} (\mathsf{valres}\ x \bullet p) \bullet q \quad \sqsubseteq \quad dec\ x \bullet (\mathsf{proc}\ X \mathrel{\widehat=} p \bullet q[X \leftarrow (\mathsf{valres}'\ x \bullet X)])$$

where

$$(\mathsf{valres}'x \bullet r)(y) \stackrel{def}{=} x := y;\ r;\ y := x$$

Proof:
Let q' be such that

$$(1)\quad q = q'[Y_1, \ldots, Yn \leftarrow X(y_1), \ldots, X(y_n)]$$

and q' contains no calls of procedure X. Clearly, for all q it is always possible to find a q' that satisfies the above equation. Then we have:

$$LHS$$
$$=\ \{\text{Definition of procedures and (1)}\}$$
$$q'[Y_1, \ldots, Yn \leftarrow (\mathsf{valres}\ x \bullet p)(y_1), \ldots, (\mathsf{valres}\ x \bullet p)(y_n)]$$
$$=\ \{\text{Theorem 5.3(Elimination of value} - \text{result parameters)}\}$$
$$q'[Y_1, \ldots, Yn \leftarrow (dec\ x \bullet x := y_1;\ p;\ y_1 := x), \ldots,$$
$$(dec\ x \bullet x := y_n;\ p;\ y_n := x)]$$

$\sqsubseteq$ {Lemma 5.3(Sharing of local variables)}

  $dec\ x\ \bullet\ q'[\,Y_1,\ldots,\ Yn\ \leftarrow\ (x := y_1;\ p;\ y_1 := x),\ldots,(x := y_n;\ p;\ y_n := x)]$

$=$ {property of substitution and (1)}

  $dec\ x\ \bullet\ q[X\ \leftarrow\ (valres'\ x\ \bullet\ p)]$

$=$ {Definition of procedures}

  RHS

$\Diamond$

5.6. Parametrised Recursion

The notation for a parametrised recursive program X is the same as before, except that now its body is a parametrised program and all the recursive calls are of the form $X(t)$, for some appropriate actual parameter t. Like parameterless recursion, the meaning of a parametrised recursive program is given by the fixed point and the least fixed point laws. For example, the fixed point law becomes

$$\mu\,X\ \bullet\ (par\ x\ \bullet\ p)\ =\ par\ x\ \bullet\ p[X\ \leftarrow\ (\mu\,X\ \bullet\ (par\ x\ \bullet\ p)]$$

The least fixed point law is also as before, except that the body of the recursive program is parametrised.

The existence of a least fixed point for a parametrised context is justified by the fact that the set of parametrised programs form a complete lattice. As presented in Section 5.4, the ordering on this lattice is defined by pointwise extension from the refinement relation on ordinary (non-parametrised) programs; recall that this relation coincides with the ordering on the lattice of predicate transformers described in Section 2.3. The meet and join of the lattice of parametrised programs is also directly obtained by pointwise extension from the meet and join of the lattice of predicate transformers.

As with procedures, our compilation strategy is to transform a parametrised recursive program into a parameterless one, and then use the reduction theorem for recursion (Theorem 5.2). The elimination of parameters proceeds as follows. Consider the program fragment:

($\star$) $\mu\,X\ \bullet\ (valres\ x\ \bullet\ \ldots X(y)\ldots)(z)$

The initial value of the formal parameter x is given by a non-recursive call which can be dealt with in the same way as procedure calls. In ($\star$), z is the argument for this initial call. Each parametrised recursive call, such as $X(y)$ above, is replaced by a program fragment (which achieves the same effect) with a parameterless recursive call:

  $var\ x;\ x := y;\ X;\ y := x;\ end\ x$

(Recall from Section 5.4 that the formal parameters (such as x above) must not be free in the argument expression, otherwise the above transformation would capture occurrences of x in y.) Perceive the use of dynamic rather than static declaration in the above case. This is essential to achieve the desired behaviour that, when the recursive call is activated, the initial value of x in the body of the recursive program is the value of y, and similarly that, when returning from the call, the current value of x is copied back into y. With the syntactic scope rules which characterise static declarations the above fragment would not have the desired effect of passing the parameter y. This is because

$$\text{dec } x \bullet x := y; \ X; \ y := x$$

is clearly equivalent to X since an occurrence of x in the body of the recursive program would not be bound to the above local declaration of x.

After parameter elimination, the program fragment $(\star)$ becomes

$$\text{dec } x \bullet x := z; \ \mu X \bullet (\ldots \text{var } x; \ x := y; \ X; \ y := x; \ \text{end } x \ldots)$$

Note that this represents precisely the way parameters of recursive procedures are implemented in practice, where for each recursive call an *activation record* [1] is created in a run time stack to store the values of the arguments (apart from other relevant values like those of local variables); in our case, this stack is being abstractly represented by the dynamic declaration of x.

The following theorem formalises the above discussion, showing how arbitrary value-result parameters can be eliminated from a recursive program. The theorems for the other parametrisation mechanisms are similar.

Theorem 5.8.   (Value-result parameters of recursion)

$$\mu X \bullet (\text{valres } x \bullet p) \ \sqsubseteq \ \text{valres } x \bullet (\mu X \bullet p[X \leftarrow (\text{valres}' \ x \bullet X)])$$

where

$$(\text{valres}' x \bullet r)(y) \ \stackrel{def}{=} \ \text{var } x; \ x := y; \ r; \ y := x; \ \text{end } x$$

Proof:

$$RHS \ \sqsubseteq \ RHS$$

$\equiv$ $\{\langle \mu \ \text{fixed point}\rangle(3.8.1)\}$

$\quad$ $\text{valres } x \bullet p[X \leftarrow \text{valres}' \ x \bullet (\mu X \bullet p[X \leftarrow (\text{valres}' \ x \bullet X)])]) \ \sqsubseteq \ RHS$

$\equiv$ $\{$From $\langle \text{dec} - (\text{var}, \text{end}) \ \text{conversion}\rangle(3.19.10)$

$\quad$ we can replace the outermost valres' with $\text{valres}\}$

$\quad$ $\text{valres } x \bullet p[X \leftarrow \text{valres } x \bullet (\mu X \bullet p[X \leftarrow (\text{valres}' \ x \bullet X)])]) \ \sqsubseteq \ RHS$

$\equiv$ $\{$Note that the left-hand side above is a function of RHS$\}$

$\quad$ $\text{valres } x \bullet p[X \leftarrow RHS] \ \sqsubseteq \ RHS$

$\Rightarrow$ $\{\langle \mu \ \text{least fixed point}\rangle(3.8.2)\}$

$\quad$ $LHS \ \sqsubseteq \ RHS$

$\diamond$

It is worth emphasising where this proof relies on the use of the dynamic (rather than the static) declaration of x on the right-hand side of the above theorem. Observe that the application of the fixed point law in the first step of the proof does not cause the renaming of x in valres$'$ x; it is because this occurrence of x is free rather than bound since the declaration is dynamic (and not static). But once the recursive call is replaced with the entire recursive program (as a result of the first step) one cannot distinguish between a static and a dynamic declaration of x, since the conditions necessary to make this conversion are satisfied at this point of the proof. The final result follows directly from the least fixed point law.

Recall that var and end operate on an implicit stack which can be made explicit by using push and pop. This fact is used below to derive the following corollary of the above theorem.

Corollary 5.1. (Stack implementation of value-result parameters)
If $\bar{x}$ is not free in p then

$$\mu \, X \bullet (\text{valres} \, x \bullet p) \;\sqsubseteq\; \text{dec} \, \bar{x} \bullet (\text{valres} \, x \bullet (\mu \, X \bullet p[X \leftarrow (\text{valres}' \, x \bullet X)]))$$

where

$$(\text{valres}' x \bullet r)(y) \stackrel{def}{=} \text{push}(x, \bar{x}); \; x := y; \; r; \; y := x; \; \text{pop}(x, \bar{x})$$

Proof: From Law $\langle(\text{var}, \text{end}) - (\text{push}, \text{pop}) \text{ conversion}\rangle(5.1.3)$ and Theorem 5.8 $\diamond$

5.7. Discussion

The main advantage of handling procedures, recursion and parameters separately is that the overall task becomes relatively simple and modular. Furthermore this imposes no practical limitation, since more complex structures can be defined by combining the basic ones. For example, we have already illustrated how parametrised procedures, parametrised recursion and multiple parametrisation can be achieved. Recursive procedures (whether parametrised or not) can also be easily introduced. Consider the procedure declaration

proc $X \mathrel{\hat{=}} p \bullet q$

where p and q may respectively contain recursive and non-recursive calls of X, and p may be a parametrised program. This can be defined as the non-recursive procedure

proc $X \mathrel{\hat{=}} (\mu \, X \bullet p) \bullet q$

whose body is a recursive program.

One aspect not fully addressed is how the reduction theorems given in this chapter can be used as compilation rules. Notice that the theorems about parametrisation establish that it can be completely eliminated by transformations at the source level. The implementation of procedures and recursion requires a more powerful target machine than the one defined in the previous chapter. Basically, new instructions are necessary to execute the call and return sequences. These instructions can be defined by the new patterns which appear in the normal form of procedures and recursion. For procedures, we have shown that the call and return sequences can be implemented by allocating temporary variables; for recursion, new instructions to model the basic stack operations are required.

In order to illustrate how these instructions can be defined, we use a sequence variable $\bar{P}$ to represent a stack of program pointers which stores the return addresses of the calling programs. The relevant instructions can be defined, in the usual way, as assignments that update the machine state. The first instruction below would be useful to save the finish address of execution of the recursive program itself. The following instruction implements procedure call: the address of the next instruction to be executed when returning from the call is saved in $\bar{P}$, and then control is transferred to the initial address, say j, where the procedure body is placed. The last instruction is necessary to resume control.

$$
\begin{aligned}
\mathsf{save}(f) &\;\stackrel{def}{=}\; \bar{P}, P := (\langle f \rangle \frown \bar{P}), P + 1 \\
\mathsf{call}(j) &\;\stackrel{def}{=}\; \bar{P}, P := (\langle P + 1 \rangle \frown \bar{P}), j \\
\mathsf{return} &\;\stackrel{def}{=}\; \bar{P}, P := \mathsf{tail}\, \bar{P}, \mathsf{head}\, \bar{P}
\end{aligned}
$$

(Recall that the result of head and tail, when applied to empty sequences, is arbitrary.) Compare the effect of the three instructions above with that of push and pop in the normal form program that implements recursion (see Theorem 5.2). Instructions to allocate temporary storage for the variables local to recursive programs can be defined in a similar way.

An additional feature of our reduction strategy is that we have allocated a separate stack to implement each recursive program. This not only simplifies the proof of the elimination of recursion, but will be essential if we decide to extend our source language with a parallel operator. In the present case of our sequential language (and for non-nested recursion), the local stacks can be replaced by a global stack. This is systematically achieved using the elimination rule for sequential composition

$$
\begin{aligned}
& v, \bar{v} : [a, b_1 \rightarrow p, c_0];\; v, \bar{v} : [c_0, b_2 \rightarrow q, c] \\
\sqsubseteq\quad & v, \bar{v} : \left[a, \left(\begin{matrix} & b_1 \rightarrow p \\ \square & b_2 \rightarrow q \end{matrix} \right), c \right]
\end{aligned}
$$

However, in the case of nested recursion, we still need a separate stack for each level of nesting (where the declarations at the same level can be shared in the way shown above). An implementation could use pointers to link the stacks in a chain representing the nesting; this technique is known as *cactus stacks* [42]. A single stack implementation is discussed in the final chapter, where it is suggested as a topic for future work. For a realistic implementation, we will need a more concrete representation of these stacks. In particular, as the storage available in any machine is finite, it is necessary to impose a limit on the size of the stacks.

The compilation of programs now including procedures and recursion (possibly with parameters) should proceed as follows. As for the simple source language considered in the previous chapter, the first step is the simplification of expressions. Recall that one result of this phase of compilation is to extend the scope of local variables as much as possible, so that they can be implemented in the same way as global variables. However, it is not possible in general to move local declarations out of a recursive program; rather, as explained before, such declarations are implemented using a stack. Also recall that for the simplified language, the order of the remaining two phases (control elimination and data refinement) is not relevant. However, the reduction theorems for procedures and parameters introduce new local variables for which storage will have to be allocated. Therefore once the expressions are simplified, it is more sensible to carry out control elimination first and leave data refinement for the very last step.

CHAPTER 6

MACHINE SUPPORT

> [...] the separation of practical and theoretical work is
> artificial and injurious. Much of the practical work done
> in computing is unsound and clumsy because people who
> do it do not have a clear understanding of the funda-
> mental principles underlying their work. Most of the ab-
> stract mathematical and theoretical work is sterile be-
> cause it has no point of contact with real computing.
> [...] this separation cannot happen.
>
> — C. Strachey

Because of the algebraic nature of this approach to compilation, it is possible to use
a term rewriting system to check the correctness of the reductions. Furthermore, the
reduction theorems can be taken as rewrite rules to carry out the compilation task.

The purpose of this chapter is to show how this can be achieved using the OBJ3
system [33]. There are three main activities involved:

- The formalisation (specification) of concepts such as the reasoning language, its
  algebraic laws, the normal form, the target machine, and so on, as a collection
  of *theories* in OBJ3.

- The verification of the related theorems.

- Compiling with theorems: the reduction theorems are collected together and
  used as a compiler prototype.

We adopt the well established algebraic approach to specifications. For a formal
presentation of the concepts involved we refer the reader to, for example, [24, 25, 89,
29]. Here we describe some of the main concepts informally.

Broadly, we will consider a specification as consisting of three parts:

- a *signature*, which comprises a family of sorts (names for carrier sets) and
  operator symbols (names for operators) with given functionalities;

- a set of *axioms*, given by equations (and inequations) relating the operators of
  the signature, and

- a set of theorems, which can be deduced from the axioms.

The idea is to construct specifications incrementally. We start with a specification whose signature is an abstract syntax for the reasoning language, and the axioms are the basic algebraic laws. The set of theorems is initially empty; it is gradually built by proving that new algebraic laws are logical consequences of the basic ones, using order sorted equational logic as the deductive system. This is one way in which a specification can be *extended*. We then proceed extending the specification in a more general way, adding sorts, operators and axioms (and proving more theorems) to describe the remaining concepts.

One important aspect not addressed by this strategy is *consistency*. In particular, how to ensure that we started with a consistent set of algebraic laws? As discussed in Chapter 3, we consider this a separate task. A reasonable alternative is to formalise a given model, such as predicate transformers, and then derive the basic laws, one by one. This is illustrated in [6], using the HOL system [36].

For simplicity, we deal with the material presented in chapters 3 and 4; the normal form theorems for procedures and recursion are not considered. The mechanisation of these features is one of the suggested topics for future work, as discussed in Chapter 7.

Our main concern here is the overall structure of the specification and proofs, rather than a detailed description of all the steps and technicalities of the verification of the theorems in OBJ3. The specification of most concepts used (together with the complete verification of some of the main theorems) is given in Appendix C.

6.1. OBJ3

OBJ3 is the latest in a series of OBJ systems, all based upon first order equational logic. A detailed description of OBJ3 can be found in [33]. In this section we give a brief overview of the system (based on Release 2) and discuss how it supports the strategy presented above. More specific features are explained when necessary.

OBJ3 is a general-purpose declarative language, especially useful for specification and prototyping. A specification in OBJ3 is a collection of modules of two kinds: *theories* and *objects*. A theory has a *loose* semantics, in the sense that it defines a variety of models. An object has a *tight* or *standard* semantics; it defines, up to isomorphism, a specific model—its initial algebra [32]. For example, we use objects to define abstract data types such as lists and maps; the reasoning language and its algebraic laws are described as a theory, since we are not concerned with a particular model.

A module (an object or a theory) is the unit of a specification. It comprises a signature and a set of (possibly conditional) equations—the axioms. The equations are regarded as rewrite rules and computation is accomplished by term rewriting, in the usual way.

An elaborate notation for defining signatures is provided. As OBJ3 is based upon *order sorted algebra* [30], it provides a notion of subsorts which is extremely convenient in practice. For instance, assuming that Var and Exp are sorts representing variables and expressions, we can introduce the subsort declaration subsort Var < Exp to indicate that the set of variables is a subset of that of expressions. This allows us to use variables both as the left- and right-hand sides of an assignment statement; no conversion function is needed to turn a variable into an expression.

A general *mixfix* syntax can be used to define operators. In our case, we use names for operators which coincide with the LaTeX [58] representation of the desirable mathematical symbols. This allows us to use the same notational conventions introduced in earlier chapters, with the hope that this will make the encoding in OBJ3 more comprehensible.

Moreover, operators may have attributes describing useful properties such as associativity, commutativity and identity. This makes it possible to document the main properties of a given operator at the declaration level. As a consequence, the number of equations that need to be input by the user is considerably reduced in some cases. Most importantly, OBJ3 provides rewriting modulo these attributes.

Modules may be parametrised by theories which define the structure and properties required of an actual parameter for meaningful instantiation. The instantiation of a generic module requires a *view*—a mapping from the entities in the requirement theory to the corresponding ones in the actual parameter (module). As a simple example, an object to describe lists of arbitrary elements, say LIST, should be parametrised by a theory which requires the argument module to have (at least) one sort. In this simple case, we may instantiate LIST with a sort, since the view is obvious. Thus, assuming that Var and Exp are sorts as described above, we can create the instances LIST[Var] and LIST[Exp] to obtain lists of variables and lists of expressions[1]. A more interesting example is the parametrisation of the module describing the reasoning language by a theory of expressions; this is further discussed in the next section.

Apart from mechanisms for defining and instantiating generic modules, OBJ3 provides means for modules to import other modules and for combining modules. For example, A + B creates a new module which combines the signature and the equations of A and B. This support is essential for our incremental strategy to specifications.

OBJ3 can also be used as a theorem prover. In particular, computation is accomplished by term rewriting which is a widely accepted method of deduction. If the rewrite rules of the application theory are *confluent* (or *Church-Rosser*) and *terminating*, the exhaustive application of the rules works as a decision procedure for the theory: the equivalence of two expressions can always be determined by reducing each one to a *normal form*; the equivalence holds if the two normal forms are the same (syntactically speaking). This proof mode is normally called *automatic*, and is supported by OBJ3.

In our case, this proof mode is useful to discharge side conditions about nonfreeness and to perform substitution. Furthermore, once the reduction theorems are proved, this mode can be used to carry out compilation automatically, since these reduction theorems are complete in that they allow the reduction of an arbitrary

---

[1]Recall from above that we introduced the subsort declaration subsort Var < Exp. So the reader might expect that the sort representing lists of variables will be considered as a subsort of that representing lists of expressions. This is not inferred automatically by OBJ3; as will be illustrated soon, it has to be explicitly declared by the user.

source program to a normal form; this will be illustrated later in this chapter. Unfortunately, the proof of these theorems cannot be carried out automatically, since there is no decision procedure for our algebraic system; as is well-known, there is no decision procedure to determine the equivalence of programs written in a language which includes recursion. As a consequence, automatic term rewriting may fail to decide whether two program fragments are equivalent; the process may even fail to terminate, like, for example, if the system repeatedly applies the fixed point law to unfold a recursive program. Therefore there is the need for a mechanism for applying rules in a controlled way, as we have done in the manual proofs presented in earlier chapters. OBJ3 supports the *step by step* application of rewrite rules either forwards (from left to right) or backwards (from right to left).

Proofs in OBJ3 are confined to these two modes. There is no built-in support for proof by induction or by case analysis of any other kind. But the most serious limitation concerning our application is the lack of a mechanism to deal with inequational rewriting. We encode inequations as equations whose right-hand sides refine the corresponding left-hand sides, but as will be discussed later this is far from satisfactory. A possible solution to this problem is discussed in Section 6.6.2.

Other limitations are related to proof management. OBJ3 does not distinguish between units of information such as an axiom, a conjecture and a theorem. Although specifications and proofs can be stored in files, the management must be done by the user.

6.2. Structure of the Specification

We use the module facilities of OBJ3 to structure the specification in such a way that each concept is described by a separate module. Fig. 6.1 shows the hierarchy of the main modules, where an arrow from module A to module B indicates that B imports A. First we explain part (a) of the figure. The module which describes the reasoning language is generic with respect to the expression language. This can be elegantly described in OBJ3 by defining a theory of expressions and parametrising the module REASONING-LANGUAGE with this theory. Then the commands (and their algebraic laws) can be instantiated with different expression languages, according to the particular needs.

The module describing the normal form is equally independent of a particular expression language (and in particular of a way of encoding control state). Clearly, it needs to import the previous module so that the normal form operator can be defined and the associated reduction theorems can be proved.

Part (b) of the figure presents the structure of the specification of our simple compiler, where each phase of compilation is described by a separate module. It also shows how the previous modules are instantiated for this application. For example, the module describing the simplification of expressions is concerned with the notation of expressions of the source language. To reason about this phase of compilation, we instantiate the module REASONING-LANGUAGE with this particular kind of expression. Similarly, the module concerned with control elimination instantiates NORMAL-FORM

NORMAL-FORM [X :: EXP]

↑

REASONING-LANGUAGE [X :: EXP]

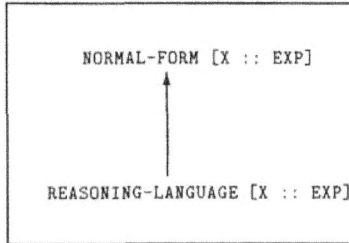

(a) Generic Modules

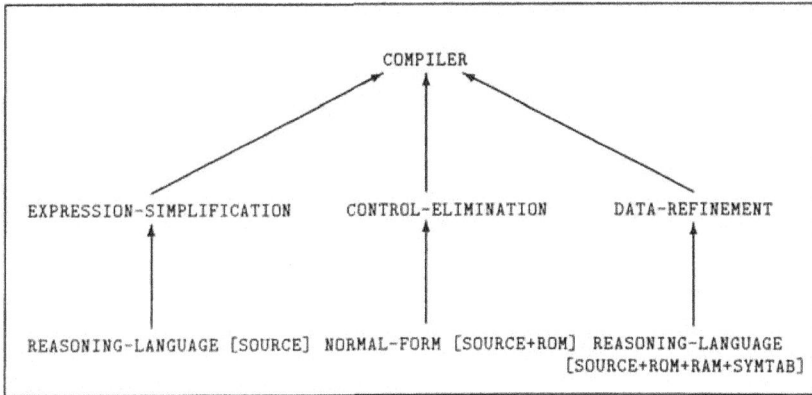

COMPILER

EXPRESSION-SIMPLIFICATION   CONTROL-ELIMINATION   DATA-REFINEMENT

REASONING-LANGUAGE [SOURCE]   NORMAL-FORM [SOURCE+ROM]   REASONING-LANGUAGE
[SOURCE+ROM+RAM+SYMTAB]

(b) Structure of the Compiler

Fig. 6.1. Structure of the Specification.

with the combination (+) of two kinds of expressions: the expressions of the source language and the ones used to represent addresses in the memory ROM of our target machine.

The module concerned with data refinement instantiates REASONING-LANGUAGE with a complex expression language formed from the two kinds discussed above and (map) expressions to represent the memory RAM and the symbol table. The compiler is formed from the modules describing the three phases of compilation.

The internal structure of these modules is described in the remaining sections, and further details are given in Appendix C.

6.3. The Reasoning Language

In the previous chapters we dealt with expressions in an informal way; new operators were introduced as we needed them. For example, to describe the data refinement phase of compilation we used map expressions to model the symbol table and the store of the target machine; in the control elimination phase we used arithmetic expressions to encode control state. This was possible because the algebraic laws are independent of a particular expression language. As mentioned above, this can be captured in OBJ3 by defining a theory of expressions and parametrising the module describing the reasoning language with this theory.

The theory of expressions must include the boolean values with the usual operators. This is necessary to enable us to describe the algebraic laws of conditional commands. The boolean expressions (conditions) are described by the following module:

```
obj COND is

    sorts CondVar CondExp .
    subsorts CondVar < CondExp .

    op true  : -> CondExp .
    op false : -> CondExp .
    op _V_ : CondExp CondExp -> CondExp [assoc comm idem id: false] .
    op _∧_ : CondExp CondExp -> CondExp [assoc comm idem id: true] .
    op ¬_  : CondExp -> CondExp .

    var a : CondExp .

    eq true V a   true .
    eq false ∧ a = false .
    eq ¬true = false .
    eq ¬false = true .

endo
```

The subsort relation states that boolean expressions may contain variables (elements of sort CondVar). The symbol _ which appears in the declaration of the operators determines the position of their arguments. The attributes of a given operator are given inside square brackets. For example, ∨ is associative, commutative, idempotent and has identity false. The additional properties of the operators are described by equations.

The module describing our theory of expressions declares sorts Var and Exp to represent arbitrary variables and expressions. The requirement that the expression language must include boolean expressions is captured by subsort relations.

```
th EXP is

    protecting COND .

    sorts Var Exp .
    subsorts Var < Exp
    subsorts CondVar < Var
    subsorts CondExp < Exp

endth
```

The module COND is imported using protecting. This mode of importation is used to state that EXP does not add or identify elements of sorts from COND.

The above theory is then used to parametrise the module which describes the reasoning language. This means that any actual parameter used for instantiation must be a *model* of the above theory. Informally, any particular expression language must be equipped with (at least) what is stated by the theory EXP. A partial description of the module describing the operators of the reasoning language is given below; see Appendix C for the complete specification of this module.

```
th REASONING-LANGUAGE[X :: EXP] is

    sorts Prog ProgId .
    subsorts ProgId < Prog .

    define ListVar is LIST[Var] .
    define ListExp is LIST[Exp] .
    subsorts ListVar < ListExp

*** Source language
    op skip : -> Prog .
    op-as _:=_ : ListVar ListExp -> Prog
        for x := e if (len x == len e) and (disj x) [prec 52] .
    op _;_ : Prog Prog -> Prog [assoc prec 56] .
    op _⊓_ : Prog Prog -> Prog [assoc comm idem id: ⊤ prec 57] .
    op _◁    ▷_ : Prog CondExp Prog -> Prog [prec 58] .
    op _*_ : CondExp Prog -> Prog [prec 54] .
    op dec _ •_ . ListVar Prog -> Prog [prec 60] .
```

```
*** Additional specification features
  op ⊥ : -> Prog .
  op ⊤ : -> Prog .
  op _⊑_ : Prog Prog -> Bool [prec 70] .
  op μ _ •_ . ProgId Prog -> Prog [prec 59] .
      . . .        . . .
endth
```

The sort ProgId declared above stands for program identifiers, used to name recursive programs. Furthermore, by declaring ProgId as a subsort of Prog we can use program identifiers as call commands. Following the sort declarations, the define clause is used to instantiate the module LIST[2] to create lists of variables and lists of expressions. The effect of define ListVar is LIST[Var] is to import LIST[Var] (using protecting) and rename the sort List of LIST to ListVar. Similarly, the second define clause renames List to ListExp; in this way we avoid name clash that would otherwise happen due to the two instantiations of the same parametrised module. The sorts ListVar and ListExp are used, for instance, in the declaration of the multiple assignment command, which is a partial operator[3] defined only for equal-length lists of variables and expressions. In addition, the list of variables must be disjoint: no variable may appear more than once in the list. The declaration of most operators includes an attribute which determines their precedence. The lower the precedence, the tighter the operator binds.

Some auxiliary operators are needed to implement the concepts of non-freeness, non-occurrence and substitution. The non-occurrence operator is used to state that a given identifier does not occur in a program, not even bound. Their declaration is given below.

```
op _\_    : ListVar Prog -> Bool [memo]      *** non-freeness
op _\\_   : ListVar Prog -> Bool [memo] .    *** non-occurrence
op-as _[_<-_] : Prog ListVar ListExp -> Prog *** substitution
    for p[x <- e] if (len x == len e) and (disj x) [memo] .
```

Notice that the last operator allows multiple substitution, and therefore it has the same precondition as that of the assignment operator. Overloaded versions of the above operators deal with expressions.

Especially when using the rewrite rules to carry out compilation, these operators are applied to the same arguments, over and over again. The number of rewrites is substantially reduced by giving them the memo attribute which causes the results of

---

[2]This parametrised module is omitted here as it does not illustrate any new feature of OBJ3. It is generic with respect to the sort of the elements (Elem) of the list (represented by the sort List). The empty list is represented by <>, a singleton list is represented by the element itself (note that this is possible using subsorts), and comma (,) is used to denote list concatenation.

[3]In Release 2 of OBJ3 partiality is only syntactic. The semantics and prototype implementation of partial operators are described in [91]; unfortunately, this implementation has not been integrated into the OBJ3 system.

evaluating a term headed by any of these operators to be saved; thus the evaluation is not repeated if that term appears again.

These operators are defined in the usual way. The complete definition requires a large number of equations, one to deal with each operator of the language, and therefore is omitted here. However, the implementation of safe substitution as a set of rewrite rules deserves some attention, due to the need to rename local variables to avoid variable capture. This is actually an instance of the more general problem of creating fresh identifiers using a formalism with a stateless semantics[4]. A possible (although cumbersome) solution is to pass a (virtually) infinite list of unique identifiers as parameter, or the finite list of already-used identifiers. As we never use substitution in a context which requires renaming, we solve the problem by using the following conditional equation

```
cq (dec x • p) [y <- f]  =  (dec x • (p[y <- f]))
if x \\ (y,f) .
```

where the condition that x does not occur in the list (y,f) prevents variable capture.

Another observation regarding these auxiliary operators is that they must be defined in a context separate from that of the algebraic laws. Their equations entail syntactic transformations, whereas the laws express semantic properties. While a formal distinction between the syntactic and the semantic natures of programs is necessary in principle, it would require the explicit definition of some kind of semantic function which would make the mechanisation extremely laborious. We avoid a formal distinction between these two views of programs by defining the equations of the auxiliary operators in a separate module. As OBJ3 allows one to specify the context for a given reduction, we can ensure that syntactic and semantic transformations are never intermixed.

The algebraic laws are described as labelled equations. The labels are used in the verification phase as references to the equations. We use the same name conventions introduced earlier. For example, Law ⟨:= skip⟩(3.15.1) is coded as

```
[:=~skip]  eq  (x := x) = skip .
```

The codification of most of the laws is straightforward, although there is a drawback concerning the laws which are inequalities. Although, for example, $b_\perp \sqsubseteq$ skip can be precisely described by the equation

```
eq  (b⊥ ⊑ skip) = true
```

this encoding is not convenient for use in proofs. This equation allows us to rewrite the left-hand side with true, or vice-versa; but we are concerned with reducing nondeterminism (by rewriting $b_\perp$ to skip) or, conversely, increasing nondeterminism, by rewriting in the opposite direction. The way we overcome this problem is coding

---

[4]Actually, OBJ3 allows *built-in* equations which provide direct access to Lisp (and therefore the possibility of modelling a global state), but we have avoided the use of this feature in order to keep the presentation purely algebraic.

inequations as equations whose left-hand sides are less deterministic than the corresponding right-hand sides. We document this fact by adding the ordering relation as an additional label to the equations. The above then becomes

$$[b_\perp \tilde{}\,skip \sqsubseteq] \quad eq \quad b_\perp = skip$$

But this is clearly unsatisfactory, as OBJ3 treats it as an ordinary equation; we have the obligation to check (with the aid of the annotations) whether an application of a rule makes sense in a given context. For example, in a refinement process, a left to right application of the above rule is valid, but an application in the opposite direction is obviously invalid.

An appropriate solution is to use a logic which supports inequational rewriting. An example of such a logic is *rewriting logic* [61, 62], developed by Meseguer. Unfortunately, no implementation of this logic was available at the time of writing this book. Rewriting logic is further discussed in Section 6.6.2. In this same section we briefly describe a system based on OBJ3, namely 2OBJ, which accepts as input an OBJ3 specification and treats the rules annotated with the ordering relation as inequations. The facilities provided by 2OBJ are similar to those of rewriting logic; but, unlike rewriting logic, it has not been given a formal semantics.

The laws of recursion also deserve some attention. OBJ3 is based on first order logic, and therefore we cannot quantify over functions, as implicitly done in the fixed point and least fixed point laws. However, this can be easily overcome using substitution:

$$[\mu\tilde{}\,fp] \qquad eq \quad (\mu\ X \bullet p) = p[X \leftarrow (\mu\ X \bullet p)] \ .$$
$$[\mu\tilde{}\,lfp \Leftarrow] \quad eq \quad (\mu\ X \bullet p) \sqsubseteq q = (p[X \leftarrow q]) \sqsubseteq q \ .$$

Note that the second equation should have been coded as an implication, with its left-hand side implied by its right-hand side.

It is convenient to define instances of the above laws to deal with iteration commands, as in this particular case we can get rid of the substitution operator.

$$[*\tilde{}\,fp] \qquad eq \quad b * p = (p\ ;\ b * p \lhd b \rhd skip) \ .$$
$$[*\tilde{}\,lfp \Leftarrow] \quad eq \quad (b * p) \sqsubseteq q = (p\ ;\ q \lhd b \rhd skip) \sqsubseteq q \ .$$

These are easily derived from the definition of iteration and the laws of recursion.

6.3.1. An Example of a Proof

To illustrate how proofs are carried out in OBJ3, we chose a simple example which highlights both some positive points and some limitations. Other proofs are presented in Appendix C.

The example used here is the first part ($RHS \sqsubseteq LHS$) of the proof of Law 3.17.6:

$$(b * p);\ q = \mu\ X \bullet (p;\ X \lhd b \rhd q)$$

OBJ3 supports the step by step style of proof that we have used in the manual proofs. First we define constants LHS and RHS to stand for the respective sides of the above equation. Then we start the proof process with

```
start   (b * p) ; q ⊑ LHS .
```

which is equivalent to `true` (by the reflexivity of ⊑). The proof strategy is to gradually transform the term (b * p) ; q into RHS by requesting OBJ3 to *apply* equations which encode the appropriate laws. For example, the following is a request to apply the fixed point law

```
OBJ> apply .*~fp within term .
```

where `within term` is used to apply a given equation to all possible subterms of the term in focus. In our case there is only one match for the left-hand side of the fixed point equation, and the system replies with the expected result:

```
result Bool: (p ; b * p ◁ b ▷ skip) ; q ⊑ LHS
```

In a similar way, we apply equations to move q inside the conditional and to eliminate skip (and then we rewrite b * p ; q to LHS), resulting in

```
result Bool: (p ; LHS ◁ b ▷ q) ⊑ LHS
```

which suggests the backward (right to left) application of the least fixed point equation (see the equation with label μ~lfp in the previous section). Note, however, that the right-hand side of that equation mentions the substitution operator explicitly, and therefore cannot be matched by the above term. The desired form can be achieved by using the equations of substitution. For the moment, we add an equation which allows us to perform the desired transformation:

```
[subst1] eq (p ; LHS ◁ b ▷ q) = (p ; X ◁ b ▷ q)[X <- LHS] .
```

Then we have

```
OBJ> apply .subst1 within term .
result Bool: (p ; X ◁ b ▷ q)[X <- LHS] ⊑ LHS
```

which enables us to apply the least fixed point equation:

```
OBJ> apply -.μ~lfp with within term .
result Bool: μ X • (p ; X ◁ b ▷ q) ⊑ LHS
```

where the minus sign preceding a label requests backward application of the corresponding equation. The final result follows directly from the definition of RHS.

But we still need to discharge the proof obligation introduced by the added equation subst1. As the equations defining substitution are confluent and terminating, we can prove this equation automatically, rather than step by step. In OBJ3 this is achieved by

```
OBJ> select SUBST .
OBJ> reduce (p ; LHS ◁ b ▷ q) == (p ; X ◁ b ▷ q)[X <- LHS] .
rewrites: 4
result Bool: true
```

where the command select is used to specify the context in which the reduction is carried out. The module SUBST contains the relevant equations of substitution. Recall that we need to collect these equations in a separate module, since a reduction involving substitution entails syntactic transformations; the algebraic laws express semantic properties and their use must be disallowed in such a proof. A similar technique is employed to reduce side conditions about non-freeness.

This simple reduction has actually uncovered one hidden assumption in the manual proof: the law being verified is true only if X is not free in p or q. So, in order to prove the above equation, we must add this as an assumption:

```
eq X \ p = true
eq X \ q = true .
```

Although the mechanical proof closely corresponds to its manual version, some limitations can be observed. One has already been discussed earlier and relates to reasoning with inequations. Note that we have no means to tell the system that the term resulting from the application of least fixed point is implied by (rather than equivalent to) the term that precedes the application. This is only informally documented in the definition of the corresponding equation.

First order logic is sufficient to express most of the algebraic system we use, but higher-order matching would enable a more convenient description (and application) of the laws of (least) fixed point, without mentioning substitution explicitly. As illustrated above, the use of substitution requires the user to provide the matching; this turns out to be cumbersome if the laws are repeatedly used. We tried to minimise the problem by defining instances of these laws to deal with iteration, since these instances do not mention the substitution operator.

Concerning proof management, no support is provided. For example, there is no facility to deal with assumptions; to be used as rewrite rules, they have to be added by the user as ordinary equations, as shown above. Also, it would be useful if the theorem we have just proved were automatically added to the module in question, and made available in later proofs. In OBJ3 this has to be carried out by the user.

6.4. The Normal Form

The module describing the normal form extends that describing the reasoning language with a new operator and its defining equation:

```
op as (_:[_, _->_, _]) : ListVar Cond Cond Prog Cond -> Prog
      for v :[a, b -> p, c] if pwd(b,c) [prec 50]

[nf~def] eq v :[a, b -> p, c]  =  dec v • v :∈ a ; b * p ; c⊥ .
```

where the precondition states the required disjointness of the conditions b and c.

The reduction theorems can then be proved from the above definition and the equations describing the algebraic laws, in much the same way as illustrated in the previous section. Then they can be added to the module as ordinary equations. For example, the reduction of sequential composition is captured by the following equation

```
[T:sequential˜composition ⊑]
    cq   v :[a, b1 -> p, co]  ;  v :[co, b2 -> q, c]  =
            v :[a, (b1 ∨ b2) -> (b1 → p □ b2 → q), c]
    if pwd(b1,b2,c) .
```

which is true only under the condition that b1, b2 and c are pairwise disjoint. Recall that these disjointness conditions were implicit in the manual proofs.

6.5. A Compiler Prototype

Here we formalise the design of the compiler presented in Chapter 4. The components of the target machine are gradually introduced by the modules describing the phases of compilation: simplification of expressions, control elimination and data refinement; these are the concern of the first three subsections. Apart from these phases, an additional step is necessary to replace the assignment statements (used as patterns to define instructions) with the corresponding instruction names. This is discussed in Subsection 6.5.4. In the last subsection we illustrate how compilation is carried out using equations which encode the reduction theorems. The complete description of the modules concerned with the compilation phases (and the verification of some of the related theorems) is given in Appendix C.

6.5.1. Simplification of Expressions

Rather than defining a particular notation of expressions in our source language, we want to illustrate how to simplify expressions involving arbitrary binary and unary operators:

```
sorts SourceVar SourceExp .
subsorts SourceVar < SourceExp .

op uop_  : SourceExp -> SourceExp .
op _bop_ : SourceExp SourceExp -> SourceExp
```

The only machine component relevant to this phase is the general purpose register. It is represented here by the following constant

```
op A  : -> SourceVar .
```

which must be of the same sort as an ordinary source variable because, during the process of simplification, A is assigned expressions of the source language.

The theorems related to this phase can be verified (and then introduced as equations) in the way already explained. But one aspect to be addressed is the creation of fresh local variables that may be required during the simplification of expressions. Like the implementation of safe substitution (mentioned before) this is an instance of the more general problem of creating fresh identifiers using a formalism with a stateless semantics.

One approach is to generate a fresh identifier every time a temporary variable is needed (which is confined to the equation concerned with the simplification of binary operators). While this obviously works, it does not optimise the use of space. An optimisation is to create distinct identifiers for variables in nested blocks, but identify variables (with the same name) which appears in disjoint blocks. This can be accomplished with

```
let n = depth(e bop f) in
  cq (A := e bop f) = dec tₙ • A:=f ; tₙ:=A ; A:=e ; A:=A bop tₙ
  if (A,tₙ) \\ (e bop f) .
```

where we use the depth[5] of a given expression as the basis to generate fresh identifiers. The term t_n comprises an operator which from an identifier t and a natural number n generates a new identifier t_n. The let clause above was used to improve readability; in OBJ3 it is available only for defining constants.

Observe that the local variables of the nested blocks generated by the simplification of a given expression are guaranteed to be distinct, as the depth of the expression decreases during the simplification process. However, the same identifiers may be generated to simplify another expression; in particular, we always use the same *base* identifier t to ensure the maximum reuse of temporaries.

Recall that an optimisation of the above rule is possible when the expression f is a variable, in which case the allocation of temporary storage is unnecessary:

```
cq (A := e bop x) = A:=e ; A:=A bop x
if A \\ (e bop x) .
```

As variables are also expressions, any assignment which matches the left-hand side of this rule also matches that of the previous rule. Of course, we always want the optimising rule to be used in such cases. But OBJ3 does not provide means to express rule priorities (one cannot even rely on the fact that the system will attempt to apply rules in the order in which they are presented). To ensure application of the optimising rule, we need to add an extra condition to the previous rule, say is-not-var(f), where is-not-var is a boolean function which yields true if and only if the expression to which it is applied is not a variable.

6.5.2. Control Elimination

The steps to formalise this phase of compilation are very similar to those of the previous phase. Expressions are further extended to include natural numbers which

---

[5]From a tree representation of an expression, we define its depth to be the number of nodes in the longest path of the tree.

are used to represent addresses in the memory ROM. Furthermore, the program counter is declared as a special (program) variable to which expressions representing ROM addresses may be assigned. These are specified as follows:

```
sorts RomAddrVar RomAddrExp .
subsorts RomAddrVar < RomAddrExp .
subsorts Nat < RomAddrExp .

op P : -> RomAddrVar .
```

where Nat is built-in to OBJ3; the usual numerical representation is available, thus we do not need to write large numbers in terms of a successor function.

The theorems for control elimination are easily verified by instantiating the normal form theorems. Additional transformations are required in some cases, but they do not illustrate any new aspect.

A problem similar to the generation of fresh identifiers is the allocation of distinct addresses for the machine instructions yielded by the compilation process. The solution we have adopted is to preprocess the source program to tag each construct with a distinct natural number representing an address in ROM. Then the reduction theorems are encoded as, for example:

```
cq {s}(x:=e) = P:[s, (P=s) -> (x,P := e,P+1), (s+1)]
    if P \\ e .
```

where s is the address allocated to place the instruction generated by x := e. We carry out the tagging after simplifying expressions, since each simple assignment will give rise to a single instruction.

It is worth stressing that tagging is merely a syntactic annotation to ensure the disjointness of the addresses allocated for the machine instructions. It has no semantical effect; more precisely, {s} p = p, for all programs p.

6.5.3. Data Refinement

This phase entails more sophisticated components such as the symbol table and the store for variables; they are represented as maps, rather than as single variables:

```
define SymTab is MAP[SourceVar,RamAddr] .
define Ram is MAP[RamAddr,SourceExp]

op M : -> Ram .
var Ψ : SymTab .
```

This formalises the fact that a symbol table is a map from identifiers to addresses of locations in Ram, which is itself a map from addresses to expressions denoting the corresponding values. In practice we use natural numbers to represent addresses; this is possible by making Nat a subsort of RamAddr.

As the other machine components, M was introduced as a constant of the appropriate sort. The symbol table, on the other hand, may change from program to program, and is therefore declared as a variable.

The simulation used to carry out data refinement can then be defined. Below we give the declaration and the definition of its first component:

```
op-as ^_  :  SymTab ListSourceVar -> Prog
        for Ψ̂w if elts(w) == (dom Ψ) and disj(w) .


eq Ψ̂w = var w ; w := M[Ψ[w]] ; end M .
```

where the precondition requires that each variable in the domain of Ψ occurs exactly once in the list of global variables w. Note the similarity between the above equation and the original definition of $\hat{\Psi}_w$ given in Section 4.6. In particular, we have implemented list application (among other map operations) to allow a straightforward encoding.

The distributivity properties of the simulation $\hat{\Psi}_w$ can be verified in the usual way. Perhaps the most interesting is the one which allocates space for the local variables:

```
cq Ψ̂w(dec v,P,A • p) = dec P,A • Φ̂(w,v)(p)
   if disj(v,w) and disj(Φ[v],Ψ[w]) .
```

where $\Phi = \Psi \cup \{v \mapsto (base + len(w) + 1 \;..\; base + len(w,v))\}$.

It is required that the global variables w are distinct from the local variables v, and that the new addresses $\Phi[v]$ are different from the ones already used, $\Psi[w]$. We have already discussed how to satisfy the first condition. The other one can be easily satisfied by allocating for the global variables the addresses $base + 1 \;..\; base + len(w)$, where $base$ is an arbitrary natural number; the definition of Φ then guarantees that the addresses allocated for the local variables are distinct from those.

The complete verification of the above theorem is given in Appendix C.

6.5.4. Machine Instructions

The machine instructions are defined as assignments that update the machine state. Therefore the instructions should also be regarded as elements of the sort Prog. However, to make it clear that we are introducing a new concept, we declare a subsort of Prog whose elements are the machine instructions:

```
sort Instruction
subsort Instruction < Prog

op load    : RamAddr -> Instruction .
eq (A,P := M[n],P + 1) = load(n) .
     ⋮      ⋮
```

The reason to order the equations in this way is that they are used as (left to right) rewrite rules at the last stage of the compilation process, to translate the semantics to the syntax of the assembly language. In other words, when the assignment statements (used as patterns to define the instructions) are generated, they are automatically replaced by the corresponding instruction names; numeric values could be used instead, if the purpose was to produce binary code.

6.5.5. Compiling with Theorems

Now we present one of the main achievements of the mechanisation: the provably correct reduction theorems can be used effectively as rewrite rules to carry out the compilation task. All that needs to be done is to input the source program with a symbol table that allocates addresses for its global variables **w**, and ask OBJ3 to reduce this program using the reduction theorems[6]. The output is a normal form program which represents the target machine executing the corresponding instructions.

The process is carried out automatically. Every subterm matching the left-hand side of a one of the reduction theorems is transformed in the way described by the right-hand side of the theorem. As we have ordered the theorems in such a way that their right-hand sides refine the corresponding left-hand sides, each application can only lead to refinement. Therefore compilation is itself a proof that the final normal form program is a refinement of the initial source program. A very simple example (actually, the same one used in Chapter 4 to illustrate the compilation process) is given below.

Example 6.1. (A simple assignment)

```
OBJ> let w = x,y,z .
OBJ> let Ψ = {x ↦ 101} ∪ {y ↦ 102} ∪ {z ↦ 103} .
OBJ> reduce Ψ̂_w(x := y bop (uop z))
rewrites: 386
result:  P,A :[0, (P=0 ∨ P=1 ∨ P=2 ∨ P=3 ∨ P=4 ∨ P=5) ->
                              (P=0) → load(103)
                          □ (P=1) → uop-A
                          □ (P=2) → store(104)
                          □ (P=3) → load(102)
                          □ (P=4) → bop-A(104)
                          □ (P=5) → store(101),
                 6]
OBJ> show time .
10.367 cpu       20.033 real
```

                                                                                    ◇

The application of the simulation function to the source program ensures that the data refinement phase will be accomplished by using the associated distributivity equations. Note in particular that the new address 104 was allocated to hold the value of a temporary variable created during the simplification of the expression. The last line shows the time (in seconds) consumed to carry out this reduction on a Sun 4/330 with 32 MB RAM.

---

[6]Recall that the algebraic laws play no role here; they were needed only to prove the reduction theorems, and not to carry out compilation.

The guarded command set of a normal form program is an abstract representation of m (the store for instructions). We have not mechanised the actual loading process, which corresponds to extracting (from the guarded command set) the mapping from addresses to instructions, and use this to initialise m. For the above example this mapping is

$$\{0 \mapsto \text{load}(103)\} \cup \{1 \mapsto \text{uop-A}\} \cup \{2 \mapsto \text{store}(104)\} \cup$$
$$\{3 \mapsto \text{load}(102)\} \cup \{4 \mapsto \text{bop-A}(104)\} \cup \{5 \mapsto \text{store}(101)\}$$

and the value of m outside the range 0..5 is arbitrary. In this case, the execution of the guarded command set has the same effect as the execution of m[P].

Although not apparent to the user of the compiler, the code generation is carried out phase by phase. For the above example, the result of each phase is given below.

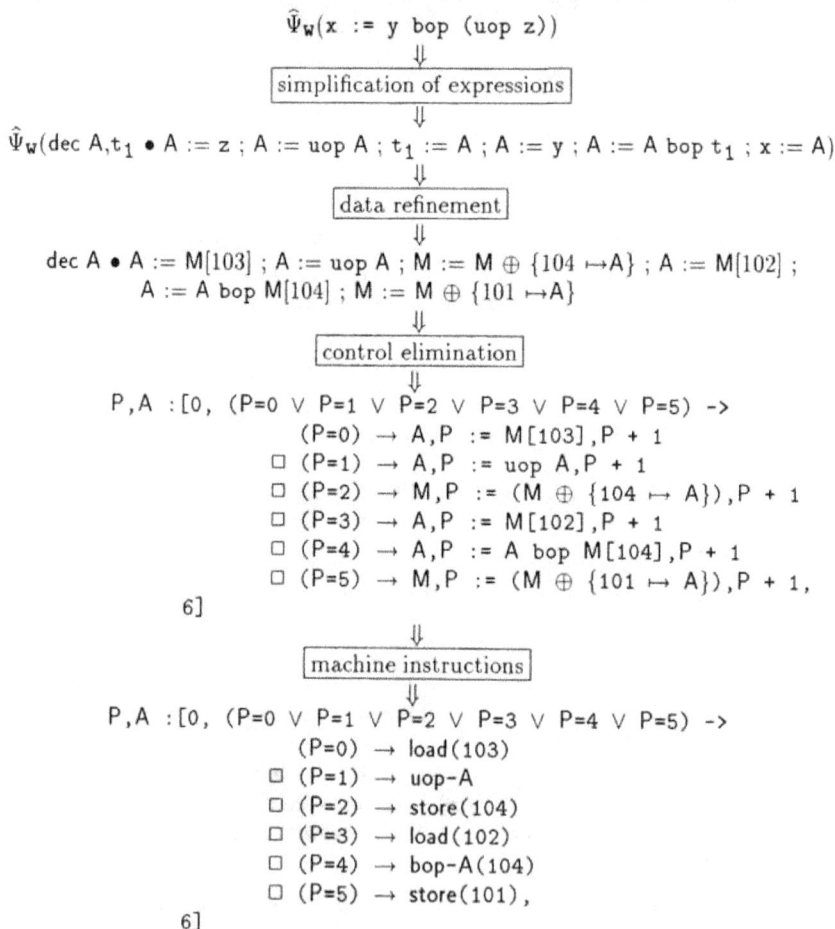

$$\hat{\Psi}_w(x := y \text{ bop } (\text{uop } z))$$
$$\Downarrow$$

simplification of expressions

$$\Downarrow$$

$\hat{\Psi}_w(\text{dec } A, t_1 \bullet A := z ; A := \text{uop } A ; t_1 := A ; A := y ; A := A \text{ bop } t_1 ; x := A)$

$$\Downarrow$$

data refinement

$$\Downarrow$$

dec A $\bullet$ A := M[103] ; A := uop A ; M := M $\oplus$ {104 $\mapsto$ A} ; A := M[102] ;
        A := A bop M[104] ; M := M $\oplus$ {101 $\mapsto$ A}

$$\Downarrow$$

control elimination

$$\Downarrow$$

```
P,A :[0, (P=0 ∨ P=1 ∨ P=2 ∨ P=3 ∨ P=4 ∨ P=5) ->
              (P=0)  →  A,P := M[103],P + 1
         □  (P=1)  →  A,P := uop A,P + 1
         □  (P=2)  →  M,P := (M ⊕ {104 ↦ A}),P + 1
         □  (P=3)  →  A,P := M[102],P + 1
         □  (P=4)  →  A,P := A bop M[104],P + 1
         □  (P=5)  →  M,P := (M ⊕ {101 ↦ A}),P + 1,
      6]
```

$$\Downarrow$$

machine instructions

$$\Downarrow$$

```
P,A :[0, (P=0 ∨ P=1 ∨ P=2 ∨ P=3 ∨ P=4 ∨ P=5) ->
              (P=0)  →  load(103)
         □  (P=1)  →  uop-A
         □  (P=2)  →  store(104)
         □  (P=3)  →  load(102)
         □  (P=4)  →  bop-A(104)
         □  (P=5)  →  store(101),
      6]
```

The last step above entails a simple syntactic transformation of the patterns used to define instructions with the corresponding instruction names.

As discussed in Chapter 4, the simplification of expressions must be performed first; no restriction was imposed regarding the order of the other two phases of compilation. In practice, however, it turned out to be much more efficient to carry out data refinement before control elimination. One reason is that the transformations associated with this last phase increase the size of the program significantly, with expressions involving the program counter which are irrelevant for data refinement. But most importantly, the normal form uses the operator $\Box$ which is both associative and commutative, and the matching of associative-commutative operators is an exponential problem. As data refinement is carried out by applying distributivity equations all the way down to the level of variables, the matching involved becomes very expensive, and (performing it after control elimination) makes the process impractical even for prototyping purposes.

It is possible to control the sequence of application of rules in OBJ3 using *evaluation strategies*. For example, by declaring the simulation function $\hat{\Psi}_w$ as *strict*, we ensure that its argument is fully reduced before any of the distributivity equations are applied; this means that the simplification of expressions is carried out before data refinement. As explained before, the equations related to control elimination are not applied before the program is tagged (this is easily controlled by pattern matching). We also use evaluation strategies to ensure that the tagging is performed only when the data refinement is complete. As a consequence, control elimination is the last phase to be accomplished.

As another example, we present the normal form reduction of a simple conditional.

Example 6.2. (A simple conditional)

```
OBJ> let w = x,y,z
OBJ> let Ψ = {x ↦ 101} ∪ {y ↦ 102} ∪ {z ↦ 103} .
OBJ> reduce Ψ̂w(z := x ◁ x bop y ▷ z := y)
rewrites: 458
result:  P,A :[0, (P=0 ∨ P=1 ∨ P=2 ∨ P=3 ∨ P=4 ∨ P=5 ∨
                   P=6 ∨ P=7) ->
                      (P=0) → load(101)
                 □ (P=1) → bop-A(102)
                 □ (P=2) → cjump(6)
                 □ (P=3) → load(101)
                 □ (P=4) → store(103)
                 □ (P=5) → cjump(8)
                 □ (P=6) → load(102)
                 □ (P=7) → store(103),
         8]
```

Compare the above to Example 1.2 of Chapter 1.

6.6. Final Considerations

We have shown how to use the OBJ3 term rewriting system to mechanise a non-trivial application. In particular, we believe to have successfully achieved three main results using a single system:

- A formal specification of all the concepts involved in this approach to compilation.

- Verification of some of the related theorems.

- Use of the theorems as a compiler prototype.

Although we have not verified all the theorems (as this was not the main purpose) the verification of a relevant subset gives some evidence that the task is feasible and relatively straightforward, especially considering that a complete framework is now in place.

Below we present a more detailed analysis of the mechanisation. First we discuss general aspects, and then we consider more specific features related to the use of OBJ3; finally we discuss some related works which report on the use of other systems to automate similar applications.

6.6.1. The Mechanisation

Even a simple attempt to automate an application gives (at least) a better insight into the problem. This is because many aspects are usually left out of (or implicit in) an informal presentation. For example, the OBJ3 presentation formally records the fact that the algebraic laws are independent of a particular expression language, provided this language includes the boolean expressions; explicit instantiations were defined when necessary.

We also had to deal with three related aspects not addressed initially: the creation of fresh local variables for the simplification of expressions, allocation of distinct addresses for local variables (also distinct from the ones used for the global variables), and, similarly, the allocation of distinct addresses for the machine instructions yielded by the compilation process.

Another major aim of a mechanisation is to check the correctness of hand proofs. With this respect, no serious error or inconsistency was found; but the mechanisation helped to uncover a few hidden assumptions (especially concerning non-freeness conditions) as well as the omission of references to laws necessary to justify some proof steps.

The only proof steps carried out completely automatically were the simplification of terms involving substitution, and the reduction of non-freeness conditions. Application of the laws required our full guidance. This is a consequence of the fact that our algebraic system is non-confluent and, furthermore, it includes non-terminating rules. Even so, the automated proofs are less laborious (and safer) than their manual versions in that the user is freed from handwriting the results of application of laws, especially regarding long terms which occur as intermediate steps in the proofs.

On the other hand, in a manual proof we sometimes allow ourselves to justify a given transformation by citing the necessary laws, leaving implicit the details of how the laws are actually used to achieve the transformation. But in a mechanical verification, every single step has to be explicitly justified, and the process may become extremely tedious. Therefore the encoding of new laws which combine the effect of more basic ones deserves special consideration. They play an increasingly important role as the number of theorems to be verified grows.

For example, the combination of assignments to distinct variables can be achieved by first normalising the left-hand sides (by adding identity assignments and using the symmetry law of multiple assignments), and then applying the law to combine assignments to the same variables. However, this process may require many applications of these laws; the same effect can be achieved using the law

```
cq  (x := e ; y := f) = (x,y := e,f[x <- e])  if x \\ y .
```

which is easily derived from the ones mentioned above. Similarly, it is possible (in some cases) to swap the order of two assignments using only the basic laws of assignment. But the process is more concisely captured by the law

```
cq  (x := e ; y := f) = (y := f[x <- e] ; x := e)
    if y \\ (x := e) .
```

Another simple example is the instantiation of the (least) fixed point laws to deal with iteration. This saved us from rewriting iteration in terms of recursion only to apply these laws and then rewrite the result back to the iteration form. Further investigation may reveal more powerful strategies to combine laws.

One of the main benefits of the mechanisation is the possibility of compiling with theorems. Once the compiling specification (given by a set of reduction theorems) was in place, no additional effort was required to produce a (prototype) implementation. This was a consequence of the fact that the reduction theorems have the form of rewrite rules.

The only unexpected result of carrying out all the work was to realise that data refinement could be performed before control elimination. This was motivated by the fact that an initial version of the prototype which executed data refinement after control elimination was extremely inefficient, as discussed in the previous section.

One final aspect we wish to address is the reliability of our mechanisation. As mentioned before, programs have both a syntactic and a semantic nature, and we have not formally distinguished between them. Rather, we have grouped the equations which define the syntactic operators in a separate context (module) from that of the algebraic laws. But this does not prevent an unadvised (or badly intentioned) user from combining the modules and deriving an inconsistency. This is illustrated by the following derivation, where we assume that the variables x, y and z are distinct.

```
      false
    = {from equations defining non-freeness}
      y \ (x:=y; x:=z)
    = {combine assignments}
      y \ (x:=z)
    = {from equations defining non-freeness}
      true
```

This is a consequence of applying a semantic transformation (the combination of assignments) to a program which should have been treated as a purely syntactic object. Such derivations would be automatically disallowed if these syntactic operators (non-freeness and substitution) were built-in to OBJ3, since in this case the user would not have access to their equations. In principle, this could be implemented in OBJ3 using (built-in) equations which provide direct access to LISP.

6.6.2. OBJ3, 2OBJ and Rewriting Logic

The normal form approach to compilation was conceived as a carefully structured hierarchy of concepts which is worth preserving in any attempted mechanisation. The parametrised modules of OBJ3 were a fundamental tool to achieve this objective.

For example, we have used distinct instantiations of the module describing the reasoning language to deal with each phase of compilation, since each phase has its own requirements regarding expressions. But clearly, the reasoning language may serve many other useful purposes such as to prove properties about programs, to perform optimisations or to reduce programs to a different normal form. The module describing the reasoning language could actually be part of a library concerning program development. The module which groups the normal form reduction theorems is equally generic and can be instantiated to deal with different target machines.

We have also demonstrated the convenience of subsorting and the operation declaration facilities of OBJ3. The fact that associativity, commutativity and identity properties can be declared (rather than stated by explicit equations) substantially simplifies the proof process. Apart from rewriting modulo these properties, OBJ3 provides mechanisms for selecting subterms (for the purpose of localised transformations) which take them into account. For example, as sequential composition is associative, the term

$$p \; ; \; q \; ; \; r$$

stands for an equivalence class containing (p ; q) ; r and p ; (q ; r). Furthermore, in this case a direct selection of any contiguous subterm is possible, as (p ; q) or (q ; r). For terms with a top operator which is both associative and commutative, a subset selection mechanism is available. Consider the term

$$p \sqcap q \sqcap r$$

We can apply a given transformation to the subterm (p ⊓ r) by directly selecting this subterm using the notation provided.

Our experience [82] with systems which do not include such facilities showed that the proofs are (at least) twice as long as the ones carried out using OBJ3. The explicit application of associativity and commutativity laws is very laborious and diverts the user's attention from more relevant proof steps.

As a language to describe theories, the only significant limitation of OBJ3 for our application is the lack of inequational rewriting. Higher-order logic would allow a more natural encoding and use of the (least) fixed point laws, but this was overcome by using substitution. Although not as convenient, it was not a major problem in practice.

The main drawbacks of OBJ3 are related to proof support, as extensively discussed in Section 6.3.1. A more pragmatic limitation is efficiency. Although the speed of the rewrites is reasonable for interactive theorem proving, it is not as satisfactory for automatic reductions involving a large number of rewrites. In particular, the use of the theorems to carry out compilation is only acceptable for prototype purposes, as illustrated in the previous section.

Most of the problems discussed above are being taken into account in the development of the 2OBJ system [31] which is being built on top of OBJ3. Broadly, this is a meta-logical framework theorem prover in the sense that it is independent of a particular logical system. The desired logical system can be programmed by the user by encoding it in equational logic. 2OBJ has a user-friendly interface and allows user-defined tactics for the particular application domain. One of the logical systems available supports order sorted, conditional, (in)equational rewriting. In particular, the inequational rewriting module of 2OBJ accepts as input an OBJ3 specification and treats the rules annotated with the ordering relation (as illustrated earlier) as inequations.

Still regarding inequational rewriting, noteworthy is the work of Meseguer [61, 62] who developed a logic called *rewriting logic* and a language, Maude, based on this logic. Maude contains OBJ3 as a functional sublanguage and provides additional features to support concurrency and object orientation. Particularly relevant to our application is what Meseguer calls *system modules*, where rewrite rules are used instead of equations. Consider, for instance, the law $b_\perp \sqsubseteq$ **skip**. It can be precisely expressed in Maude by the rule

```
rl b⊥ => skip .
```

where rl stands for rule and the sign => suggests that a rule must not be understood as an equation in the usual sense. Semantically, the main difference between equational and rewriting logic is that the former includes symmetry as a rule of deduction, whereas the latter does not.

A closer investigation of 2OBJ (or any other system based on a logic which supports inequations, such as rewriting logic) is one of the suggested topics for future work; not only more confidence will be gained in the proofs (because of a proper account of inequations), but user-defined tactics can be defined to improve the proof process.

6.6.3. Other systems

In a previous study [82], we explored the suitability of some systems to formalise a small subset of this approach to compilation. Apart from OBJ3, we considered the B-Tool [27], the Veritas[+] Environment [40] and the occam Transformation System [34]. A summary of our experience with each system is given below. Related experience of others, using the Larch Prover (LP) [28] and Higher-Order Logic (HOL) [36] is also discussed.

A specification in the B-tool is formed of a collection of units called *theories*. Unlike OBJ3, these units do not embody any idea of a module—they are just "rule containers" The lack of constructions for type definition and variable as well as operator declarations is another drawback of the B-tool. A helpful feature is the built-in implementation of non-freeness and substitution. Not only this saves a substantial specification effort in our case, but the associated reductions are carried out very efficiently. As discussed previously, this also avoids the need to distinguish between the syntactic and the semantic views of programs. Regarding theorem proving, the rewriting facilities are similar to those available in OBJ3, but there is no support for dealing with associativity, commutativity or identity.

As a specification language, Veritas includes some interesting features. Although *signatures* (the specification unit) may not be parametrised, similar facilities may be obtained by using higher-order functions and polymorphic datatypes. Besides polymorphism, the type system includes subtypes and dependent types. This allows us to express the precise domain of partial operators such as multiple assignment statements. The main drawback for our application is the difficulty of coding the algebraic laws. Defining the reasoning language as a datatype, it is impossible to postulate or prove any of the algebraic laws. The reason is that a datatype is a free algebra, and therefore terms built from the constructors cannot be equated. The laws have to be established as theorems, from a semantic function which expresses their effect, through a very laborious process.

The occam Transformation System implements an application similar to ours. Its purpose is to allow transformations of occam processes; the transformations are justified by the algebraic laws obeyed by the language [81]. As occam includes some of the operators of our reasoning language, it is possible to use the system, for example, to prove some derived laws. In principle, it is even possible to extend the system (which is implemented in the ML [79] functional programming language) with additional features which would allow us to reason about the whole compilation process. For example, new operators (especially the specification ones) with their algebraic laws would be necessary. While most of the desirable features can be easily coded in ML, the implementation of theorem proving facilities such as mechanisms to deal with associativity and commutativity is a complex task.

A work closely related to ours is reported in [83]. It investigates the use of LP to verify the proof of a compiler for a small subset of occam, not including parallelism or communication. As in our case, the reasoning framework is an extension of the source language with its algebraic laws. The proofs of the compilation rules for expressions, for the primitive operators of the source language, and for sequential composition are automated using LP.

As LP is also based on term rewriting, the specification described in [83] shares many features with ours; but it is relatively less concise and readable since LP provides no module facilities, and is based on multi-sorted, rather than order sorted, logic; therefore subsorting is not available. Also, the operation declaration facilities are not as flexible as in OBJ3. There is a mechanism to deal with associative-commutative operators, but nothing is provided for operators which are only associative. Identity properties also have to be stated by explicit equations. On the theorem proving side, LP incorporates more elaborate mechanisms than OBJ3; apart from term rewriting, it supports proof by induction, case analysis and contradiction, although the support for an interactive (step by step) application of rules is not as flexible as in OBJ3.

The work reported in [6] deals with an important aspect that we have not addressed: the correctness of the basic algebraic laws. A specification language (similar to ours) with weakest precondition semantics is formalised using the HOL system, and a number of refinement laws are (mechanically) proved. Although in principle we could do the same in OBJ3 (or perhaps 2OBJ), a system based on higher-order logic like HOL seems more appropriate for this purpose. The reason is that in the predicate transformer model, programs are regarded as functions on predicates, and therefore the reasoning is essentially higher order. Notwithstanding, it is our view that, for the purpose of using the laws for program transformation, a system like OBJ3 is more suitable, as it provides powerful rewriting capabilities.

CHAPTER 7

CONCLUSIONS

> There is a great danger associated with people's percep-
> tion of new concepts. If improved methods are used to
> tackle the same sort of problems previously handled by
> *ad hoc* methods, the systems created could be far safer.
> If, on the other hand, the improved methods are used to
> justify tackling systems of even greater complexity, no
> progress has been made.
>
> — C.B. Jones

We have presented an innovative approach to compilation, and showed how it can
be used to design a compiler which is correct by construction. The compilation
process was characterised as a normal form theorem where the normal form has the
same structure as the target executing mechanism. The whole process was formalised
within a single (and relatively simple) semantic framework: that of a procedural
language which extends the source language with additional specification features.

The specification (reasoning) language was defined as an algebraic structure whose
axioms are equations and inequations (laws) characterising the semantics of the language. The advantage of this semantic style is abstraction; it does not require the
construction of explicit mathematical models, as with denotational or operational
semantics. As a consequence, extensions or modifications to the semantics may require the alteration of only a few laws, unlike, for example, a denotational description
which would require alterations to the mathematical model and consequent revision
of every semantic clause. In the operational style, proofs are typically by structural
induction and/or by induction on the length of derivations or on the depth of trees.
Therefore if the language is extended, the proofs need to be revised. In the approach
we have adopted, we hardly use induction; this is implicitly encoded in the fixed point
laws. A purely algebraic reasoning gives some hope concerning the modularity of the
approach.

By no means are we claiming a general superiority of the algebraic approach over
the other approaches to semantics. Each style has its appropriate areas of application.
For example, postulating algebraic laws can give rise to complex and unexpected
interactions between programming constructions; this can be avoided by linking the
algebraic semantics with a mathematical model in which the laws can be verified, as
briefly illustrated in Chapter 3. Similarly, an operational semantics is necessary to
address practical aspects of the implementation and efficiency of execution. A general

theory of programming dealing with these three semantic approaches is suggested in
[51]. In particular, it is shown how an algebraic presentation can be derived from
a denotational description, and how an operational presentation is derived from the
former.

The identification of compilation as a task of normal form reduction allowed us
to capture the process in an incremental way, by splitting it into three main phases:
simplification of expressions, control elimination and data refinement. The ideas are
not biased to a particular source language or target machine. Notable are the theorems for control elimination which can be instantiated to deal with a variety of ways
of encoding control state. The independence from a source language is not so evident,
as we had to adopt a particular notation in order to formulate the mathematical laws
and illustrate the task of designing a compiler. On the other hand, our source language
includes features commonly available in existing procedural languages. It can serve as
a target for a *front-end* compiler for languages which use more conventional notations.

We initially dealt with a very simple source language to illustrate how a complete
compiler can be designed. The source language was then extended with more elaborate features (procedures, recursion and parameters), and the associated reduction
theorems were proved. This extension gave some evidence about the modularity of
the approach; each new feature was treated in complete isolation from all the other
constructions of the language. The reuse of laws, lemmas and theorems is of particular relevance. For example, the (derived) laws of iteration and the lemmas used
to prove the reduction theorem for sequential composition have been of more general
utility; they were used somehow to prove the reduction theorems for all the language
features treated subsequently.

The whole approach has been carefully structured to simplify its mechanisation.
We have illustrated the process for the simple version of the source language, using
the OBJ3 term rewriting system. The concepts were formalised as a collection of
algebraic theories, and some of the related theorems were verified and used as rewrite
rules to carry out compilation automatically. The mechanisation preserves the original structure of the algebraic theories. As discussed in the previous chapter, it
can be useful for many other purposes, such as proving properties about programs,
performing optimisations or reducing programs to a different normal form.

In summary, we believe this book to be a modest contribution to three important
fields of software engineering:

- formal methods and techniques—with a relatively large application of refinement algebra;

- compiler design and correctness—with the exploration of a new approach com-
  prising aspects such as abstraction, simplicity and modularity; and

- mechanical theorem proving—particularly, the use of term rewriting systems as
  a tool for specification, verification and (prototype) implementation.

But there is much more to be done before we can claim that this approach will generalise to more complex source languages or target machines. In the following section

we discuss related work. Some extensions to our work are discussed in Section 7.2. We finish with a critical analysis of the overall approach to compilation.

7.1. Related Work

In the previous chapter we compared OBJ3 to some other theorem provers. In Chapter 2 we gave a brief overview of refinement calculi and techniques. Regarding compiler design and correctness, some classical approaches based on operational, algebraic and denotational semantics were considered in Chapter 1. There is an extensive, and expanding, literature related to the latter topic (see Chapter 1 for some examples) and we have no intention of covering the field. Rather, the aim here is to consider closely related work and comment on a few approaches to the correct design of compiler generators and partial evaluators.

Closely Related Approaches

Nelson and Manasse [75] have previously characterised the compilation process as a normal form theorem. But the authors formalise the reduction process in more concrete terms, using a program pointer to indicate the location in memory of the next instruction to be executed. By using assumptions, assertions and generalised assignments, we have abstracted from a particular way of encoding control state; the use of a program pointer is one possible instantiation. Another difference is the reasoning framework used. They justify the correctness of the transformations by appealing to the weakest precondition calculus. We have formalised the normal form reduction process as an algebra where the central notion is a relation of refinement between programs. The use of algebraic laws seem to allow conciser and more readable proofs, apart from the fact that it makes the mechanisation easier. We have also dealt with programming features not addressed by them; these include procedures, recursion and parameters.

The first approach to prove correctness of compiling specifications using algebraic laws (in the style we have used here) was suggested by Hoare [49]. In this approach, compilation is captured by a predicate $\mathcal{C} \, p \, s \, f \, m \, \Psi$ stating that the code stored in m with start address s and finish address f is a correct translation of the source program p; Ψ is a symbol table mapping the global variables of p to their addresses. $\mathcal{C}$ is defined by

$$\mathcal{C} \, p \, s \, f \, m \, \Psi \; \stackrel{\text{def}}{=} \; \hat{\Psi}(p) \sqsubseteq \mathcal{I} \, s \, f \, m$$

where $\hat{\Psi}(p)$ is a simulation function defined in the usual way and $\mathcal{I}$ is an interpreter for the target code which can be considered a specialisation of the normal form for a particular machine. Compilation is specified by a set of theorems, one for each program construction. For example,

If $m[s] \; = \; \mathsf{load}(\Psi y)$ and $m[s + 1] \; = \; \mathsf{store}(\Psi x)$, then
$\mathcal{C} \, (x := y) \, s \, (s + 2) \, \Psi$

The reasoning is conducted in much the same way as we have illustrated in previous chapters. As the theorems have the form of Horn Clauses, they can be easily translated into a logic program [11], although a formal proof of correctness of this translation has not been attempted. Despite the similarities between the two approaches, there is a significant conceptual difference. As discussed above, the idea of an abstract normal form allowed us to capture compilation in an incremental way. The separation of the process into phases allowed the formalisation of control elimination independently of a target machine. Furthermore, as the theorems have the form of rewrite rules, we could use a term rewriting system both to verify the proofs and to carry out compilation.

Work has been undertaken to transform programs written in a subset of occam into a normal form suitable for an implementation in hardware [45]. A circuit is described in a way similar to that we have represented a stored program. Broadly, the state of a synchronous circuit is formed from a variable representing its control path and a list of variables representing its data path. The normal form comprises an assumption about the activation of the circuit; a loop (executed while the circuit is activated) which specifies state changes; and an assertion which determines the final control state of the circuit, if the loop terminates. An extra feature is the use of timed processes to specify the execution time (in clock cycles) of assignments which are used to model the state change of both the control path and the data path of the circuit. The authors show how an arbitrary source program can be reduced to normal form. However, the translation from the normal form to a *netlist* (a list of gates and latches, which is a standard form of hardware description) is addressed only informally.

Compilation as regarded in this book is an application of program transformation based on a refinement algebra. Several other applications can be characterised in a similar way. For example, in joint work with Hoare and He [54] we prove the correctness of an operational semantics for a version of Dijkstra's language. We define the meaning of the operational semantics as a program (normal form) which repeatedly executes a step of the operational semantics, until reaching a state in which there is no further transition. Each possible step is an assignment that updates two components: one to hold the data state (as *text*) and another to hold the program state (also as text). Then we prove that the interpretation of the text of any program has the same meaning as the program itself.

As another application, in joint work with Barros [8] we present some ideas towards an approach to provably correct hardware/software partitioning. We use occam as the source programming language and perform the partitioning by applying a series of algebraic transformations on the source program, using the laws of occam [81]. The result is still an occam program; its structure reflects the hardware and software components, and how they interact to achieve the overall goal.

Although the above two applications and compilation have different natures, essentially the same framework of a procedural language and its algebraic laws was used in each case: both to characterise the problem and to conduct the relevant reasoning.

Compiler Generation and Partial Evaluation

Although our approach is not biased towards a source language or a target machine, we have not gone as far as addressing the design of compiler generators. Many such systems (based on distinct semantic approaches) have been developed. As an example we can cite the classical work of Mosses [72], using denotational semantics.

Only recently, the correctness of such systems has gained some attention. The Cantor system [78, 77] generates compilers for imperative languages defined using a subset of action semantics [73]. Many imperative features can be expressed, but the considered subset of action semantics is not powerful enough to express recursion. An algebraic framework was used to design the system and prove its correctness. Another compiler generator based on action semantics is the OASIS system [76], capable of generating efficient, optimising compilers for procedural and functional languages with higher order recursive functions

Partial evaluation is a very powerful program transformation technique for specialising programs with respect to parts of its input. Applications of partial evaluation include compilation, compiler generation or even the generation of compiler generators. We quote an explanation from [56]:

> Consider an interpreter for a given language S. The specialisation of this interpreter to a known source program s (written in S) *already* is a target program for s, written in the same language as the interpreter. Thus, partial evaluation of an interpreter with respect to a fixed source program amounts to compiling. [...]
>
> Furthermore, partially evaluating a partial evaluator with respect to a fixed interpreter yields a compiler for the language implemented by the interpreter. And even more mind-boggling: partially evaluating the partial evaluator with respect to itself yields a compiler generator, namely, a program that transforms interpreters into compilers.

Partial evaluation is a very active research topic, and some powerful systems have been developed. For example, Jones *et al* [57] implemented a self-applicable partial evaluator, called λ-mix, for the untyped lambda calculus. It has been used to compile, generate compilers and generate a compiler generator. Furthermore, it is perhaps the first partial evaluator which has been proved correct [35]. The mechanical verification of an offline partial evaluator is reported in [41].

7.2. Topics for Further Research

Our work can be extended in several ways, from the treatment of more elaborate source languages and/or target machines to a provably correct compiler combining both software and hardware compilation.

More on Control Structures

In Chapter 5 our strategy to implement recursion was to allocate a separate stack
for each recursive program. This stack was represented by a local variable in the
resulting normal form program. In the case of nested recursion, the normal form
reduction process generates stacks of stacks. This can be implemented using the
cactus stack technique, as previously discussed.

For a single stack implementation, further work is necessary. One possibility is to
use the reduction rule for recursion as it stands now and then perform an additional
refinement step to implement the nested stacks using a single stack. As this is by
no means a trivial data refinement problem, it might be easier to avoid nested stacks
from the beginning. In this case, the theorem for recursion has to be modified to reuse
a stack variable which may have been allocated for compiling an inner recursion.

A further topic of investigation is the extension of our source language with even
more complex structures such as parallelism, communication and external choice (as,
for example, in occam). An initial attempt to handle these features is described in
[43], where a a communication-based parallel program is transformed into another
(yet parallel) program whose components communicate via shared variables.

Because of the high-level of abstraction of constructions to implement concurrency,
it seems more appropriate to carry out their elimination at the source level, rather
than generate a normal form directly. If the target program yielded by the process of
eliminating concurrency is described solely in terms of our source language, then we
can reduce this program to normal form and thus obtain a low level implementation
of concurrency.

Types

We have taken the simplified view of not dealing with type information. It is possible
to extend our reasoning language with data types in the usual way. For example,
typed variables can be introduced by

$$\text{dec } x : T \bullet p$$

where x is a list of variables and T an equal-length list of type names, and the
association of types with variables is positional.

Types restrict the values that can be assigned to variables. As a consequence,
they introduce a proof obligation to check if these restrictions are respected. This is
known as *type checking*. Therefore our algebraic system must ensure a consistent use
of types.

Most of the algebraic laws do not need to be changed, as their use would not give
rise to type inconsistences, provided the term to be transformed is *well-typed* to start
with. Only a few laws would require extra conditions. For example, the law

$$\text{dec } x : T \bullet p \sqsubseteq \text{dec } x : T \bullet x := e; \ p$$

(when used from left to right) allows the introduction of the assignment $x := e$.
Clearly, e must have type T in this case (or at least a type compatible with T if the

type system supports subtypes or any form of type conversion). The laws which allow the introduction of free (meta-)variables, such as x and e in the above case, are the only ones which can violate type information. One way to deal with the problem is by carrying type information around; for example, by tagging occurrences of variables and expressions with their types.

The introduction of types also affects compiler design. More specifically, it increases the complexity of the data refinement phase—we have to show how the various types of the source language can be represented in a usually untyped (or single-typed) target machine.

The implementation of *basic* types is normally achieved by very simple translation schemes. For example, there is a standard technique for translating booleans using a numerical representation [1]. Type constructors such as arrays and records are more difficult to implement. In Appendix A, we suggest a scheme for compiling static arrays and discuss its (partial) implementation in OBJ3, with a small example.

The scheme to implement arrays was designed in complete isolation from the remaining features of our language. None of the previous results needed to be changed. This gives some more evidence about the modularity of our approach to compilation. But further investigation concerning the compilation of basic types and type constructors is required. For example, non-static types such as dynamic arrays or linked lists will certainly require a much more elaborate scheme than the one devised for static arrays.

Code Optimisation

We have briefly addressed store optimisation when dealing with the creation of temporary variables for the elimination of nested expressions. Regarding code optimisation, only a very simple rule was included in connection with the compilation of boolean expressions. An important complement to our work would be the investigation of more significant optimising transformations which could be performed both on the source and on the target code.

The most difficult optimisations are those which require data flow analysis. The main problem is the need to generate (usually) complex structures to store data flow information, as well as carrying these structures around so that the optimisation rules can access them. In our algebraic framework, a promising direction seems to be the encoding of data flow information as assumptions and assertions. For example, the fact that the final values of the variables $x_1, \ldots, x_n$, produced by a given program fragment, are $e_1, \ldots, e_n$ could be encoded as an assertion of the form

$$(x_1 = e_1 \wedge \ldots \wedge x_n = e_n)_\perp$$

Similarly,

$$(x_1 = e_1 \wedge \ldots \wedge x_n = e_n)^\top$$

could be used as an assumption of the initial values of $x_1, \ldots, x_n$ in another program fragment. As described in Section 3.11, assumptions and assertions satisfy a wide set of laws which allow them to be flexibly manipulated within a source program.

Local optimisations are much easier to describe and prove. Some algebraic laws can be used directly to perform optimisations on the source code. For example,

$$(x := e;\ x := f) = (x := f[x \leftarrow e])$$

may be useful for eliminating consecutive assignments to the same variable. Another example is the law which allows the transformation of tail recursion into iteration:

$$\mu X \bullet ((p;\ X) \lhd b \rhd q) = (b * p);\ q$$

Local optimisations on a target program are known as *peephole optimisations*. The general aim is to find sequences of instructions which can be replaced by shorter or more efficient sequences. The (very abstract) normal form representation of the target machine may provide an adequate framework to carry out optimisations and prove them correct. As a simple example, the following equation allows the elimination of *jumps to jumps*:

$$P : \left[s, \begin{pmatrix} & (P = j) \rightarrow \mathsf{jump}(k) \\ \Box & (P = k) \rightarrow \mathsf{jump}(l) \\ \Box & q \end{pmatrix}, f\right] = P : \left[s, \begin{pmatrix} & (P = j) \rightarrow \mathsf{jump}(l) \\ \Box & (P = k) \rightarrow \mathsf{jump}(l) \\ \Box & q \end{pmatrix}, f\right]$$

where q stands for an arbitrary context containing the remaining instructions. The aim of this transformation is to eliminate all jumps to k, one at a time. When there are no jumps to k then it is possible to eliminate the guarded command

$$(P = k) \rightarrow \mathsf{jump}(l)$$

provided it is preceded by an unconditional jump instruction of the form

$$(P = k - 1) \rightarrow \mathsf{jump}(n)$$

with n different from k. Notice that associative and commutative matching as provided in OBJ3 allows the above rule to cover cases where one jump instruction is not textually followed by the other, as apparently required by the left-hand side of the rule.

It would also be interesting to investigate some machine-dependent optimisations such as register allocation and the replacement of sequences of machine instructions with other sequences known to execute more efficiently. But this only makes sense in the context of a more complex target machine than the one we have considered here. Information necessary to optimise register allocation can be encoded as assumptions and assertions, following the style suggested in [44].

More on Mechanisation

As described in the previous chapter, a significant amount of work concerning the mechanisation of our approach to compilation has been carried out; but much more could be done. For example, we have not considered procedures, recursion or parameters. Extending our OBJ3 specification with rewrite rules to eliminate these features would produce a prototype for a more interesting language. Clearly, it would be necessary to extend the target machine with stacks and related operations in order to support recursion.

The more complex the theorems and their proofs are, the more likely the occurrence of errors is. The complete verification of the reduction theorem for recursion would be a worthwhile exercise.

The ideal would be to mechanise any new translation scheme which is designed. Apart from the benefit of verification, the mechanisation (as we have addressed in this work) helps to ensure that the scheme is described in sufficient detail to be implemented.

As this will eventually become a relatively large application of theorem proving, a good deal of proof management is required. A promising direction seems to be "customising" a system like 2OBJ for this application, as discussed in the previous chapter, or any other system based on a logic (for instance, rewriting logic) which supports inequations.

Compiler Development

The only limitation that prevents the specification of the compiler (written in OBJ3) to be used as an actual implementation is efficiency. As discussed in the previous chapter, one reason for its inefficient execution is the use of commutative and associative matching, which is an exponential problem. Therefore the elimination of these features from the present specification is an essential step towards improving efficiency.

A more serious constraint is imposed by the implementation of OBJ3 itself; currently the language is interpreted and term rewriting is carried out at a speed which is acceptable only for prototyping purposes. A possible solution might be to compile the rewrite rules into efficient code, as done by the ASF+SDF system [87, 88]. The development of an efficient compiler for (a subset of) OBJ3 is reported in [39, 38]. According to the author, the code generated by this compiler runs an order of magnitude faster than the OBJ3 interpreter. Unfortunately, we use features of OBJ3 not implemented by this compiler, such as associative/commutative matching and rewriting modulo these properties. In order to benefit from the efficiency of this compiler we need to eliminate these features from our rewriting system.

An alternative is to develop an implementation of the compiler in some other programming language that is implemented efficiently. As our reference against which to check the implementation is a declarative specification of the compiler (given by a set of rewrite rules), it might be easier to develop a functional implementation. A language such as ML [79] could be useful for this purpose.

The main task is therefore to derive a compilation function, say C, from the rewrite rules. It is possible to develop the implementation with a similar structure as the OBJ3 specification; C is defined by the composition of three functions, one for each phase of compilation (simplification of expressions, control elimination and data refinement):

$$C\ p\ \Psi\ s\ \overset{def}{=}\ \hat{\Psi}(\mathit{ControlElim}(\mathit{ExpSimp}(p),s))$$

where p is a source program, Ψ its symbol table and s the start address of code. The definition of each of the above functions can be systematically generated from the rewrite rules in the corresponding OBJ3 modules. For example,

$$\mathit{ExpSimp}(x := e)\ =\ \mathsf{dec\,A} \bullet \mathit{ExpSimp}(\mathsf{A} := e);\ x := \mathsf{A}$$
$$\mathit{ExpSimp}(\mathsf{A} := \mathsf{uop}\ e)\ =\ \mathit{ExpSimp}(\mathsf{A} := e);\ \mathsf{A} := \mathsf{uop}\ e$$
$$\vdots \qquad \vdots$$

The aim of this transformation is to end up with a functional program still in OBJ3, but including only features available, say, in ML; so a *simple* syntactic transformation would produce an ML program which could then be translated to machine code using an efficient ML compiler [2].

Although this is a relatively simple way of producing an efficient compiler from the specification in OBJ3, not all the transformations are as straightforward as the ones illustrated above. For example, associative/commutative matching is built-in to OBJ3, whereas this is not the case in ML. Another aspect is that the approach is rigorous rather than completely formal. One source of insecurity is that even an apparently trivial syntactic transformation from OBJ3 into ML (more generally, from a language to any other language) may be misleading; the other is the ML compiler itself (unless its correctness had been proved).

An approach which avoids the need for an already verified compiler is suggested in [14] and further discussed in [16]. It is based on the classical technique of *bootstrapping*. The main goal is to obtain an implementation of the compiler written in the source language itself. The work reported in [14] describes an implementation of a compiler for an occam-like language extended with parameterless recursive procedures. The implementation (in the source language itself) is formally derived from a specification of the compiler given in an inductive function definition style that uses a subset of LISP.

In principle, we could adopt a similar technique to derive an implementation of our compiler (written in our source language) from the specification in OBJ3. In this case, we could run the specification to automatically translate the implementation of the compiler into machine code. But as pointed out in [14], the formal derivation of the implementation from the specification is by no means a simple task.

Hardware and Software Co-design

Software compilation is cheap but produces code which is usually slow for many of the present applications; hardware compilation produces components which execute fast, but are expensive. A growing trend in computing is the design of systems which are partially implemented in software and partially in hardware. This of course needs the support of compilers which give the choice of compiling into software or hardware (or both).

We have addressed software compilation and, as discussed in the previous section, some work has been done for hardware compilation using a similar approach. A very ambitious project is to develop a common approach to support the design (and correctness proof) of a hardware/software compiler. The main challenge is to discover an even more general normal form which would be an intermediate representation of code describing hardware or software. Broadly, the structure of such a compiler would be as in Fig. 7.1. Normal form reduction here can be considered as an abstract

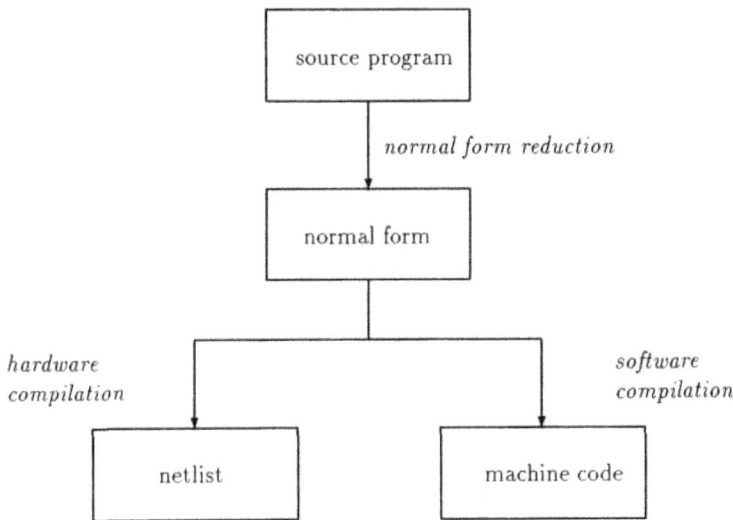

Fig. 7.1. Hardware and software co-design.

characterisation of a hardware/software partitioning algorithm. For this application, it is important that the reasoning language provide parallelism and communication so that the normal form is expressed as the parallel composition of the software and the hardware components. A language like occam is particularly suitable for this purpose, since it obeys a large set of algebraic laws [81]. A formal approach to hardware/software partitioning using occam is described in [8].

7.3. A Critical View

In this final section we present a critical analysis of our work and try to answer the following questions:

- Will this ever be a practical way to write compilers?

- If not, is there any independent reason for pursuing research of this kind?

- To what extent should we believe in provably correct compilers (and systems in general)?

In the previous section and in Chapter 1 we briefly described a few approaches to compiler correctness, some based on different formalisms, but these are only a small fraction of the enormous effort that has been dedicated to the field.

We have defended the use of yet another approach. We believe it is very uniform and is based on a comparatively simple semantic framework. In spite of that, the overall task of constructing a correct compiler was not at all trivial. Many frustrating alternatives were attempted until we could discover reasonable ways of structuring the proofs. On the positive side, there is the hope that these will be of more general utility. The main purpose was not to show that a particular compiler correctly translates programs from a particular source language to a particular target language; but rather, to build a set of transformations that may be useful for tackling the problem in a more general sense.

Uniformity was achieved by reducing the task of compilation to one of program refinement. Although this is extremely difficult in general, it is much more manageable when dealing with a particular class of problems, such as compiler design. Our understanding of and intuition about compilation helped us to achieve a modular design; our knowledge about programming helped us in the reasoning (using algebraic laws) necessary to discharge the related proof obligations.

But the approach is not sufficiently mature yet. It is too early to tell whether this (or a similar) approach will ever be widely adopted by practical compiler writers. Although the mathematics involved is not very deep, the amount of reasoning required to assert the correctness of the design might scare professionals with a more practical background.

Here we definitely need a division of labour. It should be the task of computer scientists to continue the search for general theorems to support the design of compilers for more powerful languages. Ideally, the result of this search should be an interface appealing to practical use, where particular compilers could then be designed as specialisations of the more abstract theorems, as illustrated in this book.

Whereas we do not have enough grounds yet to affirm that our approach will allow a systematic development of provably correct (realistic) compilers, we hope that this book will be useful as a reference for further work in the field.

Concerning the problem of provably correct systems in general, there will always be a gap between any mathematical model and its implementation. Even if compilers, assemblers, loaders and the actual hardware are provably correct, it is actually mathematical models of these objects that are verified [16]. The transition from the models to reality can never be formalised, let alone reasoned about. The purpose of pursuing formal verification is to gain a better insight into the problem and reduce the occurrence of errors; their total absence can never be proved.

APPENDIX A

A SCHEME FOR COMPILING ARRAYS

In order to illustrate how type constructors can be handled, we suggest a scheme for compiling arrays. We will confine ourselves to one-dimensional arrays. Furthermore, we will illustrate the process using a global array variable a and will assume that it has length l. But the scheme can be easily extended to cover an arbitrary number of multi-dimensional array variables.

We extend the source language to allow two operations on arrays: update of an element and indexing. We adopt the map notation, as described in Chapter 4:

$$a := a \oplus \{i \mapsto e\} \quad \text{update the } i^{th} \text{ element of } a \text{ with } e$$
$$a[i] \qquad\qquad\qquad \text{yield the } i^{th} \text{ element of } a$$

Arrays are indexed from 0. Thus given that the length of a is l, its elements are $a[0], \ldots, a[l-1]$. We will assume that indexing a with a value out of the range $0..(l-1)$ will lead to abortion; this avoids the need of runtime tests that indices are in bounds, as the implementation cannot be worse than abort.

In addition to the above, we will use lambda expressions in assignments to the entire array a; but this will be used only for reasoning, and will not be considered a source construction.

Our first task is to extend the symbol table Ψ to include the array variable a.

$$\Phi \stackrel{def}{=} \Psi \cup \{a \mapsto n\}$$
$$\text{where} \quad \forall i : 0..(l-1) \bullet (n+i) \notin \text{ran } \Psi$$

In practice, the symbol table must record the length of static arrays. As we are treating a single array, and are assuming that its length is l, we can stick to the same structure of our simple symbol table which maps identifiers to addresses. The address n associated with a determines the memory location where the element $a[0]$ will be stored; this is usually called the *base* address. The locations for an arbitrary element is calculated from n, using the index as an *offset*. Therefore the location associated with element $a[i]$ is given by $n+i$, for $0 \le i < l$. The condition on the above definition requires that the addresses allocated for a must not have been used previously. In the case of more than one array variable, this condition would be extended to each one. Furthermore, an extra condition would be required to guarantee non-overlapping of the addresses allocated to distinct arrays.

We can then define the *encoding* program $\hat{\Phi}_{a,w}$ which *retrieves* the abstract state (formed from the array variable a and the other global variables w) from the concrete store of the target machine.

$$\hat{\Phi}_{a,w} \stackrel{def}{=} \mathbf{var}\ a;\ a := \lambda\, i : 0..(l-1) \bullet \mathsf{M}[i+n];\ \hat{\Psi}_w$$

Recall that $\hat{\Psi}_w$ was defined in Chapter 4 to deal with the global variables w. The following *decoding* program maps the abstract state down to the concrete machine state.

$$\hat{\Phi}_{a,w}^{-1} \stackrel{def}{=} \hat{\Psi}_w^{-1};\ \mathsf{M} := \mathsf{M} \oplus \lambda\, i : n..(n+l-1) \bullet a[i-n];\ \mathbf{end}\ a$$

The following proposition establishes that the pair $(\hat{\Phi}_{a,w}, \hat{\Phi}_{a,w}^{-1})$ is a simulation.

Proposition A.1. $((\hat{\Phi}_{a,w}, \hat{\Phi}_{a,w}^{-1})$ simulation$)$

$$\hat{\Phi}_{a,w};\ \hat{\Phi}_{a,w}^{-1} \;=\; \mathbf{skip} \;\sqsubseteq\; \hat{\Phi}_{a,w}^{-1};\ \hat{\Phi}_{a,w}$$

◇

We already know how to carry out the data refinement of programs involving ordinary variables; now this is extended to cover the array operations.

Proposition A.2.   (data refinement of array operations)
(1) $\hat{\Phi}_{a,w}(a := a \oplus \{i \mapsto e\}) \sqsubseteq \mathsf{M} := \mathsf{M} \oplus \{\hat{\Phi}_{a,w}(i) + n \mapsto \hat{\Phi}_{a,w}(e)\}$
(2) $\hat{\Phi}_{a,w}(a[i]) \sqsubseteq \mathsf{M}[\hat{\Phi}_{a,w}(i) + n]$

◇

The remaining task is the simplification of expressions involving arrays.

Proposition A.3.   (Simplification of expressions)
If neither A nor t occur in i or e
(1) $(a := a \oplus \{i \mapsto e\}) \;=\; \mathbf{dec}\,\mathsf{A}, t \bullet \mathsf{A} := e;\ t := \mathsf{A};\ \mathsf{A} := i;\ a := a \oplus \{\mathsf{A} \mapsto t\}$
(2) $(\mathsf{A} := a[i]) \;=\; (\mathsf{A} := i;\ \mathsf{A} := a[\mathsf{A}])$

◇

By structural induction, it is possible to show that the above two rules, together with the ones given in Chapter 4, are sufficient to simplify an arbitrary expression.

Applying data refinement to a simple assignment of the form

$$a := a \oplus \{\mathsf{A} \mapsto t\}$$

leads to

$$\mathsf{M} := \mathsf{M} \oplus \{\mathsf{A} + n \mapsto \mathsf{M}[\Psi\, t]\}$$

which can be taken as the definition of an update instruction for arrays. If preferred, we can store the value to update the array in a new register, say B, rather than in the auxiliary variable t. In this case, the update instruction would be defined by

$$\text{update–array–at}(n) \stackrel{def}{=} M := M \oplus \{A + n \mapsto B\}$$

Similarly, the assignment

$$A := a[A]$$

will eventually be data refined to

$$A := M[A + n]$$

which can be taken as the definition of a read instruction

$$\text{read–array–at}(n) \stackrel{def}{=} A := M[A + n]$$

We have actually added the rules for expression simplification to our OBJ3 prototype and performed some reductions. For example,

```
OBJ> reduce a := a ⊕ {(a[i bop j]) bop k -> a[dop i]}
rewrites: 178
result Prog: dec A,B • A := i ; A := dop A ; A := a[A] ;
                       B := A ; A := i ; A := A bop j ;
                       A := a[A] ; A := A bop k ;
                       a := a ⊕ {A -> B}
```

The original assignment updates array a at position (a[i bop j]) bop k with the value of a[dop i]. The resulting program declares variables A and B to play the roles of two registers. Before the final assignment, A and B hold, respectively, the value of the index and the element to update array a.

In the case of arrays local to a recursive program, a similar scheme could be adopted; but storage would be allocated in the runtime stack, rather than in the fixed memory M.

APPENDIX B

PROOF OF LEMMA 5.1

The proof of Lemma 5.1 uses the following abbreviations, as introduced in Chapter 5.

$$MID = v, \bar{v} : [a_0 \wedge \text{empty } \bar{v}, S, c_0 \wedge \text{empty } \bar{v}]$$

$$\text{where} \quad S = \begin{pmatrix} b \rightarrow (v :\in r; \ \text{push}(v, \bar{v}); \ v :\in a_0) \\ \square \quad (c_0 \wedge \neg\text{empty } \bar{v}) \rightarrow \text{pop}(v, \bar{v}) \\ \square \quad b_0 \rightarrow p \end{pmatrix}$$

$$T = \begin{pmatrix} a \rightarrow (v :\in c; \ \text{push}(v, \bar{v}); \ v :\in a_0) \\ \square \quad b \rightarrow (v :\in r; \ \text{push}(v, \bar{v}); \ v :\in a_0) \\ \square \quad c_0 \rightarrow \text{pop}(v, \bar{v}) \\ \square \quad b_0 \rightarrow p \end{pmatrix}$$

$$U = \begin{pmatrix} b \rightarrow (v :\in r; \ \text{push}(v, \bar{v}); \ v :\in a_0) \\ \square \quad (c_0 \wedge \#\bar{v} > 1) \rightarrow \text{pop}(v, \bar{v}) \\ \square \quad b_0 \rightarrow p \end{pmatrix}$$

We also need the following lemma. It establishes that a normal form program with guarded command set S (operating initially on an empty sequence) is refined by a normal form program obtained from this one, by replacing S with U and the empty sequence with a singleton sequence.

Lemma B.1. (Lift of sequence variables) If S and U are as defined above, and k occurs only where explicitly shown below, then

$$v, \bar{v} : [(a_0 \wedge \text{empty } \bar{v}), S, (c_0 \wedge \text{empty } \bar{v})]$$

$$\sqsubseteq$$

$$v, \bar{v} : [(a_0 \wedge \bar{v} = \langle k \rangle), U, (c_0 \wedge \bar{v} = \langle k \rangle)]$$

Proof: we can regard the above as a data refinement problem: although the data space of the two programs are apparently the same, note that the right-hand side requires the stack $\bar{v}$ to be non-empty. Therefore, in order to compare the above programs we define a simulation.

$$\text{Let} \quad \Theta \quad \overset{def}{=} \quad \text{var } \bar{w}, w; \ (\neg\text{empty } \bar{v})_\perp; \ (\bar{w}, w) := (\text{front } \bar{v}, \text{last } \bar{v}); \ \text{end } \bar{v}$$

$$\text{and} \quad \Theta^{-1} \quad \overset{def}{=} \quad \text{var } \bar{v}; \ \bar{v} := \bar{w} \frown \langle w \rangle; \ \text{end } \bar{w}, w$$

149

As before, we use $\Theta(p)$ to denote Θ; p; Θ^{-1} The following facts are true of Θ and Θ^{-1}:

(1) (Θ,Θ^{-1}) is a simulation.
(2) $\Theta(\text{push}(v, \bar{w})) \sqsubseteq \text{push}(v, \bar{v})$
(3) $\Theta(\text{pop}(v, \bar{w})) \sqsubseteq \text{pop}(v, \bar{v})$
(4) $\Theta((\neg\text{empty } \bar{w})^{\top}) \sqsubseteq (\#\bar{v} > 1)^{\top}$
(5) Let $d_1 = (b \vee (c_0 \wedge \neg\text{empty } \bar{w}) \vee b_0)$ and $d_2 = (b \vee (c_0 \wedge \#\bar{v} > 1) \vee b_0)$. Then
$\Theta(d1 * S[\bar{v} \leftarrow \bar{w}]) \sqsubseteq (d_2 * U)$

> **(1)** $\quad \Theta; \Theta^{-1}$
>
> $=$ $\{\langle\text{end} - \text{var skip}\rangle(3.19.7), \langle:= \text{combination}\rangle(3.15.4)$ and
> $\quad \langle\text{laws of sequences}\rangle(5.1.1)\}$
> $\quad \textsf{var } \bar{w}, w; \ (\neg\text{empty } \bar{v})_{\perp}; \ (\bar{w}, w) := (\text{front } \bar{v}, \text{last } \bar{v}); \ \textsf{end } \bar{w}, w$
>
> $\sqsubseteq$ $\{\langle\text{end}- := \text{ final value}\rangle(3.19.5), \langle\text{end} - \text{var simulation}\rangle(3.19.6)$ and
> $\quad b_{\perp} \sqsubseteq \ \textsf{skip}\}$
> $\quad \textsf{skip}$
>
> $=$ $\{\langle\text{end}- := \text{ final value}\rangle(3.19.5), \langle\text{end} - \text{var skip}\rangle(3.19.7)$ and
> $\quad \langle\text{void } b_{\perp}\rangle(3.16.4)\}$
> $\quad \textsf{var } \bar{v}; \ \bar{v} := \bar{w} \frown \langle w \rangle; \ (\neg\text{empty } \bar{v})_{\perp}; \ \textsf{end } \bar{v}$
>
> $=$ $\{\langle\text{end} - \text{var skip}\rangle(3.19.7), \langle:= \text{combination}\rangle(3.15.4)$ and
> $\quad \langle\text{laws of sequences}\rangle(5.1.1)\}$
> $\quad \Theta^{-1}; \Theta$

> **(2)** $\quad \Theta(\text{push}(v, \bar{w}))$
>
> $=$ $\Theta; \text{push}(v, \bar{w}); \Theta^{-1}$
>
> $=$ $\{\langle\text{end change scope}\rangle(3.19.2)$ and $\langle\text{end} - \text{var skip}\rangle(3.19.7)\}$
> $\quad \textsf{var } \bar{w}, w; \ (\neg\text{empty } \bar{v})_{\perp}; \ (\bar{w}, w) := (\text{front } \bar{v}, \text{last } \bar{v}); \ \text{push}(v, \bar{w});$
> $\quad \bar{v} := \bar{w} \frown \langle w \rangle; \ \textsf{end } \bar{w}, w$
>
> $=$ $\{\langle:= \text{combination}\rangle(3.15.4)$ and $\langle\text{end} - \text{var simulation}\rangle(3.19.6)\}$
> $\quad (\neg\text{empty } \bar{v})_{\perp}; \ \text{push}(v, \bar{v})$
>
> $\sqsubseteq$ $\{b_{\perp} \sqsubseteq \ \textsf{skip}\}$
> $\quad \text{push}(v, \bar{v})$

> **(3)** $\quad$ Similar to (2).

> **(4)** $\quad$ Similar to (2).

> **(5)** $\quad$ From $(1) - (4)$ and the distributivity of Θ over iteration.

Then we have:

RHS

$\sqsupseteq$ $\{\langle \text{end} - \text{var skip}\rangle(3.19.7) \text{ and } (5)\}$

$\quad \text{dec } v, \bar{v} \bullet v :\in a_0; \ \bar{v} := \langle k \rangle; \ \text{var } \bar{w}, w; \ (\neg \text{empty } \bar{v})_\perp;$

$\quad (\bar{w}, w) := (\text{front } \bar{v}, \text{last } \bar{v}); \ d_1 * S[\bar{v} \leftarrow \bar{w}]; \ \bar{v} := \bar{w} \frown \langle w \rangle;$

$\quad \text{end } \bar{w}, w; \ (c_0 \wedge \bar{v} = \langle k \rangle)_\perp$

$=$ $\{\langle \text{void } b_\perp \rangle(3.16.4) \text{ and } \langle := \text{ combination}\rangle(3.15.4)\}$

$\quad \text{dec } v, \bar{v} \bullet v :\in a_0; \ \bar{v} := \langle k \rangle; \ \text{var } \bar{w}, w; \ (\bar{w}, w) := (\langle \rangle, k);$

$\quad d_1 * S[\bar{v} \leftarrow \bar{w}]; \ \bar{v} := \bar{w} \frown \langle w \rangle; \ \text{end } \bar{w}, w; \ (c_0 \wedge \bar{v} = \langle k \rangle)_\perp$

$=$ $\{\langle := \text{ combination}\rangle(3.15.4), \langle \text{end} - := \text{ final value}\rangle(3.19.5) \text{ and}$

$\quad \langle \text{end} - \text{var simulation}\rangle(3.19.6)\}$

$\quad \text{dec } v, \bar{v} \bullet v :\in a_0; \ \bar{v} := \langle k \rangle; \ \text{var } \bar{w}; \ \bar{w} := \langle \rangle;$

$\quad d_1 * S[\bar{v} \leftarrow \bar{w}]; \ \bar{v} := \bar{w} \frown \langle k \rangle; \ \text{end } \bar{w}; \ (c_0 \wedge \bar{v} = \langle k \rangle)_\perp$

$=$ $\{\langle := -b_\perp \text{ commutation}\rangle(3.15.8) \text{ and } \langle \text{dec} - := \text{ final value}\rangle(3.18.6)\}$

$\quad \text{dec } v, \bar{v} \bullet v :\in a_0; \ \bar{v} := \langle k \rangle; \ \text{var } \bar{w}; \ \bar{w} := \langle \rangle;$

$\quad d_1 * S[\bar{v} \leftarrow \bar{w}]; \ (c_0 \wedge \text{empty } \bar{w})_\perp; \ \text{end } \bar{w}$

$\sqsupseteq$ $\{\langle \text{dec} - :\in \text{ initial value}\rangle(3.18.5) \text{ and } \langle \text{dec elim}\rangle(3.18.3)\}$

$\quad \text{dec } v \bullet v :\in a_0; \ \text{var } \bar{w}; \ \bar{w} := \langle \rangle; \ d_1 * S[\bar{v} \leftarrow \bar{w}]; \ (c_0 \wedge \text{empty } \bar{w})_\perp; \ \text{end } \bar{w}$

$=$ $\{\langle \text{dec} - (\text{var}, \text{end}) \text{ conversion}\rangle(3.19.10) \text{ and } \langle \text{dec rename}\rangle(3.18.4)\}$

$\quad LHS$

$\diamondsuit$

Now we can prove Lemma 5.1. First we repeat the inequation to be proved. Let $d_1 = (b \vee (c_0 \wedge \neg \text{empty } \bar{v}) \vee b_0)$, then we have:

$$b^\top; \ d_1 * S \ \sqsupseteq \ (\text{empty } \bar{v})_\perp; \ MID; \ v :\in r; \ d_1 * S$$

Proof:

$\quad b^\top; \ d_1 * S$

$\sqsupseteq$ $\{\langle * - \square \text{ unfold}\rangle(3.17.3) \text{ and } b^\top \sqsupseteq \text{ skip}\}$

$\quad v :\in r; \ \text{push}(v, \bar{v}); \ v :\in a_0; \ d_1 * S$

$=$ $\{\langle * \text{ sequence}\rangle(3.17.7) \text{ and Let } d_2 = (b \vee (c_0 \wedge \#\bar{v} > 1) \vee b_0)\}$

$\quad v :\in r; \ \text{push}(v, \bar{v}); \ v :\in a_0; \ d_2 * U; \ d_1 * S$

$\sqsupseteq$ $\{b_\perp \sqsubseteq \text{ skip and } \langle * - \square \text{ unfold}\rangle(3.17.3)\}$

$\quad v :\in r; \ \text{push}(v, \bar{v}); \ v :\in a_0; \ d_2 * U; \ (c_0 \wedge \#\bar{v} > 1)_\perp; \ \text{pop}(v, \bar{v}); \ d_1 * S$

$=$ $\{\langle \text{dec introduction}\rangle(3.19.11) \text{ and Definition } 4.1(\text{Normal form})\}$

$v :\in r;\ \mathsf{push}(v,\bar v);\ v : [a_0,\ U,\ (c_0 \wedge \#\bar v > 1)];\ \mathsf{pop}(v,\bar v);\ d_1 * S$

$=$ {⟨dec rename⟩(3.18.4), assuming w is fresh and $t' = t[v \leftarrow w]$}

$v :\in r;\ \mathsf{push}(v,\bar v);\ w : [a_0',\ U',\ (c_0' \wedge \#\bar v > 1)];\ \mathsf{pop}(v,\bar v);\ d_1 * S$

$\sqsupseteq$ {$(c_0' \wedge \#\bar v > 1)_\perp \sqsupseteq (c_0' \wedge \#\bar v > 1)_\perp;\ (\bar v = \langle v\rangle)_\perp = (c_0' \wedge \bar v = \langle v\rangle)_\perp$}

$v :\in r;\ \mathsf{push}(v,\bar v);\ w : [a_0',\ U',\ (c_0' \wedge \bar v = \langle v\rangle)];\ \mathsf{pop}(v,\bar v);\ d_1 * S$

$=$ {Definition of push and pop}

$v :\in r;\ \bar v := \langle v\rangle \frown \bar v;\ w : [a_0',\ U',\ (c_0' \wedge \bar v = \langle v\rangle)];\ \bar v := \langle\rangle;\ d_1 * S$

$\sqsupseteq$ {$b_\perp \sqsubseteq \mathsf{skip}$}

$v :\in r;\ (\mathsf{empty}\ \bar v)_\perp;\ \bar v := \langle v\rangle;\ w : [a_0',\ U',\ (c_0' \wedge \bar v = \langle v\rangle)];\ \bar v := \langle\rangle;\ d_1 * S$

$=$ {⟨dec introduction⟩(3.19.11) and $(\mathsf{empty}\ \bar v)_\perp;\ \bar v := \langle\rangle = (\mathsf{empty}\ \bar v)_\perp$}

$v :\in r;\ (\mathsf{empty}\ \bar v)_\perp;\ w, \bar v : [(a_0' \wedge \bar v = \langle v\rangle),\ U',\ (c_0' \wedge \bar v = \langle v\rangle)];\ d_1 * S$

$\sqsupseteq$ {Lemma B.1(Lift of sequence variables) and ⟨dec rename⟩(3.18.4)}

$v :\in r;\ (\mathsf{empty}\ \bar v)_\perp;\ MID;\ d_1 * S$

$\sqsupseteq$ {⟨$x :\in b;\ p$ commute⟩(3.16.9)}

$(\mathsf{empty}\ \bar v)_\perp;\ MID;\ v :\in r;\ d_1 * S$

APPENDIX C

SPECIFICATION AND VERIFICATION IN OBJ3

Here we give further details about the mechanisation. Following the same structure as that of Chapter 6, we give the complete description of the main modules together with the automated proofs of some of the theorems.

C.1. The Reasoning Language

The reasoning language and its algebraic laws (including the derived ones) are described by the following theory. The next two sections illustrate the verification of two laws of while.

```
th REASONING-LANGUAGE [X :: EXP] is

  sorts Prog ProgId .
  subsorts ProgId < Prog

  define ListVar is LIST[Var]
  define ListExp is LIST[Exp]
  subsorts ListVar < ListExp

*** Program constructs
  op skip   -> Prog
  op dec   •_ : ListVar Prog -> Prog [prec 60]
  op-as _:=_   ListVar ListExp -> Prog
         for x := e if (len x == len e) and (disj x) [prec 52]
  op _;_ : Prog Prog -> Prog [assoc prec 56]
  op _∩_ : Prog Prog -> Prog [assoc comm idem id: ⊤ prec 57]
  op _◁  ▷_   Prog CondExp Prog -> Prog [prec 58]
  op _*_   CondExp Prog -> Prog [prec 54] .

*** Additional reasoning features
  op ⊥ : -> Prog .
  op ⊤ : -> Prog .
  op _⊔_ : Prog Prog -> Prog [assoc comm idem id: ⊥ prec 57]
  op _⊑_   Prog Prog -> Bool [prec 70] .
  op μ _ •_   ProgId Prog -> Prog [prec 59] .
  op _⊔⁝_   Prog Prog -> Prog [prec 56]      *** Inverse of ;
  op _._   ProgId ListVar -> ProgId .
  op  ⊤   CondExp -> Prog
  op _⊥   CondExp -> Prog
  op _→_ : CondExp Prog -> Prog [prec 53]
```

153

```
   op _□_ : Prog Prog -> Prog [assoc comm idem id: T prec 57]
   op _:∈_ : ListVar CondExp -> Prog [prec 52] .
   op var_   ListVar -> Prog .
   op end_   ListVar -> Prog .

*** auxiliary operators ***
   op _\_    ListVar Prog -> Bool [memo] .         *** Non-freeness
   op _\_  : ProgId  Prog -> Bool [memo]
   op _\\_   ListVar Prog -> Bool [memo]           *** Non-occurrence
   op-as _[_<-_]   Prog ListVar ListExp  -> Prog   *** substitution
      for p[x <- e] if (len x == len e) and (disj x) [memo] .
   op _[_<-_]   Prog ProgId Prog  -> Prog [memo]

*** variables declaration (for use in equations)
   var X Y Z : ProgId
   var p q r   Prog
   var x y z : ListVar .
   var a b c : CondExp
   var e f g : ListExp .

*** Sequential composition
[;-skip~Lunit]  eq  (skip ; p) = p .
[;-skip~Runit]  eq  (p ; skip)   p
[;-⊥~Lzero]     eq  (⊥ ; p)    ⊥
[;-T~Lzero]     eq  (T ; p)    T .

*** Demonic nondeterminism
[∩-⊥~zero] eq  (p ∩ ⊥)   ⊥
[∩-T~unit] eq  (p ∩ T)   p .

*** The ordering relation
[⊑-⊥~bottom ⊑] eq  ⊥   p .
[⊑-T~top ⊑]    eq  p   T
[⊑-∩~lb ⊑]     eq  (p ∩ q)  p
[⊑-⊔~ub ⊑]     eq  p  (p ⊔ q)

*** Angelic nondeterminism
[⊔-⊥~unit] eq  (p ⊔ ⊥)   p .
[⊔-T~zero] eq  (p ⊔ T) = T

*** Recursion
[μ~fp]      eq  (μ X • p) = p[X <- (μ X • p)]
[μ~lfp ⇐] eq  (μ X • p) ⊑ q   (p[X <- q]) ⊑ q

*** Strongest inverse of sequential composition
[;-;~1]    eq (p ; q ⊑ r)   (p ⊑ r ⊔; q)
[;-;~2 ⊑]  eq (p ⊔; q) ; q   p .

*** Assumption and Assertion
[b^T~true~cond]     eq  true^T   skip
[b⊥~true~cond]      eq  true⊥    skip .
```

[b$^\top$⁻false⁻cond]   eq false$^\top$ $\top$.
[b$_\perp$⁻false⁻cond]   eq false$_\perp$ $\perp$.
[b$^\top$⁻conjunction]   eq (a$^\top$; b$^\top$) = (a $\wedge$ b)$^\top$.
[b$_\perp$⁻conjunction]   eq (a$_\perp$; b$_\perp$) = (a $\wedge$ b)$_\perp$.
*** The law of simulation gives rise to many laws
[b$^\top$⁻void⁻b$_\perp$]   eq (b$^\top$; b$_\perp$)   b$^\top$.
[b$_\perp$⁻void⁻b$^\top$]   eq (b$_\perp$; b$^\top$)   b$_\perp$.
[b$^\top$⁻skip $\sqsubseteq$]   eq skip   b$^\top$.
[b$_\perp$⁻skip $\sqsubseteq$]   eq b$_\perp$ skip .
[b$_\perp$-b$^\top$⁻sim1 $\sqsubseteq$]   eq (b$_\perp$; b$^\top$)   skip .
[b$_\perp$-b$^\top$⁻sim2 $\sqsubseteq$]   eq skip = (b$^\top$; b$_\perp$) .

*** Guarded command
[$\rightarrow$⁻def]   eq b $\rightarrow$ p   (b$^\top$; p)
[$\rightarrow$⁻true⁻guard]   eq (true $\rightarrow$ p) = p
[$\rightarrow$⁻false⁻guard] eq (false $\rightarrow$ p) = $\top$.
[$\rightarrow$-b$^\top$⁻conversion] eq b $\rightarrow$ p   (b$^\top$; p) .
[$\rightarrow$⁻conjunction] eq a $\rightarrow$ (b $\rightarrow$ p)   (a $\wedge$ b) $\rightarrow$ p
[$\rightarrow$⁻disjunction] eq (a $\rightarrow$ p) $\sqcap$ (b $\rightarrow$ p)   (a $\vee$ b) $\rightarrow$ p .
[$\rightarrow$-$\sqcap$⁻dist]   eq b $\rightarrow$ (p $\sqcap$ q)   (b $\rightarrow$ p) $\sqcap$ (b $\rightarrow$ q)
[;-$\rightarrow$⁻Ldist]   eq (b $\rightarrow$ p) ; q   b $\rightarrow$ (p ; q)

*** Guarded command set
[$\square$⁻def]   eq (p $\square$ q)   (p $\sqcap$ q)
[$\square$⁻elim]   eq a $\rightarrow$ (a $\rightarrow$ p $\square$ b $\rightarrow$ q)   (a $\rightarrow$ p)

*** Conditional
[$\triangleleft \triangleright$⁻def]   eq (p $\triangleleft$ b $\triangleright$ q)   (b $\rightarrow$ p $\square$ $\neg$b $\rightarrow$ q)
[$\triangleleft \triangleright$⁻true⁻cond] eq (a $\wedge$ b)$^\top$; (p $\triangleleft$ b $\vee$ c $\triangleright$ q) = (a $\wedge$ b)$^\top$; p .
[$\triangleleft \triangleright$⁻false⁻cond] eq (a $\wedge$ $\neg$b)$^\top$; (p $\triangleleft$ b $\wedge$ c $\triangleright$ q)   (a $\wedge$ $\neg$b)$^\top$; q
[$\triangleleft \triangleright$⁻void⁻b$^\top$⁻1]   eq (b$^\top$; p $\triangleleft$ b $\triangleright$ q) = (p $\triangleleft$ b $\triangleright$ q)
[$\triangleleft \triangleright$⁻void⁻b$^\top$⁻2]   eq (p $\triangleleft$ b $\triangleright$ $\neg$b$^\top$; q)   (p $\triangleleft$ b $\triangleright$ q)
[$\triangleleft \triangleright$⁻idemp]   eq (p $\triangleleft$ b $\triangleright$ p)   p
[;-$\triangleleft \triangleright$⁻Ldist]   eq (p $\triangleleft$ b $\triangleright$ q) ; r   (p ; r $\triangleleft$ b $\triangleright$ q ; r) .
[guard-$\triangleleft \triangleright$⁻dist] eq a $\rightarrow$ (p $\triangleleft$ b $\triangleright$ q)   (a $\rightarrow$ p) $\triangleleft$ b $\triangleright$ (a $\rightarrow$ q) .
[$\triangleleft \triangleright$⁻cond⁻disj] eq p $\triangleleft$ b $\triangleright$ (p $\triangleleft$ c $\triangleright$ q)   (p $\triangleleft$ b $\vee$ c $\triangleright$ q) .
[$\triangleleft \triangleright$⁻cond⁻conj] eq (p $\triangleleft$ b $\triangleright$ q) $\triangleleft$ c $\triangleright$ q   (p $\triangleleft$ b $\wedge$ c $\triangleright$ q)

*** Assignment
[:=⁻skip]   eq (x := x)   skip .
[:=⁻identity]   eq (x,y := e,y)   (x := e) .
[:=⁻sym]   eq (x,y := e,f)   (y,x := f,e)
[:=⁻combination]   eq (x := e ; x := f)   (x := f[x <- e])
[$\rightarrow$-:=⁻subst]   eq (x = e) $\rightarrow$ (y := f)   (x   e) $\rightarrow$ (y := f[x <- e]) .
[:=-$\sqcap$⁻Rdist]   eq x := e ; (p $\sqcap$ q)   (x := e ; p) $\sqcap$ (x := e ; q)
[:=-$\triangleleft \triangleright$⁻Rdist]   eq x := e ; (p $\triangleleft$ b $\triangleright$ q)
                               (x := e ; p) $\triangleleft$ b[x <- e] $\triangleright$ (x := e ; q) .
*** The following 3 laws are not in Chapter 3
[:=⁻combination2] cq (x := e ; y := f)   (x,y := e,(f[x <- e])) if x \\ y
[:=⁻commute]   cq (x := e ; y := f)   (y := f[x <- e] ; x := e)
                       if y \\ (x := e) .

[:=˜split]   cq (x,y := e,f)   (x := e ; y := f) if x \\ (y := f) .

*** Generalised assignment
[:∈˜false˜cond]   eq (x :∈ false)   ⊤
[:∈˜true˜cond ⊑] eq (x :∈ true) = skip .
[:∈˜void˜bᵀ]   eq x :∈ a ; aᵀ   x :∈ a
[:∈˜void˜b⊥]   eq x :∈ a ; a⊥ = x :∈ a
[:∈-bᵀ ⊑]   eq (x :∈ b)   bᵀ .
[:∈-◁ ▷˜Rdist]   eq x :∈ a ; (p ◁ b ▷ q)   (x :∈ a ; p ◁ b ▷ x :∈ a ; q)
[:∈-:=]   cq x :∈ (x   e)   (x := e) if x \\ e

*** Iteration
[*˜def]   cq b * p   μ X • (p ; X ◁ b ▷ skip) if X \ p .
[*˜fp]   eq b * p   (p ; (b * p)) ◁ b ▷ skip .
[*˜lfp ⇐]   eq (b * p ⊑ q)   (p ; q ◁ b ▷ skip ⊑ q)
[*˜elim1]   cq x :∈ a ; b * p   x :∈ a if pwd(a,b)
[*˜elim2]   cq aᵀ ; b * p   aᵀ if pwd(a,b)
[*˜unfold]   eq x :∈ a ; (a ∨ b) * p   x :∈ a ; p ; (a ∨ b) * p
[*-□˜unfold]   cq x :∈ a ; (a ∨ b) * (a → p □ b → q)
                      x :∈ a ; p ; (a ∨ b) * (a → p □ b → q) if pwd(a,b)
[*-□˜elim]   cq a * (a → p □ b → q)   a * p if pwd(a,b) .
[*-→˜elim]   eq a * (a → p)   a * p
[*-μ˜tail˜rec]   eq (b * p) ; q   μ X • (p ; X ◁ b ▷ q) .
[*˜sequence]   eq (b * p) ; (b ∨ c) * p   (b ∨ c) * p

*** Static Declaration
[dec˜assoc]   cq dec x • (dec y • p)   (dec x,y • p) if x \\ y
[dec˜sym]   eq dec x • (dec y • p)   dec y • (dec x • p)
[dec˜elim]   cq (dec x • p)   p if x \ p .
[dec˜rename]   cq (dec x • p)   (dec y • p[x <- y])
                      if y \ p and contiguous-scope(x,p)
[dec-:=˜init ⊑]   eq (dec x • p)   (dec x • x := e ; p)
[dec-:∈˜init ⊑]   eq (dec x • p)   (dec x • x :∈ b ; p)
[dec-:=˜final]   eq (dec x • p)   (dec x • p ; x := e)
[dec-:∈˜final ⊑] eq (dec x • p)   (dec x • p ; x :∈ b)
[;-dec˜Ldist]   cq (dec x • p) ; q   (dec x • p ; q) if x \ q .
[;-dec˜Rdist]   cq q ; (dec x • p)   (dec x • q ; p) if x \ q
[dec-;˜dist ⊑]   eq (dec x • p) ; (dec x • q)   (dec x • p ; q) .
[dec-□˜dist]   cq a → (dec x • p) □ b → (dec x • q) =
                      (dec x • a → p □ b → q) if x \\ (a,b) .
[dec-◁ ▷˜dist]   cq (dec x • p) ◁ b ▷ (dec x • q)   (dec x • p ◁ b ▷ q)
                      if x \\ b
[dec-*˜dist ⊑]   cq b * (dec x • p)   (dec x • b * p) if x \\ b

*** Dynamic Declaration
[var˜assoc]   cq var x ; var y   var x,y if x \\ y .
[end˜assoc]   cq end x ; end y   end x,y if x \\ y
[var˜change˜scope] cq (p ; var x)   (var x ; p) if x \ p
[end˜change˜scope] cq (end x ; p)   (p ; end x) if x \ p .
[var-◁ ▷˜Rdist]   cq (var x ; p) ◁ b ▷ (var x ; q) = var x ; (p ◁ b ▷ q)
                      if x \\ b .

```
[end-◁ ▷⁻Rdist]      cq  (end x ; p) ◁ b ▷ (end x ; q)    end x ; (p ◁ b ▷ q)
                             if x \\ b
[var-:=⁻init ⊑]      eq  var x = (var x ; x := e)
[var-:∈⁻init ⊑]      eq  var x   (var x ; x :∈ b) .
[end-:=⁻final]       eq  end x   (x := e ; end x) .
[end-:∈⁻final ⊑]     eq  end x   (x :∈ e ; end x)
[end-var⁻sim1]       eq  (var x ; end x)   skip
[end-var⁻sim2 ⊑]     eq  (end x ; var x)   skip
[end-var⁻skip]       cq  (end x ; var x ; x := e)   (x := e) if x \\ e
[var⁻elim1]          eq  (dec x • var x ; p)   (dec x • p)
[end⁻elim1]          eq  (dec x • end x ; p)   (dec x • p)
[var⁻elim2]          eq  (dec x • p ; var x)   (dec x • p)
[end⁻elim2]          eq  (dec x • p ; end x)   (dec x • p) .
[dec-var⁻end]        cq  (dec x • p)   (var x ; p ; end x)
                             if contiguous-scope(x,p) and block-structured(p,x)

endth
```

C.1.1. Proof of Theorem 3.17.6

Here we give the complete mechanisation of the proof of the equation

```
[*-μ⁻tail⁻rec] eq (b * p) ; q   μ X • (p ; X ◁ b ▷ q)
```

which actually relies on the assumption that X is not free in p or q. Most of the features of OBJ3 used in the proof have been introduced before. Others are explained as the need arises.

First we need to specify the context in which the reasoning will be conducted. In this case, it is given by the module describing the reasoning language together with the assumptions and abbreviations used in the proof. As rewriting in OBJ3 is carried out only for *ground* terms (that is, terms involving only constants), we need to explicitly declare a constant to play the role of each variable appearing in the equation. Of course, we must not assume anything about these constants, except the conditions associated with the theorem. The context of our proof is defined by (this is omitted for the next proofs):

```
open REASONING-LANGUAGE[EXP]
op X    -> ProgId
op p    -> Prog
op q :  -> Prog
op b :  -> CondExp
[hyp1] eq X \ p = true
[hyp2] eq X \ q = true
[LHS⁻def] let LHS   (b * p) ; q
[RHS⁻def] let RHS   μ X • (p ; X ◁ b ▷ q) .
```

We also add an equation (for later use) which expresses a simple lemma about substitution. It can be automatically proved from the definition of the substitution operator:

```
[subst1]   eq (p ; X ◁ b ▷ q)[X <- LHS]   (p ; LHS ◁ b ▷ q)
***> Proof
OBJ> reduce in SUBST   (p ; X ◁ b ▷ q)[X <- LHS] == (p ; LHS ◁ b ▷ q)
rewrites: 4
result Bool: true
```

where SUBST is the module which contains the relevant equations of substitution.

We split the proof of the theorem into two steps: (RHS ⊑ LHS) and (LHS ⊑ RHS). Recall that the symbol - preceding the label of an equation (in an apply command) means that the equation is to be applied in reverse (from right to left).

```
***> Proof of (RHS ⊑ LHS)

OBJ> start (b * p) ; q ⊑ LHS
===============================================
OBJ> apply .*⁻fp within term
result Bool: (p ; b * p ◁ b ▷skip) ; q ⊑ LHS
===============================================
OBJ> apply .;-◁▷⁻Ldist within term
result Bool: p ; (b * p) ; q ◁ b ▷ skip ; q ⊑ LHS
===============================================
OBJ> apply .;-skip⁻Lunit within term
result Bool: p ; (b * p) ; q ◁ b ▷ q ⊑ LHS
===============================================
OBJ> apply  .LHS⁻def within term
result Bool: p ; LHS ◁ b ▷ q ⊑ LHS
===============================================
OBJ> apply   .subst1 within term
result Bool: (p ; X ◁ b ▷ q)[X <- LHS] ⊑ LHS
===============================================
OBJ> apply -.μ⁻lfp at term .
result Bool: μ X • p ; X ◁ b ▷ q ⊑ LHS
===============================================
OBJ> apply  .RHS⁻def within term
result Bool: RHS ⊑ LHS
```

The other part of the proof illustrates ways of selecting a particular subterm. A natural number is used to specify the desired subterm, where the arguments of a given operator are numbered from 1. For example, in LHS ⊑ RHS, (1) selects LHS. Nested selections are specified using the keyword of. The application of a given equation may require the user to provide an explicit instantiation (binding) of some of its variables. This usually happens when applying an equation in reverse and its left-hand side contains variables which do not appear on the right-hand side. The binding for these extra variables is defined using the keyword with, followed by a list of equations of the form *var = term*.

```
***> Proof of (LHS ⊑ RHS)

OBJ> start μ X • p ; X ◁ b ▷ q ⊑ RHS
===============================================
OBJ> apply .μ⁻fp at (1)
result Bool: (p ; X ◁ b ▷ q)[X <- μ X • p ; X ◁ b ▷ q] ⊑ RHS
===============================================
OBJ> select SUBST                    *** Contains equations for substitution
===============================================
OBJ> apply red at (1)                *** Does the substitution automatically
result Bool: p ; (μ X • p ; X ◁ b ▷ q) ◁ b ▷ q ⊑ RHS
===============================================
OBJ> select REASONING-LANGUAGE[EXP]  *** Back to context providing the laws
```

```
=========================================
OBJ> apply -.RHS~def within term
result Bool: p ; RHS ◁ b ▷ q ⊑ RHS
=========================================
```

```
OBJ> apply -.;-⊔⁻2 with p   RHS within (1) .
result Bool: p ; (RHS ⊔ q) ; q ◁ b ▷ q ⊑ RHS
=========================================
```

```
OBJ> apply -.;-skip~Lunit at (3) of (1)
result Bool: p ; (RHS ⊔ q) ; q ◁ b ▷ skip ; q ⊑ RHS
=========================================
```

```
OBJ> apply  .;-◁ ▷~Ldist within term
result Bool: (p ; (RHS ⊔ q) ◁ b ▷ skip) ; q ⊑ RHS
=========================================
```

```
OBJ> apply .;-⊔⁻1 at term
result Bool: p ; (RHS ⊔ q) ◁ b ▷ skip ⊑ RHS ⊔ q
=========================================
```

```
OBJ> apply .*~lfp at term
result Bool: b * p ⊑ RHS ⊔ q
=========================================
```

```
OBJ> apply -.;-⊔⁻1 at term
result Bool: b * p ; q ⊑ RHS
=========================================
```

```
OBJ> apply -.LHS~def within term
result Bool: LHS ⊑ RHS
```

C.1.2. Proof of Theorem 3.17.7

The equation to be verified is

```
[*~sequence]    eq (b * p) ; (b ∨ c) * p   (b ∨ c) * p
```

The proof strategy is very similar to the that of the last section. First we prove a simple lemma about substitution (for later use)

```
[subst1] eq (p ; X ◁ b ▷ (b ∨ c) * p)[X <- RHS] = (p ; RHS ◁ b ▷ (b ∨ c) * p) .
***> Proof
OBJ> reduce in SUBST : (p ; X ◁ b ▷ (b ∨ c) * p)[X <- RHS] ==
                       (p ; RHS ◁ b ▷ (b ∨ c) * p)
rewrites: 4
result Bool: true
```

and then split the proof in two parts, as above.

```
***> Proof of (LHS ⊑ RHS)
```

```
OBJ> start (b ∨ c) * p ⊑ RHS
=========================================
OBJ> apply  ◁ ▷~idemp at (1)
result Bool: (b ∨ c) * p ◁ b ▷ (b ∨ c) * p ⊑ RHS
=========================================
OBJ> apply .*~fp at (1) of (1) .
```

```
result Bool: (p ; (b ∨ c) * p ◁ b ∨ c ▷ skip) ◁ b ▷ (b ∨ c) * p ⊑ RHS
========================================
OBJ> apply -.RHS¯def within (1) of (1) .
result Bool: (p ; RHS ◁ b ∨ c ▷ skip) ◁ b ▷ (b ∨ c) * p ⊑ RHS
========================================
OBJ> apply -.◁ ▷¯void¯bᵀ¯2 at (1) of (1) .
result Bool: (p ; RHS ◁ b ∨ c ▷ ¬(b ∨ c)ᵀ ; skip) ◁ b ▷ (b ∨ c) * p ⊑ RHS
========================================
OBJ> apply -.*¯elim2 with b = (b ∨ c) within term
result Bool: (p ; RHS ◁ b ∨ c ▷ ¬(b ∨ c)ᵀ ; (b ∨ c) * p ; skip) ◁ b ▷
            (b ∨ c) * p ⊑ RHS .
========================================
OBJ> apply .;-skip¯Runit within term .
result Bool: (p ; RHS ◁ b ∨ c ▷ ¬(b ∨ c)ᵀ ; (b ∨ c) * p) ◁ b ▷
            (b ∨ c) * p ⊑ RHS
========================================
OBJ> apply .◁ ▷¯void¯bᵀ¯2 within term .
result Bool: (p ; RHS ◁ b ∨ c ▷ (b ∨ c) * p) ◁ b ▷ (b ∨ c) * p ⊑ RHS
========================================
OBJ> apply .◁ ▷¯cond¯conj within term
result Bool: p ; RHS ◁ (b ∨ c) ∧ b ▷ (b ∨ c) * p ⊑ RHS
========================================
OBJ> apply red at (2) of (1) .
result Bool: p ; RHS ◁ b ▷ (b ∨ c) * p ⊑ RHS
========================================
OBJ> apply -.subst1 within term
result Bool: (p ; X ◁ b ▷ (b ∨ c) * p)[X <- RHS] ⊑ RHS
========================================
OBJ> apply -.μ¯lfp at term
result Bool: μ X • p ; X ◁ b ▷ (b ∨ c) * p ⊑ RHS
========================================
OBJ> apply -.*-μ¯tail¯rec within term
result Bool: b * p ; (b ∨ c) * p ⊑ RHS
========================================
OBJ> apply -.LHS¯def within term .
result Bool: LHS ⊑ RHS
```

The above result is added to the system in the form of an "inequation"

```
[LHS¯⊑¯RHS ⊑] eq LHS    RHS .
```

which is then used in the other part of the proof.

```
***> Proof of (RHS ⊑ LHS)

OBJ> start (b * p) ; (b ∨ c) * p ⊑ LHS .
========================================
OBJ> apply .*¯fp at (1) of (1)
result Bool: (p ; b * p ◁ b ▷ skip) ; (b ∨ c) * p ⊑ LHS
========================================
OBJ> apply .;-◁ ▷¯Ldist within term
result Bool: p ; b * p ; (b ∨ c) * p ◁ b ▷ skip ; (b ∨ c) * p ⊑ LHS
========================================
```

```
OBJ> apply .;-skip~Lunit within term .
result Bool: p ; b * p ; (b ∨ c) * p ◁ b ▷ (b ∨ c) * p ⊑ LHS
=============================================
OBJ> apply .*~fp at (3) of (1) .
result Bool: p ; b * p ; (b ∨ c) * p ◁ b ▷ (p ; (b ∨ c) * p ◁ b ∨ c ▷ skip)
           ⊑ LHS
=============================================
OBJ> apply -.LHS~def within term .
result Bool: p ; LHS ◁ b ▷ (p ; (b ∨ c) * p ◁ b ∨ c ▷ skip) ⊑ LHS
=============================================
OBJ> apply -.RHS~def within term .
result Bool: p ; LHS ◁ b ▷ (p ; RHS ◁ b ∨ c ▷ skip) ⊑ LHS
=============================================
OBJ> apply -.LHS~⊑~RHS within term .
result Bool: p ; LHS ◁ b ▷ (p ; LHS ◁ b ∨ c ▷ skip) ⊑ LHS
=============================================
OBJ> apply .◁ ▷~cond~disj within term
result Bool: p ; LHS ◁ b ∨ b ∨ c ▷ skip ⊑ LHS
=============================================
OBJ> apply red at (2) of (1) .
result Bool: p ; LHS ◁ c ∨ b ▷ skip ⊑ LHS
=============================================
OBJ> apply -.*~lfp at term
result Bool: (c ∨ b) * p ⊑ LHS
=============================================
OBJ> apply .RHS~def within term .
result Bool: RHS ⊑ LHS
```

C.2. The Normal Form

The normal form definition and the related lemmas and theorems are described by the following theory. Note that this module is also independent of an expression language. The next sections illustrate the verification of some of the proofs.

```
th NORMAL-FORM [X :: EXP] is

  protecting REASONING-LANGUAGE[X]

  op-as (_:[_, _->_, _]) : ListVar CondExp CondExp Prog CondExp  -> Prog
      for v :[a, b -> p, c] if pwd(b,c) [prec 50] .

*** Variables for use in equations
  var p q   Prog
  var a ao a1 a2 b b1 b2 c co c1 . CondExp .
  var x v : ListVar
  var e f   ListExp
```

$[nf\text{-}def]$ eq v :[a, b -> p, c]   dec v • v :∈ a ; b * p ; c⌋

$[T:skip1 \sqsubseteq]$ cq skip   v :[a, b -> p, a]   if pwd(a,b)

$[L:primitive\text{-}commands \sqsubseteq]$
   cq p   v :[a, a -> (p ; v :∈ c), c]   if pwd(a,c) and v \ p .

$[T:skip2 \sqsubseteq]$ cq skip   v :[a, a -> v :∈ c, c]   if pwd(a,c)

$[T:assignment \sqsubseteq]$
   cq (x := e)   v :[a, a -> (x := e ; v :∈ c), c]   if pwd(a,c)

$[L:sequential\text{-}composition \sqsubseteq]$
   cq v :[a, b1 -> p, co] ; v :[co, (b1 ∨ b2) -> (b1 → p □ b2 → q), c]
       v :[a, (b1 ∨ b2) -> (b1 → p □ b2 → q), c]   if pwd(b1,b2)

$[L:eliminate\text{-}guarded\text{-}command \sqsubseteq]$
   cq v :[a, b1 -> p, c]   v :[a, (b1 ∨ b2) -> (b1 → p □ b2 → q), c]
   if pwd(b1,b2,c) .

$[T:sequential\text{-}composition \sqsubseteq]$
   cq v :[a, b1 -> p, co] ; v :[co, b2 -> q, c]
       v :[a, (b1 ∨ b2) -> (b1 → p □ b2 → q), c]   if pwd(b1,b2,c)

$[L:conditional \sqsubseteq]$
   cq v :[a1, (a ∨ b1) -> (a → (v :∈ a1 ◁ b ▷ v :∈ a2) □ b1 → p), c] ◁ b ▷
      v :[a2, (a ∨ b1) -> (a → (v :∈ a1 ◁ b ▷ v :∈ a2) □ b1 → p), c]

       v :[a, (a ∨ b1) -> (a → (v :∈ a1 ◁ b ▷ v :∈ a2) □ b1 → p), c]
   if pwd(a,b1)

```
[T:conditional ⊑]
  cq v :[a1, b1 -> p, c1]  ◁ b ▷ v :[a2, b2 -> q, c] =
     v :[a, (a ∨ b1 ∨ c1 ∨ b2) ->
               (  a → (v :∈ a1 ◁ b ▷ v :∈ a2) ▢ b1 → p
                  ▢ c1 → v :∈ c ▢ b2 → q), c]
   if pwd(a,b1,b2,c1,c)

[L:void¯initial¯state ⊑]
  cq v :[a, (co ∨ b) -> (co → v :∈ a ▢ b → p), c] =
     v :[co, co -> (v :∈ a ▢ b → p), c]   if pwd(co,b) .

[T:iteration ⊑]
  cq b * v :[ao, b1 -> p, co] =
     v :[a, (a ∨ b1 ∨ co) ->
               (a → (v :∈ ao ◁ b ▷ v :∈ c) ▢ b1 → p ▢ co → v :∈ a ), c]
   if pwd(a,b1,co,c)

endth
```

C.2.1. Proof of Lemma 4.2

Here we verify the inequation

```
[L:sequential¯composition ⊑]
  cq  v :[a, b1 -> p, co]  ;  v :[co, (b1 ∨ b2) -> (b1 → p ▢ b2 → q), c] =
      v :[a, (b1 ∨ b2) -> (b1 → p ▢ b2 → q), c]    if pwd(b1,b2) .
```

As usual, we assume the hypothesis by adding it in the form of an equation.

```
open NORMAL-FORM [EXP]
[hyp1] eq pwd(b1,b2)    true .
```

This is used to discharge the disjointness conditions associated with some of the laws. It is possible to tell OBJ3 that we want conditions to be discharged automatically, rather than by applying rules step by step:

```
set reduce conditions on
```

Then we proceed with the proof.

```
OBJ> start v :[a,b1 -> p,co] ; v :[co,(b1 ∨ b2) -> (b1 → p ▢ b2 → q),c] .
===========================================
OBJ> apply .nf¯def within term
result Prog: (dec v • v :∈ a ; b1 * p ; co⊥) ;
             (dec v • v :∈ co ; (b1 ∨ b2) * (b1 → p ▢ b2 → q) ; c⊥)
===========================================
OBJ> apply .dec-;¯dist at term
result Prog: dec v • v :∈ a ; b1 * p ; co⊥ ; v :∈ co ;
                    (b1 ∨ b2) * (b1 → p ▢ b2 → q) ; c⊥
===========================================
OBJ> apply .:∈-b^T with b  co within term .
result Prog: dec v • v :∈ a ; b1 * p ; co⊥ ; co^T ;
                    (b1 ∨ b2) * (b1 → p ▢ b2 → q) ; c⊥
```

```
==========================================
OBJ> apply .b⊥-bᵀ˜sim1 within term
result Prog: dec v • v :∈ a ; b1 * p ; skip ; (b1 ∨ b2) * (b1 → p □ b2 → q) ; c⊥
==========================================
OBJ> apply .;-skip˜Runit within term .
result Prog: dec v • v :∈ a ; b1 * p ; (b1 ∨ b2) * (b1 → p □ b2 → q) ; c⊥
==========================================
OBJ> apply -.*-□˜elim with b   b2 within term
result Prog: dec v • v :∈ a ; b1 * (b1 → p □ b2 → q) ;
                         (b1 ∨ b2) * (b1 → p □ b2 → q) ; c⊥
==========================================
OBJ> apply .*˜sequence within term .
result Prog: dec v • v :∈ a ; (b1 ∨ b2) * (b1 → p □ b2 → q) ; c⊥
==========================================
OBJ> apply -.nf˜def at term
result Prog: v :[a,b1 ∨ b2 -> b1 → p □ b2 → q,c]
```

C.2.2. Proof of Lemma 4.3

The proof of the lemma

```
[L:eliminate˜guarded˜command ⊑]
  cq  v :[a, b1 -> p, c]      v :[a, (b1 ∨ b2) -> (b1 → p □ b2 → q), c]
  if pwd(b1,b2,c)
```

follows directly from the lemma verified in the last section and the one of the reduction theorems for skip, as shown below.

```
open NORMAL-FORM [EXP]
[hyp1] eq pwd(b1,b2,c) = true

OBJ> start v :[a, (b1 ∨ b2) -> (b1 → p □ b2 → q), c]
==========================================
OBJ> apply -.L:sequential˜composition with co = c at term .
result Prog: v :[a,b1 -> p,c] ; v :[c,b1 ∨ b2 -> b1 → p □ b2 → q,c]
==========================================
OBJ> apply -.T:skip1 at (2) .
result Prog: v :[a,b1 -> p,c] ; skip
==========================================
OBJ> apply .;-skip˜Runit at term
result Prog: v :[a,b1 -> p,c]
```

C.2.3. Proof of Theorem 4.4

Using the above two lemmas, the proof of the reduction theorem of sequential composition

```
[T:sequential˜composition ⊑]
  cq  v :[a, b1 -> p, co]  ;  v :[co, b2 -> q, c]
      v :[a, (b1 ∨ b2) -> (b1 → p □ b2 → q), c]    if pwd(b1,b2,c)
```

is straightforward.

```
open NORMAL-FORM [EXP] .
[hyp1] eq pwd(b1,b2,c)    true

OBJ> start v : [a , (b1 ∨ b2) -> (b1 → p □ b2 → q), c] .
============================================
OBJ> apply -.L:sequential~composition at term .
result Prog: v :[a,b1 -> p,co] ; v :[co,b1 ∨ b2 -> b1 → p □ b2 → q,c]
============================================
OBJ> apply -.L:eliminate~guarded~command with b1    b2, p    q at (2) .
result Prog: v :[a,b1 -> p,co] ; v :[co,b2 -> q,c]
```

C.3. Simplification of Expressions

The following module groups the theorems related to the simplification of expressions. In order to prove them, we need to instantiate the module describing the reasoning language with the module SOURCE which describes the expression sub-language of the source language. The module SOURCE is omitted here; its relevant sorts and operators were given in Chapter 6. Each of the next two sections presents the verification of one theorem related to this phase of compilation.

```
th EXP-SIMPLIFICATION is

  protecting REASONING-LANGUAGE [SOURCE]

*** Variables for use in equations ***
    var p q        Prog .
    var b ė f    SourceExp
    var ẋ t      SourceVar
    var x y u  : ListVar

[Introduce˜A] cq (ẋ := ė)    (dec A • A := ė ; ẋ := A)
               if (A \\ ẋ) and (A \\ ė)

[simple˜bop] cq (A := ė bop f́)    dec t • A := f́ ; t := A ; A := e ;A := A bop t
               if (A,t) \\ (ė bop f́) and is-not-var(f́)

[simple˜bop˜optimisation] cq (A := ė bop ẋ) = A := ė ; A := A bop ẋ
                            if A \\ (ė bop ẋ)

[simple˜uop] cq (A := uop ė) = (A := ė ; A := uop A)    if A \\ ė


[simple˜cond1 ⊑] cq (dec x,A • p) ◁ b ▷ (dec ʌ,A • q)
                    dec x,A • A := b ; (p ◁ A ▷ q)
                    if (x,A) \\ b

[simple˜cond2 ⊑] cq b * (dec x,A • p)    (dec x,A • A := b ; A * (p ; A := b))
                    if (x,A) \\ b .

endth
```

C.3.1. Proof of Theorem 4.3

The proof of the theorem

```
[simple˜bop] cq (A := ė bop f́)    dec t • A := f́ ; t := A ; A := ė ;A := A bop t
               if (A,t) \\ (ė bop f́)
```

follows from the basic laws of assignment and declaration. Using a simple derived law to commute two assignments significantly reduces the number of proof steps. Although the equations defining substitution are used in automatic (rather than step by step) reductions, we still need to tell OBJ3 to do so. Having substitution as a built-in operator (as in the B-tool) would reduce the number of steps of this proof to a half.

A new feature to select subterms is used in this proof. A term involving only associative operators is viewed as a sequence numbered from 1; the form [n .. m] selects the subsequence delimited by (and including) the positions n and m. The hypothesis is encoded in the usual way, and is omitted here.

```
OBJ> start dec t • A := f ; t := A ; A := e ; A := A bop t .
==========================================
OBJ> apply .:=˜combination within term .
result Prog: dec t • A := f ; t := A ; A := A bop t[A <- e]
==========================================
OBJ> apply red at (2) of [3] of (2) .
result Prog: dec t • A := f ; t := A ; A := e bop t
==========================================
OBJ> apply .:=˜commute at [1 .. 2] of (2) .
result Prog: dec t • t := A[A <- f] ; A := f ; A := e bop t
==========================================
OBJ> apply red at (2) of [1] of (2) .
result Prog: dec t • t := f ; A := f ; A := e bop t
==========================================
OBJ> apply .:=˜combination within term
result Prog: dec t • t := f ; A := e bop t[A <- f]
==========================================
OBJ> apply red at (2) of [2] of (2)
result Prog: dec t • t := f ; A := e bop t
==========================================
OBJ> apply .:=˜commute within term
result Prog: dec t • A := e bop t[t <- f] ; t := f
==========================================
OBJ> apply red at (2) of [1] of (2)
result Prog: dec t • A := e bop f ; t := f
==========================================
OBJ> apply .dec-:=˜final at term
result Prog: dec t • A := e bop f
==========================================
OBJ> apply .dec˜elim at term
result Prog: A := e bop f
```

C.3.2. Proof of Theorem 4.5

Here we verify the proof of the theorem

```
[simple˜cond2 ⊑] cq b * (dec x,A • p) = (dec ʌ,A • A := b ; A * (p ; A := b))
                    if (x,A) \\ b
```

It gives one more example of the use of the (least) fixed point laws. The hypothesis is encoded in the usual way, and is omitted here.

```
OBJ> start dec x,A • A := b ; A * (p ; A := b) ⊑ RHS
==========================================
OBJ> apply .*˜fp within term
result Bool: dec x,A • A := b ; (p ; A := b ; A * (p ; A := b) ◁ A ▷ skip)
              ⊑ RHS
```

```
=========================================
OBJ> apply .:=-◁ ▷¯Rdist within term
result Bool: dec x,A • A := b ; p ; A := b ; A * (p ; A := b) ◁ A[A <- b] ▷
             A := b ; skip ⊑ RHS
=========================================
OBJ> apply red at (2) of (2) of (1) .
result Bool: dec x,A • A := b ; p ; A := b ; A * (p ; A := b) ◁ b ▷
             A := b ; skip ⊑ RHS
=========================================
OBJ> apply -.dec-◁ ▷¯dist within term .
result Bool: (dec x,A • A := b ; p ; A := b ; A * (p ; A := b)) ◁ b ▷
             (dec x,A • A := b ; skip) ⊑ RHS
=========================================
OBJ> apply -.dec¯assoc within term .
result Bool: (dec x • (dec A • A := b ; p ; A := b ; A * (p ; A := b))) ◁ b ▷
             (dec x • (dec A • A := b ; skip)) ⊑ RHS
=========================================
OBJ> apply .dec-:=¯init within term
result Bool: (dec x • (dec A • p ; A := b ; A * (p ; A := b))) ◁ b ▷
             (dec x • (dec A • skip)) ⊑ RHS
=========================================
OBJ> apply .dec¯assoc within term
result Bool: (dec ʌ,A • p ; A := b ; A * (p ; A := b)) ◁ b ▷
             (dec x,A • skip) ⊑ RHS
=========================================
OBJ> apply .dec¯elim within term .
result Bool: (dec ʌ,A • p ; A := b ; A * (p ; A := b)) ◁ b ▷ skip ⊑ RHS
=========================================
OBJ> apply .dec-;¯dist with p   p within term
result Bool: (dec ʌ,A • p) ; (dec x,A • A := b ; A * (p ; A := b)) ◁ b ▷
             skip ⊑ RHS
=========================================
OBJ> apply -.RHS¯def within term .
result Bool: (dec x,A • p) ; RHS ◁ b ▷ skip ⊑ RHS
=========================================
OBJ> apply -.*¯lfp at term
result Bool: b * (dec x,A • p) ⊑ RHS
=========================================
OBJ> apply .LHS¯def within term
result Bool: LHS ⊑ RHS
```

C.4. Control Elimination

The following theory illustrates an instantiation of the normal form theorems to deal with our particular target machine. The module NORMAL-FORM is instantiated with the *union* of the modules SOURCE (describing the expressions of the source language, as discussed above) and ROM which includes sorts and operators to model addresses in ROM, as discussed in Chapter 6. The instantiation of some of the theorems requires some additional transformations, but they are very simple and do not illustrate any interesting point.

```
th CONTROL-ELIMINATION is

  protecting NORMAL-FORM [SOURCE + ROM] .

  var p q · Prog .
  var s so s1 f fo f1 . Nat
  var ẋ : Var .
  var ė   Exp .
  var b1 b2   CondExp
  var x : ListVar

[skip˜theo ⊑] eq skip   P :[P   ə, false -> skip, P   s]

[:=˜theo ⊑] cq (ẋ := ė) = P :[P   ə, (P   s) -> (ẋ,P := ė,P + 1), P   s + 1]
            if P \\ ė .

[;˜theo ⊑] cq (P :[P = ə, b1 -> p, P   fo]) ; (P :[P = fo, b2 -> q, P   f])
              P :[P - s, (b1 ∨ b2) -> (b1 → p □ b2 → q),P   f]
            if pwd(b1,b2,(P   f))

[if˜theo ⊑]
  cq (P :[P   s + 1,  b1 -> p, P   fo]) ◁ A ▷ (P :[P   s1, b2 -> q, P = f])
     P :[P   s,((P   s) ∨ b1 ∨ (P   fo) ∨ b2) ->
           ( (P   s) → (P := P + 1 ◁ A ▷ P := s1)
             □ b1 → p □ (P   fo) → (P := f) □ b2 → q), P   f]
  if pwd((P   s),b1,b2,(P   fo),(P   f)) .

[iteration˜theo ⊑]
  cq A * (P :[P   s + 1, b1 -> p, P   fo])
     P :[P   s,((P   s) ∨ b1 ∨ (P   fo)) ->
           ( (P   s) → (P := P + 1 ◁ A ▷ P := fo + 1)
             □ b1 → p □ (P   fo) → (P := s)), P   fo + 1]
  if pwd((P   s),b1,(P   fo),(P   fo + 1)) .

endth
```

C.5. Data Refinement

The instantiation of the module describing the reasoning language shows the many kinds of expressions used to reason about this phase of compilation. The modules SYMTAB and RAM defines the symbol table and the memory RAM as instantiations of a generic module describing maps with the usual operations.

Here we omit the declaration of the operators related to this phase of compilation. Only their definitions and some of the theorems are described.

```
th DATA-REFINEMENT is

  protecting REASONING-LANGUAGE [SOURCE + ROM + RAM + SYMTAB]
```

*** Definitions
[$\dot{\Psi}$~simulation] eq $\hat{\Psi}_{\texttt{w}}$ var w ; w := M[Ψ[w]] ; end M

[Ψ^{-1}~cosimulation] eq $\hat{\Psi}_{\texttt{w}}^{-1}$ var M ; M := M $\oplus$ {Ψ[w] $\longmapsto$ w } ; end w

[$\dot{\Psi}$~simulation~function] eq $\hat{\Psi}_{\texttt{w}}(p)$ $\hat{\Psi}_{\texttt{w}}$; p ; $\hat{\Psi}_{\texttt{w}}^{-1}$.

[$\dot{\Psi}$~simulation~as~substitution] eq $\hat{\Psi}_{\texttt{w}}(\dot{e})$ $\dot{e}$ [w <- M[Ψ[w]]]

*** Theorems
[$\dot{\Psi}$-$\dot{\Psi}^{-1}$~simulation1 $\sqsubseteq$] eq $\hat{\Psi}_{\texttt{w}}$; $\hat{\Psi}_{\texttt{w}}^{-1}$ skip

[$\dot{\Psi}$-$\dot{\Psi}^{-1}$~simulation2] eq $\hat{\Psi}_{\texttt{w}}^{-1}$; $\hat{\Psi}_{\texttt{w}}$ skip .

*** Piecewise~data~refinement
[$\dot{\Psi}$-skip~dist $\sqsubseteq$] eq $\hat{\Psi}_{\texttt{w}}(\text{skip})$ skip .

[$\dot{\Psi}$-:=~dist1 $\sqsubseteq$] eq $\hat{\Psi}_{(\dot{x},\texttt{w})}(x := \dot{e})$ (M := M $\oplus$ {Ψ[x] $\longmapsto$ $\hat{\Psi}_{(\dot{x},\texttt{w})}(\dot{e})$}) .

[$\dot{\Psi}$-:=~dist2 $\sqsubseteq$] cq $\hat{\Psi}_{\texttt{w}}(x := \dot{e})$ = ($\dot{x}$:= $\hat{\Psi}_{\texttt{w}}(\dot{e})$) if $\dot{x}$ \\ w .

[$\dot{\Psi}$-;~dist $\sqsubseteq$] eq $\hat{\Psi}_{\texttt{w}}(p ; q)$ $\hat{\Psi}_{\texttt{w}}(p)$; $\hat{\Psi}_{\texttt{w}}(q)$

[$\dot{\Psi}$-$\lhd\rhd$~dist $\sqsubseteq$] eq $\hat{\Psi}_{\texttt{w}}(p \lhd b \rhd q)$ = $\hat{\Psi}_{\texttt{w}}(p) \lhd \hat{\Psi}_{\texttt{w}}(b) \rhd \hat{\Psi}_{\texttt{w}}(q)$.

[$\dot{\Psi}$-*~dist $\sqsubseteq$] eq $\hat{\Psi}_{\texttt{w}}(b * p)$ $\hat{\Psi}_{\texttt{w}}(b) * \hat{\Psi}_{\texttt{w}}(p)$.

[introducing~machine~state $\sqsubseteq$]
    cq $\hat{\Psi}_{\texttt{w}}(\text{dec } v,P,A \bullet p)$ dec P,A $\bullet$ ($\Psi \cup \widehat{\{v \longmapsto n \}}$)$_{(\texttt{w},v)}(p)$
    if disj(v,w) and disj(n,Ψ[w])

endth

C.5.1. Proof of Theorem 4.10

Below we verify the proof that $(\hat{\Psi}_{\texttt{w}}, \hat{\Psi}_{\texttt{w}}^{-1})$ is a simulation.

```
***> Ψ̂ᵥ ; Ψ̂ᵥ⁻¹ ⊑ skip

OBJ> start Ψ̂_ᵥ ; Ψ̂_ᵥ⁻¹ .
============================================
OBJ> apply .Ψ˜simulation within term
result Prog: var ᵥ ; ᵥ := M[Ψ[ᵥ]] ; end M ; Ψ̂_ᵥ⁻¹
============================================
OBJ> apply .Ψ⁻¹˜cosimulation within term
result Prog: var ᵥ ; ᵥ := M[Ψ[ᵥ]] ; end M ;
             var M ; M := M ⊕ {Ψ[ᵥ] ↦ ᵥ} ; end ᵥ
============================================
OBJ> apply .end-var˜sim2 within term
result Prog: var ᵥ ; ᵥ := M[Ψ[ᵥ]] ; skip ; M := M ⊕ {Ψ[ᵥ] ↦ ᵥ} ; end ᵥ
============================================
OBJ> apply .;-skip˜Lunit within term .
result Prog: var ᵥ ; ᵥ := M[Ψ[ᵥ]] ; M := M ⊕ {Ψ[ᵥ] ↦ ᵥ} ; end ᵥ
============================================
OBJ> apply .:=˜combination2 within term
result Prog: var ᵥ ; ᵥ,M := M[Ψ[ᵥ]],(M ⊕ {Ψ[ᵥ] ↦ ᵥ}[ᵥ <- M[Ψ[ᵥ]]]) ; end ᵥ
============================================
OBJ> apply red at (2) of [2]
result Prog: var ᵥ ; ᵥ,M := M[Ψ[ᵥ]],M ; end ᵥ
============================================
OBJ> apply .:=˜identity within term
result Prog: var ᵥ ; ᵥ := M[Ψ[ᵥ]] ; end ᵥ
============================================
OBJ> apply -.end-:=˜final within term
result Prog: var ᵥ ; end ᵥ
============================================
OBJ> apply .end-var˜sim1 within term .
result Prog: skip


***> Ψ̂_ᵥ⁻¹ ; Ψ̂_ᵥ    skip

OBJ> start Ψ̂_ᵥ⁻¹ ; Ψ̂_ᵥ .
============================================
OBJ> apply .Ψ⁻¹˜cosimulation within term
result Prog: var M ; M := M ⊕ {Ψ[ᵥ] ↦ ᵥ } ; end ᵥ ; Ψ̂_ᵥ
============================================
OBJ> apply .Ψ˜simulation within term
result Prog: var M ; M := M ⊕ {Ψ[ᵥ] ↦ ᵥ } ; end ᵥ ;
             var ᵥ ; ᵥ := M[Ψ[ᵥ]] ; end M
============================================
OBJ> apply .end-var˜skip within term
result Prog: var M ; M := M ⊕ {Ψ[ᵥ] ↦ ᵥ } ; ᵥ := M[Ψ[ᵥ]] ; end M
============================================
OBJ> apply .:=˜combination2 within term
result Prog: var M ; M,ᵥ := (M ⊕ {Ψ[ᵥ] ↦ ᵥ}),(M[Ψ[ᵥ]][M<-M ⊕ {Ψ[ᵥ] ↦ ᵥ}]);
             end M
============================================
```

```
OBJ> apply red at (2) of [2]
result Prog: var M ; M,w := (M ⊕ {Ψ[w] ↦ w}),w ; end M
==========================================
OBJ> apply .:=~identity within term .
result Prog: var M ; M := M ⊕ {Ψ[w] ↦ w} ; end M
==========================================
OBJ> apply -.end-:=~final within term
result Prog: var M ; end M
==========================================
OBJ> apply .end-var~sim1 within term
result Prog: skip
```

C.5.2. Proof of Theorem 4.14

Here we verify the inequation

```
[introducing~machine~state ⊑]
  cq Ψ̂w(dec v,P,A • p)   dec P,A • Φ̂(w,v)(p)
  if disj(v,w) and disj(n,Ψ[w]) .
```

where $\Phi = \Psi \cup \{v \mapsto n \}$. The proof uses two lemmas which are also verified below.

***> lemma1: $\hat{\Psi}_w$; var v ⊑ $\hat{\Phi}_{v,w}$

```
OBJ> start Ψ̂w ; var v .
==========================================
OBJ> apply .Ψ̂~simulation within term
result Prog: var w ; w := M[Ψ[w]] ; end M ; var v
==========================================
OBJ> apply .var~change~scope at [2 .. 4]
result Prog: var w ; var v ; w := M[Ψ[w]] ; end M
==========================================
OBJ> apply .var-:=~init with e = M[n] at [2] .
result Prog: var w ; var v ; v := M[n] ; w := M[Ψ[w]] ; end M
==========================================
OBJ> apply .var~change~scope at [ 1 .. 2 ] .
result Prog: var v ; var w ; v := M[n] ; w := M[Ψ[w]] ; end M
==========================================
OBJ> apply .var~assoc within term .
result Prog: var v,w ; v := M[n] ; w := M[Ψ[w]] ; end M
==========================================
OBJ> apply .:=~combination2 within term .
result Prog: var v,w ; v,w := M[n],(M[Ψ[w]][v <- M[n]]) ; end M
==========================================
OBJ> apply red at (2) of [2] .
result Prog: var v,w ; v,w := M[n],M[Ψ[w]] ; end M
==========================================
OBJ> apply -.list~application within term
result Prog: var v,w ; v,w := M[n,Ψ[w]] ; end M
==========================================
OBJ> apply -.map~lemma1 with x1 = v within term .
result Prog: var v,w ; v,w := M[(Ψ ∪ {v ↦ n })[v,w]] ; end M
```

```
=============================================
OBJ> apply .Φ¯def within term .
result Prog: var v,w ; v,w := M[Φ[v,w]] ; end M
=============================================
OBJ> apply -.Ψ¯simulation within term .
result Prog: Φ̂v,w


***> lemma2: end v ; Ψ̂w⁻¹ ⊑ Φ̂v,w⁻¹

OBJ> start end v ; Ψ̂w⁻¹ .
=============================================
OBJ> apply .Ψ⁻¹¯cosimulation within term .
result Prog: end v ; var M ; M := M ⊕ {Ψ[w] ↦ w } ; end w
=============================================
OBJ> apply .end¯change¯scope at [ 1 .. 3 ] .
result Prog: var M ; M := M ⊕ {Ψ[w] ↦ w } ; end v ; end w
=============================================
OBJ> apply .end¯assoc within term .
result Prog: var M ; M := M ⊕ {Ψ[w] ↦ w } ; end v,w
=============================================
OBJ> apply .var-:=¯init with e   M ⊕   n ↦ v    within term
result Prog: var M ; M := M ⊕ {n ↦ v } ; M := M ⊕ {Ψ[w] ↦ w } ; end v,w
=============================================
OBJ> apply .:=¯combination within term
result Prog: var M ; M := M ⊕ {Ψ[w] ↦ w }[M <- M ⊕ {n ↦ v }] ; end v,w
=============================================
OBJ> apply red at (2) of [2] .
result Prog: var M ; M := M ⊕ {n,Ψ[w] ↦ v,w } ; end v,w
=============================================
OBJ> apply -.map¯lemma1 with x1   v within term .
result Prog: var M ; M := M ⊕ {(Ψ ∪ {v ↦ n })[v,w] ↦ v,w } ; end v,w
=============================================
OBJ> apply -.Φ¯def within term .
result Prog: var M ; (M := M ⊕ {Φ[v,w] ↦ v,w } ; end v,w)
=============================================
OBJ> apply -.Ψ⁻¹¯cosimulation within term
result Prog: Φ̂v,w⁻¹


***> Therefore we can add inequations representing the two lemmas
[lemma1 ⊑] eq Ψ̂w ; var v   Φ̂v,w .
[lemma2 ⊑] eq end v ; Ψ̂w⁻¹   Φ̂v,w⁻¹


***> Proof of the theorem

OBJ> start Ψ̂w(dec v,P,A • p)
=============================================
OBJ> apply .Ψ¯simulation¯function at term .
```

```
result Prog: Ψ̂_w ; (dec v,P,A • p) ; Ψ̂_w^{-1}
==========================================
OBJ> apply -.dec˜assoc with x   v within term .
result Prog: Ψ̂_w ; (dec v •(dec P,A • p)) ; Ψ̂_w^{-1}
==========================================
OBJ> apply .dec-var˜end within term
result Prog: Ψ̂_w ; var v ; (dec P,A • p) ; end v ; Ψ̂_w^{-1}
==========================================
OBJ> apply .lemma1 within term
result Prog: Φ̂_{v,w} ; (dec P,A • p) ; end v ; Ψ̂_w^{-1}
==========================================
OBJ> apply .lemma2 within term
result Prog: Φ̂_{v,w} ; (dec P,A • p) ; Φ̂_{v,w}^{-1}
==========================================
OBJ> apply .;-dec˜Rdist within term .
result Prog: (dec P,A • Φ̂_{v,w} ; p) ; Φ̂_{v,w}^{-1}
==========================================
OBJ> apply .;-dec˜Ldist within term
result Prog: dec P,A • Φ̂_{v,w} ; p ; Φ̂_{v,w}^{-1}
==========================================
OBJ> apply -.Ψ˜simulation˜function within term .
result Prog: dec P,A • Φ̂_{v,w}(p)
```

C.6. Machine Instructions

The machine instructions are defined as assignments that update the machine state. Therefore, the instructions should also be regarded as elements of the sort Prog. However, to
make it clear that we are introducing a new concept, we declare a subsort of Prog whose
elements are the machine instructions.

```
th CODE is

    protecting REASONING-LANGUAGE [SOURCE + ROM + RAM] .

    sort Instruction .
    subsort Instruction < Prog

    op load   : RamAddr -> Instruction
    op store    RamAddr -> Instruction
    op bop-A : RamAddr -> Instruction
    op uop-A    -> Instruction .

    op jump  : RomAddr -> Instruction .
    op cjump : RomAddr -> Instruction

    var n    RamAddr
    var j    RomAddr

    eq (A,P := M[n],P + 1)    load(n) .
    eq (M,P := (M ⊕ {n ↦ A }),P + 1)    store(n)
    eq (A,P := A bop M[n],P + 1)    bop-A(n) .
    eq (A,P := uop A,P + 1)    uop-A .

    eq (P := j)    jump(j)
    eq (P := P + 1  ◁ A ▷ jump(j))    cjump(j)

endth
```

The reason to order the equations in this way is that they are used as rewrite rules during
the compilation process. Therefore, when the assignment statements (used as patterns to
define the instructions) are generated, they are automatically replaced by the corresponding
instructions names.

BIBLIOGRAPHY

1. A. V. Aho, R. Sethi, and J. D. Ullman. *Compilers: Principles, Techniques and Tools*. Addison-Wesley, 1986.
2. A. W. Appel and D. B. MacQueen. A Standard ML compiler. In *Functional Programming Languages and Computer Architecture*, volume 274 of *Lecture Notes in Computer Science*, pages 301–324. Springer-Verlag, 1987.
3. R. J. R. Back. Correctness preserving program refinements: Proof theory and applications. Mathematical Center Tracts 131, Mathematical Center, Amsterdam, 1980.
4. R. J. R. Back. Procedural abstraction in the refinement calculus. Reports on Computer Science and Mathematics 155, Department of Computer Science and Mathematics, Åbo Akademi, Finland, 1987.
5. R. J. R. Back and J. von Wright. Refinement calculus, part I: Sequential nondeterministic programs. In *Stepwise Refinement of Distributed Systems*, volume 430 of *Lecture Notes in Computer Science*, pages 42–66. Springer-Verlag, 1990.
6. R. J. R. Back and J. von Wright. Refinement concepts formalised in higher order logic. *Formal Aspects of Computing*, 2:247–272, 1990.
7. R. J. R. Back and J. von Wright. Combining angels, demons and miracles in program specifications. *Theoretical Computer Science*, 100:365–383, 1992.
8. E. Barros and A. Sampaio. Towards provably correct hardware/software partitioning using occam. In *Proceedings of the Third International Workshop on Hardware/Software Codesign*, pages 210–217, Grenoble, France, 1994. IEEE Computer Society Press.
9. W. R. Bevier, W. A. Hunt, J. S. Moore, and W. D. Young. An approach to systems verification. *Journal of Automated Reasoning*, 5:411–428, 1989.
10. G. Birkhoff. *Lattice Theory*. American Mathematical Society, 1961.
11. J. Bowen. From programs to object code using logic and logic programming. In R. Giergerich and S. L. Graham, editors, *Code Generation — Concepts, Tools, Techniques (Proceedings of the 1991 International Workshop on Code Generation—CODE'91)*, Workshops in Computing, pages 173–192, Dagstuhl, Germany, 1992. Springer-Verlag.
12. J. Bowen *et al.* A ProCoS II project final report: Esprit basic research project 7071. *Bulletin of the European Association for Theoretical Computer Science (EATCS)*, 59:76–99, 1996.
13. R. Burstall and P. Landin. Programs and their proofs: an algebraic approach. *Machine Intelligence*, 7:17–43, 1969.

14. B. Buth *et al.* Provably correct compiler development and implementation. In *4th International Conference on Compiler Construction*, volume 641 of *Lecture Notes in Computer Science*, pages 141–155. Springer-Verlag, 1992.

15. W. Chen and J. T. Udding. Program inversion: More than fun! Computing Science Notes CS 8903, Department of Mathematics and Computing Science of Groningen University, The Netherlands, April 1989.

16. P. Curzon. Of what use is a verified compiler specification? Technical Report TR-274, Computing Laboratory, University of Cambridge, 1992.

17. F. da Silva. *Correctness Proofs of Compilers and Debuggers: an Approach Based on Structural Operational Semantics.* PhD thesis, Department of Computer Science, University of Edinburgh, 1992. Published as LFCS Report Series ECS-LFCS-92-241 or CST-95-92.

18. B. A. Davey and H. A. Priestley. *Introduction to Lattices and Order.* Cambridge Mathematical Textbooks. Cambridge University Press, 1990.

19. J. Despeyroux. Proof of translation in natural semantics. In *First Symposium on Logic in Computer Science*, pages 193–205. IEEE Computer Society Press, 1986.

20. E. W. Dijkstra. Notes on structured programming. In O. J. Dahl, E. W. Dijkstra, and C. A. R. Hoare, editors, *Structured Programming*, pages 1–82. Academic Press, 1972.

21. E. W. Dijkstra. *A Discipline of Programming.* Prentice-Hall, Englewood Cliffs, 1976.

22. E. W. Dijkstra. Program inversion. Technical Report EWD671, University of Technology, Eindhoven, The Netherlands, 1978.

23. E. W. Dijkstra. The equivalence of bounded nondeterminacy and continuity. In *Selected Writings on Computing: A Personal Perspective*, Texts and Monographs in Computer Science, pages 358–359. Springer-Verlag, 1982.

24. H. Ehrig and B. Mahr. *Fundamentals of Algebraic Specification 1: Equations and Initial Semantics*, volume 6 of *EATCS Monographs on Theoretical Computer Science*. Springer-Verlag, 1985.

25. H. Ehrig and B. Mahr. *Fundamentals of Algebraic Specification 2: Module Specifications and Constraints*, volume 21 of *EATCS Monographs on Theoretical Computer Science*. Springer-Verlag, 1990.

26. P. Gardiner and P. K. Pandya. Reasoning algebraically about recursion. *Science of Computer Programming*, 18:271–280, 1992.

27. P. Gardiner and T. Vickers. The logic of B. PRG Monograph 92, Oxford University Computing Laboratory, 1991.

28. S. J. Garland and J. V. Guttag. An overview of LP, the Larch Prover. In N. Dershowitz, editor, *Proceedings of the Third International Conference on Rewriting Techniques and Applications*, volume 355 of *Lecture Notes in Computer Science*, pages 137–155. Springer-Verlag, 1989.

29. J. A. Goguen. *Theorem Proving and Algebra.* MIT Press, 1997. To appear.

30. J. A. Goguen and J. Meseguer. Order sorted algebra I: Equational deduction for multiple inheritance, overloading, exceptions and partial operations.

Theoretical Computer Science, 105:217–273, 1992.

31. J. A. Goguen, A. Stevens, K. Hobley, and H. Hilberdink. 2OBJ, a metalogical framework based on equational logic. In C. A. R. Hoare and M. J. C. Gordon, editors, *Mechanized Reasoning and Hardware Design*, pages 69–86. Prentice-Hall, 1992.

32. J. A. Goguen, J. W. Thatcher, E. G. Wagner, and J. B. Wright. Initial algebra semantics and continuous algebras. *Journal of the ACM*, 24(1):68–95, January 1977.

33. J. A. Goguen *et al.* Introducing OBJ. Technical Report SRI-CSL-92-03, Computer Science Laboratory, SRI International, California, USA, 1992. Revised version to appear in J. A. Goguen and G. Malcolm, editors, *Software Engineering with OBJ: Algebraic Specification in Practice*. Cambridge University Press, 1997.

34. M. Goldsmith. occam transformation at Oxford. In T. Muntean, editor, *Parallel Programming of Transputer Based Machines (Proceedings of the 7th occam User Group Technical Meeting)*, Amsterdam, 1988. IOS Press.

35. C. K. Gomard. A self-applicable partial evaluator for the lambda calculus: Correctness and pragmatics. *ACM Transactions on Programming Languages and Systems*, 14(2):147–172, April 1992.

36. M. J. C. Gordon. HOL: A proof generating system for higher-order logic. In G. Birtwistle and P. A. Subrahmanyam, editors, *VLSI Specification, Verification and Synthesis*. Kluwer Academic Publishers, 1988.

37. D. Gries. *The Science of Programming*. Springer Verlag, New York, 1981.

38. L. Hamel. *Behavioural Verification and Implementation of an Optimising Compiler for OBJ3*. PhD thesis, Oxford University Computing Laboratory, 1996.

39. L. Hamel and J. A. Goguen. Towards a provably correct compiler for OBJ3. In *Proceedings of Programming Language Implementation and Logic Programming Symposium*, volume 844 of *Lecture Notes in Computer Science*. Springer-Verlag, 1994.

40. F. K. Hanna, N. Daeche, and M. Longley. Veritas[+]: A specification language based on type theory. In M. Leeser and G. Brown, editors, *Hardware Specification, Verification and Synthesis: Mathematical Aspects*, volume 408 of *Lecture Notes in Computer Science*, pages 358–379, Mathematical Sciences Institute Workshop, Cornell University, Ithaca, New York, 1989. Springer-Verlag.

41. J. Hatcliff. Mechanically verifying the correctness of an offline partial evaluator. In M. Hermenegildo and S. D. Swierstra, editors, *Proceedings of the Seventh International Symposium on Programming Languages, Implementations, Logics and Programs*, volume 982 of *Lecture Notes in Computer Science*, pages 279–298, Utrecht, The Netherlands, 1995.

42. E. A. Hauck and B. A. Dent. Burroughs B6500 stack mechanism. In *Proceedings of the 1968 Spring Joint Computer Conference*, pages 245–251. Thomson Book Company, Inc., 1968.

43. J. He. Hybrid parallel programming and implementation of synchronised

communication. In A. M. Borzyszkowski and S. Sokołowski, editors, *Mathematical Foundations of Computer Science 1993 (MFCS'93)*, volume 711 of *Lecture Notes in Computer Science*, pages 537–546, Gdańsk, Poland, 1993. Springer-Verlag.

44. J. He and J. Bowen. Specification, verification and prototyping of an optimized compiler. *Formal Aspects of Computing*, 6:643–658, 1994.

45. J. He, I. Page, and J. Bowen. A provable hardware implementation of occam. In G. J. Milne and L. Pierre, editors, *Correct Hardware Design and Verification Methods (Advanced Research Working Conference, CHARME' 93)*, volume 683 of *Lecture Notes in Computer Science*, pages 214–225. Springer-Verlag, 1993.

46. C. A. R. Hoare. Procedures and parameters: an axiomatic approach. In *Symposium on the Semantics of Algorithmic Languages*, volume 188 of *Lecture Notes in Mathematics*, pages 102–116. Springer Verlag, 1971.

47. C. A. R. Hoare. Proof of correctness of data representations. *Acta Informatica*, 1(4):271–281, 1972.

48. C. A. R. Hoare. *Communicating Sequential Processes*. Series in Computer Science. Prentice-Hall International, 1985.

49. C. A. R. Hoare. Refinement algebra proves correctness of compiling specifications. In C. Morgan and J. C. P Woodcock, editors, *3rd Refinement Workshop*, Workshops in Computing, pages 33–48. Springer-Verlag, 1991.

50. C. A. R. Hoare. Algebra and models. In M. Broy, editor, *Program Design Calculi (Lecture Notes for the 1992 Marktoberdorf Summer School)*, volume 118 of *NATO ASI Series F: Computer and Systems Sciences*, pages 161–195. Springer-Verlag, 1993.

51. C. A. R. Hoare. Unified theories of programming. Technical report, Oxford University Computing Laboratory, 1994.

52. C. A. R. Hoare and J. He. The weakest prespecification. *Information Processing Letters*, 24(2):127–132, January 1987.

53. C. A. R. Hoare, J. He, and A. Sampaio. Normal form approach to compiler design. *Acta Informatica*, 30:701–739, 1993.

54. C. A. R. Hoare, J. He, and A. Sampaio. Algebraic derivation of an operational semantics. In G. D. Plotkin, editor, *Milner Festschrift*. MIT Press, 1997. To appear.

55. C. A. R. Hoare *et al.* Laws of programming. *Communications of the ACM*, 30(8):672–686, August 1987.

56. N. D. Jones, P. Sestoft, and H. Søndergaard. An experiment in partial evaluation: the generation of a compiler generator. In J.-P. Jouannaud, editor, *Rewriting Techniques and Applications*, volume 202 of *Lecture Notes in Computer Science*, pages 124–140. Springer-Verlag, 1985.

57. N. D. Jones *et al.* A self-applicable partial evaluator for the lambda calculus. In *1990 International Conference on Computer Languages*, IEEE Computer Society, 1990.

58. L. Lamport. LaTeX: A Document Preparation System. Addison-Wesley, 1986.

59. H. Langmaack and A. P. Ravn. The ProCoS project: Provably correct systems.

In J. Bowen, editor, *Towards Verified Systems*, volume 2 of *Real Time Safe Critical Systems*, appendix B. Elsevier, 1994.

60. J. McCarthy and J. Painter. Correctness of a compiler for arithmetic expressions. In *Proceedings of Symposium on Applied Mathematics*, pages 33–41. American Mathematical Society, 1967.

61. J. Meseguer. A logical theory of concurrent objects and its realization in the Maude language. In G. Agha, P. Wegner, and A. Yonezawa, editors, *Object-Oriented Programming*, pages 314–390. MIT Press, 1993.

62. J. Meseguer. Rewriting logic as a semantic framework for concurrency: a progress report. In U. Montanari and V. Sassone, editors, *Proceedings of CONCUR '96*, volume 1119 of *Lecture Notes in Computer Science*, pages 331–372. Springer-Verlag, 1996.

63. R. Milner. *A Calculus of Communicating Systems*, volume 92 of *Lecture Notes in Computer Science*. Springer-Verlag, 1980.

64. C. Morgan. Procedures, parameters, and abstraction: Separate concerns. *Science of Computer Programming*, 11:17–27, 1988.

65. C. Morgan. The specification statement. *Transactions on Programming Languages and Systems*, 10:403–419, 1988.

66. C. Morgan. *Programming from Specifications*. Series in Computer science. Prentice-Hall International, 1990.

67. C. Morgan and P. Gardiner. Data refinement by calculation. In *On the Refinement Calculus* (by C. Morgan, K. Robinson and P. Gardiner), volume 70 of *PRG Monographs*, pages 103–134. Oxford University Computing Laboratory, 1988.

68. F. Morris. Advice on structuring compilers and proving them correct. In *SIGACT/SIGPLAN Symposium on Principles of Programming Languages*, pages 144–152. ACM, 1973.

69. J. M. Morris. A theoretical basis for stepwise refinement and the programming calculus. *Science of Computer Programming*, 9:287–306, 1987.

70. J. M. Morris. Invariance theorems for recursive procedures. Technical report, Department of Computer Science, University of Glasgow, June 1988.

71. J. M. Morris. Laws of data refinement. *Acta Informatica*, 26:287–308, 1989.

72. P. D. Mosses. SIS—Semantics Implementation System. Technical Report DAIMI MD-30, Computer Science Department, Aarhus University, 1979.

73. P. D. Mosses. *Action Semantics*. Number 26 in Cambridge Tracts in Theoretical Computer Science. Cambridge University Press, 1992.

74. M. Müller-Olm. *Modular Compiler Verification*. PhD thesis, Technische Facultät der Christian-Albrechts-Universität, Kiel, Germany, 1996.

75. G. Nelson and M. Manasse. The proof of a second step of a factored compiler. In F. L. Bauer, M. Broy, E. W. D. Dijkstra, and C. A. R. Hoare, editors, *Programming and Mathematical Method (Lecture Notes for the 1990 Marktoberdorf Summer School)*, volume 88 of *NATO ASI Series F: Computer and Systems Sciences*. Springer-Verlag, 1992.

76. P. Ørbæk. OASIS: An optimising action-based compiler generator. In

Compiler Construction (Proc. 5th Intl. Conf., CC'94, Edinburgh, U.K., April 1994), volume 786 of *Lecture Notes in Computer Science*, pages 1–15. Springer-Verlag, 1994.

77. J. Palsberg. *Provably Correct Compiler Generation.* PhD thesis, Computer Science Department, Aarhus University, 1992.

78. J. Palsberg. A provably correct compiler generator. In *ESOP'92, Proc. European Symposium on Programming, Rennes*, volume 582 of *Lecture Notes in Computer Science*, pages 418–434. Springer-Verlag, 1992.

79. L. Paulson. *ML for the Working Programmer.* Cambridge University Press, 1991.

80. W. Polak. *Compiler Specification and Verification*, volume 124 of *Lecture Notes in Computer Science*. Springer-Verlag, 1981.

81. A. Roscoe and C. A. R. Hoare. The laws of occam programming. *Theoretical Computer Science*, 60:177–229, 1988.

82. A. Sampaio. A comparative study of theorem provers: Proving correctness of compiling specifications. Technical Report PRG-TR-20-90, Oxford University Computing Laboratory, 1990.

83. E. Scott. Automated proof of the correctness of a compiling specification. In *Proceedings of the Third International Conference on Algebraic Methodology and Software Technology*, Workshops in Computing. Springer-Verlag, 1993. Extended version published as technical report CS-93-01, Department of Computer Science, University of Surrey.

84. A. Tarski. On the calculus of relations. *Symbolic Logic*, 6:73–89, 1941.

85. A. Tarski. A lattice theoretical fixed point theorem and its applications. *Pacific Journal of Mathematics*, 5, 1955.

86. J. W. Thatcher, E. G. Wagner, and J. B. Wright. More on advice on structuring compilers and proving them correct. *Theoretical Computer Science*, 15:223–249, 1981.

87. A. van Deursen. Introducing ASF+SDF: Using the λ-calculus as example. Technical report, CWI, Amsterdam, The Netherlands, August 1994. Available by ftp: ftp.cwi.nl:/pub/gipe/reports/Deu92.ps.Z.

88. A. van Deursen, J. Heering, and P. Klint. *Language Prototyping: An Algebraic Specification Approach*, volume 5 of *Algebraic Methodology and Software Technology*. World Scientific, 1996.

89. M. Wirsing. Algebraic specification: Semantics, parameterization and refinement. In E. J. Neuhold and M. Paul, editors, *Formal Description of Programming Concepts*, pages 259–318. Springer-Verlag, 1991.

90. N. Wirth. Program development by stepwise refinement. *Communications of the ACM*, 14(4):221–227, 1971.

91. H. Yan. *Theory and Implementation of Sort Constraints for Order Sorted Algebra.* PhD thesis, Oxford University Computing Laboratory, 1995.

INDEX

www.ingramcontent.com/pod-product-compliance
Lightning Source LLC
Chambersburg PA
CBHW050640190326
41458CB00008B/2359